V. T. Fernan

DEDICA

For Ach

CONTENTS

	Acknowledgments	v
	Introduction	vi
1	Pronounciation	1
2	Description	16
3	Non-Past Verbs	41
4	Past Tense Verbs	66
5	Animate Nouns	94
6	Inanimate Nouns	121
7	Pronouns	139
8	Complex Sentences	168
9	Numbers	199
10	Time	221
11	Vocabulary	240
12	Loanwords	258
13	The Sinhala Alphabet	267
	Answers to End-of-Chapter Exercises	286
	English-Sinhala Vocabulary	326
	Sinhala-English Vocabulary	360
	Glossary	400

ACKNOWLEDGMENTS

The Sinhala dialogues in this book were composed and edited in consultation with my family, especially my parents, G.W. and S. K. Fernando

INTRODUCTION

The purpose of this book is to thoroughly teach spoken Sinhala. The emphasis on "spoken" here is not because this book is exceptionally focused on conversation, per se, but rather due to an odd historical situation.

In English, we write and speak formally using a slightly different language than the one we use with our friends and family, but the difference isn't that significant. Compare "Are you injured?" vs. "Are you OK?". One is more formal than the other, but both would probably be acceptable in most situations. They are certainly more similar to each other than to a four hundred year old sentence out of Romeo and Juliet: "[...] Art thou hurt?" Of course, such an antiquated way of speaking has little relevance to modern people, at least outside of an academic environment.

In Sinhala, the situation is different, to say the least. Some 800 years ago, a grammar of Sinhala called the *Sidath Sangarawa* was composed. Some parts of it were probably archaic even at that point in time; it may well be merely the oldest surviving exposition on a considerably older tradition. In any case, the rules expounded upon the *Sidath Sangarawa* are, more or less, those used in what is commonly called "literary Sinhala." In spite of the name, it is used not only for literature, but nearly all forms of written communication, as well as poetry and songs. Given its age, the gulf between literary Sinhala and the colloquial variety is, if anything, greater than the difference between Shakespearean and modern English.

The colloquial language, also called spoken Sinhala, is the subject of this book. It must be noted that, given the contexts in which the literary variety is used, this knowledge will only get you so far. Even if you consult the final chapter in this book and learn the Sinhala script, you will not be able to write proper Sinhala essays, read Sinhala books that are for audiences other than young children, understand much of Sinhala music, or compose Sinhala poetry. In short, knowledge of the spoken language will teach you how to speak and listen, not read and write.

Prior to the publication of this book, anyone trying to learn to speak the Sinhala language and lacking easy access to a Sinhala speaker was basically out of luck. The best educational materials available were designed for use with a Sinhala-speaking instructor. Many others just consist of collections of phrases; these may be useful in their own way, but they do not go too far in teaching the fundamental rules behind the language, which would allow students to express themselves more flexibly instead of parroting some memorized lines. There are number of older works in English that deal with the literary language; for the reasons mentioned above, these are of little use for a person looking to speak and understand Sinhala. Some substandard works actually confuse the two, presenting information from both varieties mixed together, sometimes in ways not generally used by anyone.

This book, on the other hand, presents both a large quantity of examples, mostly in the form of translation exercises, and the grammatical rules governing them. It was composed in 2017, and thus is considerably less outdated than most of the other texts available. A final advantage is that this book does not require knowledge of the Sinhala script, although a chapter focused on teaching it is available at the end.

The first chapter explains how to pronounce Sinhala. This book uses a transliteration scheme that an English speaker should find reasonably intuitive, though reading the pronunciation rules carefully is recommended, especially for vowels and sounds which do not exist in English. Chapters 2 - 8 introduce the grammar of Spoken Sinhala; covering adjectives, verbs, nouns, pronouns, and several other parts of speech, some of which do not have exact English analogs. Chapters 9-12 introduce various vocabulary items, and particulars governing their use. Chapter 13 teaches the Sinhala script. Going through the chapters in order is recommended, though after chapter 8, the remaining chapters should be equally accessible with the exception of Chapter 10, which, due to the nature of the material, builds off of Chapter 9. All of the main chapters have exercises at the end, though only 2-10 contain these in significant numbers. The latter subset of chapters have example problems throughout as well.

There are also three appendices for reference. The first gives the answers to the exercises at the end of each chapter (answers to examples within the chapters are provided therein). The second is a (basic) English-Sinhala dictionary, and the third is a somewhat more detailed Sinhala-English dictionary.

In this book, Sinhala words are always presented in bold text and in the transliteration scheme described, with the only exceptions being Sinhala words that are being used as English proper nouns. Thus this introduction refers to the *Sidath Sangarawa*, but if that book's title were rendered in the style of this book, it would be **Siḋath Sa^{n}gárává**. Sinhala words which are literary or archaic are preceded by a parenthetical indication of that fact. Cases where this transliteration deviates from Sinhala orthography are indicated with the faithful transcription in curly brackets:

evvā vs. {**evuvā**}

The only prerequisite for this book is knowledge of American English, which aside from the actual text is also used to provide the sound values in the pronunciation guide. These values are also provided in their IPA notations. Data from other languages is cited when there is no good English equivalent, but an approximation based only on the knowledge of English sounds is provided.

That said, knowledge of certain other languages may prove helpful. The Indic languages (that is, the Indo-Aryan, Dravidian, and Munda languages) generally contain a set of sounds found in Sinhala but not in English; knowledge of one of these would certainly make accent elimination much easier. Knowledge of Swahili, certain other Bantu languages, the Yi language of China, or especially Dhivehi, would be helpful with regard to another group of sounds, found in no Indic languages other than Sinhala and Dhivehi.

With respect to grammar, anyone who has studied an inflected Indo-European language like Sanskrit, Latin, Greek, Lithuanian, Russian, or German will be prepared for dealing with certain aspects of Sinhala grammar which would otherwise be rather unintuitive for an English speaker. Knowledge of the former will be quite helpful for learning vocabulary, as the great bulk of Sinhala words are either cognate to, or borrowed from Sanskrit or its close relative, Pali. Knowledge of Tamil, Portuguese, and Dutch will be helpful due to the presence of loans from these languages (The largest source of loanwords these days is English, but knowledge of it is of course assumed).

1
PRONUNCIATION

This book does not require knowledge of the Sinhala script; instead, it will use a transliteration scheme not unlike those used by many Sinhalese people in their day-to-day use. However, in order to represent the sounds as clearly as possible, certain letters will be modified with diacritics.

A big difference between this script and that of normal English is that letters *do not* change their pronunciation according to various rules; instead, all of the letters / digraphs shown here will *always* have the values indicated given.

1.1 Pronunciation Guide

This book uses the Latin alphabet with diacritics to write the Sinhala script. If you wish to focus less on accurate pronunciation, you can simply assume the consonant sounds take the values they commonly do in English. This will result in accented but understandable speech. Even if you choose to take this approach, it is recommended that you look at the vowel table below.

In Sinhala, vowels can be long or short. Long vowels are approximately twice the length of short ones.

Letter	English Equivalent	IPA Symbol
a	Like the first "a" in "mama"	[ɑ]
ā	Like "ah"	[ɑ:]
á	Like the "a" in "around."	[ə]
ā́	Like the "uhh" in "uhh..."	[ə:]
æ	Like the "a" in "fat"	[æ]
ǣ	Like the "aa" of a sheep's "baa"	[æ:]
i	Like the "i" in "dim"	[i]
ī	Like the "ee" in "deem"	[i:]
u	Like the "u" in "computer"	[u]
ū	Like the "oo" in zoo"	[u:]
e	Like the "e" in "pet"	[e]
ē	Like the "e" in "bed"	[e:]
o	Like the "o" in "sow"*	[o]
ō	Like the "oe" in "foe"&	[o:]

*The English equivalents given for **o** and **ō** are diphthongs, but the Sinhala sounds are not.

All vowels other than **á** may start diphthongs (two vowels in the same syllable of a word, i.e. **ai**, **au**, **æi**, etc) (if **á** would be made into a diphthong by some grammatical process, it becomes **a** instead, i.e. **á** + **i** = **ai**), but only **i** or **u** may end them. In this book, diphthongs are written as above except when an **i** precedes a **y**, or a **u** precedes a **v**.

The following consonants have good, sometimes identical, approximations in English:

Letter	English Equivalent	IPA symbol
k	The “k” in skate	[k]
g	The “g” in “gate”	[g]
ṅ	The “ng” in sing	[ŋ]
ch	The “ch” in “purchase”	[tʃ]
j	The “dg” in “dodge”	[dʒ]
n, ṇ	The “n” in “ten”	[n]
p	The “p” in “spend”	[p]
b	The “b” in “bat”	[b]
m	The “m” in “man”	[m]
y	The “y” in “yet”	[j]
l, ḷ	The “l” in “let”	[l]
s	The “s” in “set”	[s]
sh, ṣh	The “sh” in “‘shop”	[ʃ]
h	The “h” in “how”	[h]
f	The “f” in “fair”	[f]

Note that characters with dots underneath them, namely **ṇ**, **ḷ**, and **ṣh** are not pronounced any differently than their un-dotted counterparts. These letters represent historical spellings, and are maintained here mostly for orthographic accuracy.

The following sounds do not have good English equivalents. In addition to a rough English approximation, advice is included to make the pronunciation more accurate. Additionally, sounds from other scripts or languages that are identical or nearly so are indicated.

Letter	English Approximation	Notes	Better Equivalents
ñ	The "gn" in "gnu"	Pronounced as a single sound, not as an "n" followed by a "y"	IPA [ɲ], Spanish "ñ", Portuguese "nh", Hindi ञ्, Tamil ஞ்
t	The "t" in "part"	Pronounced with the tongue curled back	IPA [ʈ], Hindi ट्, Tamil ட்
d	The "d" in "hard"	Pronounced with the tongue curled back	IPA [ɖ], Hindi ड्
th	The "th" in "bath"	Pronounced more strongly, with less breath	IPA [t̪], French, Spanish, and Portuguese "t", Hindi त्, Tamil த்
ḋ	The "th" in "teethe"	Pronounced more strongly, with less breath	IPA [d̪], Hindi द्
r	The "r" in "red"	Flapped	IPA [ɾ], Spanish and Portuguese "r", Hindi र्
v	The "w" in "wood"	Articulated more like English "v"	IPA [ʋ], Hindi व्, Tamil வ்

The **v**, **t**, and **d** sounds are typical of Indic languages; and often associated with the stereotypical Indian accent.

The difference between the **th** and **ḋ** sounds and their English approximations is that the former are strongly pronounced ***stops***, comparable to sounds like **t**, **d**, **p**, **b** etc, while the English sounds are ***fricatives***, like **f** or **s**.

Letter	Components	Other Representations
^{n}g	ṅ + g	IPA [^{ŋ}g], Dhivehi ންގ, Shona, Swahili "ng," Yi Pinyin "mg"
^{n}d	ṇ + d	IPA [^{n}d], Dhivehi ންދ, can be approximated with Shona, Swahili, Yi Pinyin "nd"
^{n}ḋ	n + ḋ	IPA [^{n}ɖ], Dhivehi ންޑ
^{m}b	m + b	IPA [^{m}b], Dhivehi ންބ, Shona, Swahili "mb," Yi Pinyin "nb"

A special category of Sinhala sounds are the ***half nasals***, which are also known as pre-nasalized consonants.

These sounds have no comparable equivalent in English, and moreover, Sinhala appears to be one of the most widely spoken language that has these sounds in the first place. Thus, we will describe how these sounds are pronounced in detail.

Pre-nasals are made up of the two component sounds shown in the table above, but are pronounced faster than the sequence of the corresponding nasal and stop. For example, the sequence **mb** is about twice as long as the pre-nasal **^{m}b**. However the ***nasal*** (m-or-n-like) sound is not as long as the sound after it; instead, it lasts for about 1/4 of the time the second sound does. As such, Sinhala speakers usually think of these sounds as different versions of **b**, **d**, **ḋ**, and **g**, rather than combinations of sounds.

Note that although **n** and **ṇ** are not distinct sounds in modern times, their half nasal counterparts are still distinct.

A less important category of sounds are the sounds called ***aspirates***, or **mahaprānā́** in Sinhala. These are found in loanwords from Sanskrit and Pali, and as such are relatively rare, but not nonexistent in the spoken language. Less educated speakers may pronounce them identically with their unaspirated (Sinhala: **alpáprāná**) counterparts, and you may choose to follow suit, if you are less focused on pronunciation.

Aspirates are indicated here with small "h"s: **k^h**, **g^h**, etc. The difference between **k** and **k^h** is demonstrated by the difference between the "k" of "skit" and the "k" of "kit." If you place your hand near your mouth while saying those words, you will notice that with "kit," there is a significant amount of breath released with the "k." This additional breath is represented by **^{h}** in the book.

1.2 Notes and Caveats

Through the use of diacritics, this script represents the Sinhala language in an unambiguous way. When Sinhala speakers write their language in the Roman script in various situations, they generally do not use such a notation, with the result that various sounds can be confused. The **á** sound is usually just written as "a," because it's not written differently from **a** in the Sinhala script. But in standard spoken Sinhala, **a** and **á** aren't freely mixed up; each is pronounced in certain places, and it sounds unnatural if the wrong one is said. As such, this book will use different symbols for both.

Although the **a** and **æ** sounds are completely different letters in Sinhala, in casual romanizations they are usually both written as "a," which can lead to significant confusion. Likewise, **ḋ** and **d** are both typically written as "d."

Also common is to write ^{m}**b**, ^{n}**d**, ^{n}**ḋ**, and ^{n}**g** as "mb", "nd", "nd", and "ng," **ñ** and **ṇ** as "n," **ṅ** as "ng" or "n," and **v** as "w." That last one is just a choice on our part; since the real sound is neither "v" nor "w," but something kind of in-between, we could have just as easily used "w." The others, however, are ambiguous, so they are not suitable for a book like this. Some vowels are written this way too: "oo" for **ū**, "ee" for **ī**, "a," "e," or "ae" for **æ**. In some positions, **á** is may be written using "e" or "o".

There are a few cases where sounds may be ambiguous in the spoken language itself, with two sounds alternating even in the speech of one person. Word final nasals (**m** or **n**) may be pronounced **ṅ** instead. Sometimes the latter pronunciation is more common than the first, this book will only explicitly write a nasal as **ṅ** if that is the case.

Similarly, word final long vowels are usually pronounced as their short counterparts. Long vowels are only ambiguous in the final position, or before one of the (animate) ***case endings***.

Note that the alteration of **m**/**n** with **ṅ** is common, so two forms of many words that end in m or n may be found. Words that are written with final long vowels, on the other hand, are only rarely pronounced with them; they are written this way in this book for historical reasons. Pronouns (see ch. 7) are typically exceptions, their final vowels, especially before case endings, are more commonly fully pronounced.

In the middle of words, **á** is often pronounced as **e**.

Most consonants can double. A doubled consonant is pronounced for twice the length of a single consonant. For most sounds, this is represented by writing the letter or digraph representing the sound twice, i.e. **th** doubled is **thth**, **j** doubled is **jj**. When pre-nasals would double, however, they are replaced by their corresponding full nasal-stop sequence, that is, ^{m}**b**, ^{n}**d**, ^{n}**ḋ**, and ^{n}**g** just become **mb**, **ṇd**, **nḋ**, and **ṅg**, respectively.

Three other sounds, **h**, **r**, and **ḷ**, do not double either. If **h** would double, it becomes **ss** instead; while the latter two are simply not found doubled at all.

The **h** and **s** sounds are related in other ways as well. The **s** sound has, in many positions, changed to the **h** sound; but the older pronunciation is maintained by some speakers. Thus a word may have alternate forms: **raha** and **rasá**, for instance, both mean "tasty." The pronunciation with **s** is usually more refined. This book will list both variants if they are colloquial.

Another is that native words do not end in **h**. As such, when a word changes to cause a medial **h** to become final, it becomes **s**. This often occurs when forming Sinhala noun stems, which for some nouns are equivalent to the plural. The plural of **pothá** ("book"), is **poth**, for instance. The plural of **gaha** (tree) is formed the same way, but it becomes **gas** due to the rule above.

The **h** sound has one final peculiarity; it tends to disappear, causing the vowels before and after to fuse. This can result in pairs of words with the same meaning; for instance, an alternative version of **mahaprāná** is **māprāná**. The **h**-less version is usually less formal.

1.3 Summary and Supplementary information

Transliteration:

The romanization scheme used here is very similar to the IAST, which is typically used to transliterate Sanskrit. The main differences are:

The letter **á** here corresponds with the letter "a" in the IAST.

The letters **e** and **o** here represent short vowels; their long versions are represented with bars, as with other vowels.

The letter **ḷ** represents a no-longer-differentiated pronunciation of l, not the syllabic l.

The letters **th**, **ḋ**, **t**, **d**, **sh**, and **ṣh** correspond with IAST t, d, t, d, ś, and ṣ.

Aspirates are written with a superscript h, not a full sized h.

The anusvara (or the **binḋuvá**, as it is known in Sinhala) and visarga are not given special characters, the sounds of the former are represented "as is;" the latter is not pronounced differently from **h** in Sinhala.

The following technical terms were introduced in this chapter:

Half-nasal/prenasalized consonant: A consonant which consists of a ***nasal*** (**m** or **n** like) sound quickly followed by a ***stop*** sound (**g**, **ḋ**, **d**, or **b**). These are very common in Sinhala, and it is important to distinguish them from full nasal-stop sequences, eg. **nd**, **mb**. In this book, they are written with a small nasal followed by a regular stop, eg. ^{m}**b**. Unlike most consonants, which ***double*** simply (b x 2 = bb) a half nasal doubles like so: ^{m}**b** x 2 = **mb**.

Aspirate: A consonant with extra breath at release. In Sinhala, these are fairly rare, and sometimes not differentiated from their ***unaspirated*** counterparts even by native speakers. In this book, aspirated consonants are indicated by an ^{h}.

Sinhala also has four ***fricative*** sounds: **s**, **sh**, **f**, and **h**, and seven vowels (which can be long or short), **a**, **á**, **æ**, **o**, **e**, **u**, and **i**. The last two have ***semivowel*** counterparts **v** and **y**. Sequences of semivowels and vowels sometimes have a pronunciation different from their nominal transcription in Sinhala; this book will write these sounds as they are pronounced, rather than how they are traditionally written.

Here are some more conventions used in this book:

Vowels take only the values given in the table above; long vowels are indicated by a line above them.

Consonants are pronounced according to their normal English values. The letter **ḋ** is pronounced like the "th" in "seethe," while **th** only represents the "th" of "math." The letter "v" represents a sound close to, but not exactly English "w" or "v." A small "n" or "m" indicates a briefer version of the sound almost fused with the sound after it.

A small "h" indicates the sound before it is released with extra breath; the plain versions of these sounds are pronounced with less breath than in English. This pronunciation is not always followed by Sinhala speakers. The same applies to "sh," which is sometimes pronounced as "s."

Some letters have dots under them. These are pronounced just like the undotted versions; the dots are just there to represent Sinhala spelling accurately.

Compared to traditional Sinhala orthography, this representation differs in a few ways. Aside from differentiating between the different "a" and "d" sounds, the biggest thing is the treatment of diphthongs. The sequences written **iu**, ou, **ei**, **ui**, would, in Sinhala, be written {**ivu**}, {**ovu**}, {**eyi**}, and {**uyi**}, respectively. The former convention is used because in speech, **oi** is a single syllable that rhymes with "boy," not two syllables, i.e. "bo-yee." The only case in which this simplification would not be made is if the same semivowel occurs in the next syllable, so {**ayiyā**} "elder brother" is written **ayyā** here.

Another difference between half nasals and full nasal-stop sequences, that is, between ^{m}**b** and **mb**, is that the former is always part of one syllable, while the latter's nasal sound, **m**, is part of the previous syllable, and its stop sound, **b**, is part of the next syllable.

Incidentally, when **ā** is shortened at the end of a word, it becomes **a**, never **á**; and aside from this shortening, native Sinhala words almost never end in short **a**, only **ā** or **á**. (the exception is words that end in **-ha**; the "short a" sound after **h** is usually pronounced **a** in native Sinhala words (see section 13.7).

1.4 Exercises

These problems are designed to test your mastery of this transliteration scheme; they may be skipped if no such testing is needed.

1-3: Match each Sinhala word with the English word it rhymes best with.

1.

Īrī (sow), **Minihā** (man), **Gollō** (guys), **Eḷu** (an archaic name of Sinhala)

Shoe, Shiny, Show,
Pizza

2.

hædi (messy), **gedi** (fruits), **podi** (small)

Cody, paddy, ready

3.

Nil "blue," **kakul** "feet," **mal** "flowers," **thel**, "oil"

null, pull, fell, kill

4-6: The following are samples of casually romanized Sinhala. Convert them to the format used in this book.

4. Wei

5. Beelā

6. Ooru

7-9: The following words are written in a casual romanization scheme like those commonly used in Sri Lanka. Identify the sounds which are ambiguous:

7. Hondai

8. Parissameng

9. Duka

The following Sinhala words form stems by removing the final vowel. Predict the stem or stems that would result, given the standard sound changes discussed in this chapter.

10. **Paha** (five)

11. **Æ^{n}ḋumá** (article of clothing)

12. **Bathá** (rice)

Below are some words with the semivowel **v**, faithfully transcribed from Sinhala. How would they be simplified in this book?

13. {**rilav**} (monkeys)

14. {**uḋavuvá**} (help)

15. {**uḋavu**} pl. of 14

Do not assume forming Sinhala plurals is as simple as the above rule would suggest; there are several different ways to form them, and the most straightforward way to deal with them is simply memorization.

Note: Sinhala has nothing analogous to capital or simple letters. These appear in transcription here so purely for stylistic reasons.

2
DESCRIPTION

Dialogue 1: Greetings

The phrase **āyubōvan** is described as the Sinhala word for hello in many places, but it is an archaic word which is not commonly used in non-formal situations. In fact, the English word "hello" is frequently used, especially in more urban environments. Another popular greeting is **kohomáḋá**. Its use is illustrated below:

A - **Kohomáḋá.** How (are you)?

B - **Prashnáyak næ.** Everything's fine. (Lit. a problem-not)

Sinhala is a rather compact language; many pieces of information are conveyed by context. Thus, when **kohomáḋá** is used by itself, to address someone, it is assumed that the inquirer is asking after the condition of the addressee.

Aside from **prashnáyak nǣ**, another potential response would be **ho^{n}ḋin innávā** "(I) am well". If someone is not, in fact, feeling well, it is acceptable to give an alternate response. Afterwards, people will usually ask after each other's families:

Kohomáḋá "wife"tá? "how (is your) wife?

In urban areas, the English words "husband" and "wife" are commonly used, more so than other words. In a rural environment, one might instead say **kohomáḋá geḋárekenātá**, literally, "how is the one at home?" **Geḋárekenā** can technically refer to anyone dwelling in one's home, but usually refers to a spouse of either gender. **Geḋárá ayá**, "the people at home," is most commonly used to refer to a person's family.

The **-tá** ending marks a noun in the dative case, which in Sinhala, is used in several contexts, one of which is talking about people's temporary feelings.

To specifically ask after a person's children, one might ask:

Ḷamai ho^{n}ḋin innávāḋá? Are (your) children well?

There is no **-tá** ending here because **ḷamai** is the subject of the sentence, that is, the noun that the verb **innávā** ("are," more generally, "be") is referring to. The subject of a sentence, as in English, will be in the nominative case, which isn't marked.

Notice also that this statement is quite similar to **ho^{n}ḋin innávā** above, aside from the presence of **ḋá**. **Ḋá** is the question particle, adding it to the end of a sentence will transform a plain statement into a question. When combined with **ḋá**, **prashnáyak næḋḋá** means "Everything's ok, isn't it?".

It is also acceptable to talk about your family's problems in a context like this:

A- **Kohomáḋá ḷamáyā?**

B- **Mage ḷamáyek(u)tá asanipai.** One of my children is sick. Using **ḷamáyātá** here would cause the sentence to mean "my child is sick."

A- **Mokaḋḋá asanīpe?** What's wrong? Lit. What illness? **Mokaḋḋá** is an informal version of **mokak** "what" combined with **ḋá**

B- **Eyātá hembirisāvá**. She's (got) a cold.

Sickness is also a temporary condition which warrants the dative **-tá** ending. Upon hearing that a family member is ill, the questioner will inquire about the person's condition:

A- **Eyātá uná.** She (is) running a temperature.

B- **Hu^{n}gak unáḋá? Ḋosthárá balanná/la^{n}gátá giyāḋá? Beheth gaththāḋá?** Is it a high temperature? Did you see/go to the doctor? Did she take medicine?

A- **Behethválátá** (**eyātá**) **ho^{n}ḋá vēgáná enávā.** With the medicine she's getting better.

B- (**Ēká**) **Ho^{n}ḋai.** (That's) good.

Hu^{n}gak is a superlative, like the English words "much," "many," "high," or "great." It could be used as a substitute for any of those words. B's second question depicts the other major use of the dative case, to mark the indirect object of the sentence. It frequently corresponds to the English preposition "to."

Notice that there are three different forms of the word for "good":

Ho^{n}ḋai, which stands by itself.

Ho^{n}ḋá, which is used to modify nouns, just like English adjectives.

Ho^{n}ḋin, which is used to modify verbs.

The latter two are simply the adjective and adverb forms, respectively. The first, however, is a form peculiar to Sinhala.

Adjectives and the i-Form

Sinhala is a highly inflected language. This means that the meaning of words can (and often must) be changed by altering (inflecting) their endings.

For example, the word for "cold" is **sīthálá.**

Sīthálá vathurá- : cold water-

Like the English translation, the Sinhala above is not a complete sentence, as indicated by the dash. The other possibility,

Vathurá sīthálai. Water is cold.

is a complete sentence, because **sīthálá** has been inflected with the addition of **i**. This ***i-form*** is an inflection which effectively adds the verb "to be" to the sentence.

An **i** is added only for adjectives that end in vowels. Thus:

Ē pothá aluth. That book is new.

Mamá pohosath. I'm rich.

Example Problems:

Translate the following sentences into Sinhala

1. The tea is warm. (The word for tea is **thē eká**; the word for warm is **rasne**)

2. The new book is good.

3. He's odd (the word for odd is **amuthu**, the most common word for "he" is **eyā**).

4. The green book is new. (The word for green is here is **koḷá pātá**)

Answers:

1. **Thē eká rasnei**.

2. **Aluth pothá ho^{n}ḋai.**

3. **Eyā amuthui**. Recall that in the dialogue at the start of the chapter, the word **eyā** was translated as "she." What's going on here? Simply put, spoken Sinhala does not make a fundamental gender distinction between masculine and feminine nouns, that is, the word for "he" and "she" is the same.

4. **Koḷá pātà pothá aluth**.

Nouns and Animacy

The situation can get more complex:

Budágini minihā- : the hungry man-

Minihātá budáginī. the man is hungry.

In the second example above, the noun is inflected as well, with the dative suffix **-tá**, yet this did not occur in the example with **vathurá**. Why?

Remember that the dative case is used to mark feelings. Obviously, water cannot feel anything, and this, as it turns out, is reason for this difference. It is a consequence of the ***animacy*** of the noun. In Sinhala, ***animate*** nouns are humans, animals, supernatural beings, and in general, things that can experience events for themselves. All other things, even nouns that make up animates, are said to be ***inanimate***. These objects, like houses, but also plants, bacteria, organizations, and anything not under the animate category, behave in a fundamentally different way from words for objects.

Not all adjectives require **-tá**, even for animate nouns. For instance:

Mamá suḋḋai. I'm clean.

But:

Matá niḋimathai. I'm sleepy / I feel sleepy.

For most nouns, the dative is formed by adding **-tá**, but **mamá** ("I") is irregular; its dative form is **matá**.

Which type of adjective you're dealing with can't be absolutely determined by any rule, but the following generalization seems to hold for most of them:

Adjectives that describe temporary feelings generally require **-tá**. The rest usually do not.

Thus, things like cleanliness, age, or blindness do not need **-tá**, while things like hunger, happiness, and tiredness do. This is a generalization, however, and so there are some exceptions. Whether an adjective needs **-tá** with its i-form for animate nouns is indicated in the vocabulary lists in the back of this book.

All of these considerations are only important if the adjective has an i-form, of course, so for those that don't (these end in consonants), these considerations are unimportant. The same goes for using adjectives with inanimate nouns, since none of these need **-tá** anyway.

Example Problems:

Animacy in Sinhala is basically grammatical gender, like the masculine, feminine, and neuter distinctions found in many languages. Fortunately for those studying Sinhala, it is a natural form of gender, meaning that you don't have to memorize the animacy of a noun; you can determine it using the meaning of the noun and the definition given above.

1-8: Would the following English nouns be classified as animate or inanimate in Sinhala?

Rock

Dog

Tree

Crowd

Arm

God

Trick questions:

Coral

Planet

Translate the following sentences into Sinhala:

9. I'm hungry.

10. That man is thirsty.(the word for thirsty is **thibáhá**).

11. She's tired (the word for tired is **mānsi**, the most common word for "she" is **eyā**).

12. I'm ugly(the word for ugly is **kathá**).

13. She's old (a word for old is **vayásá**).

14. The tree is old (the appropriate word for old here is **paráṇá**, the word for "tree is **gaha**).

15. The room is warm. (the word for room is **kāmáráyá/ kāmárē**, pl. **kāmárá**).

16. I'm feeling warm.

Answers:

Inanimate. The Sinhala word is **galá**, pl. **gal**

Animate, the Sinhala word is **ballā**, pl. **ballō**

Inanimate. Do not mistake the animate / inanimate distinction for a living / non-living distinction. The Sinhala word is **gaha**, pl. **gas**

Animate, since a group of people can certainly be considered sentient, if not quite the same as a person thinking alone. The Sinhala word for crowd is **sená^{n}gá**.

Inanimate. A body part is not a sentient being, even though it may be part of one. The Sinhala word is **athá**, pl. **ath**. Since the role of the brain in cognition was presumably not known to the Sinhalese people at the time these conventions developed, even that word (**molē**, formally **moláyá**, pl. **molá**) is inanimate.

Animate, the Sinhala word is **ḋeviyā**, pl. **ḋeviyō**

Muhuḋu galá, inanimate. While modern science recognizes that coral is, in fact, an animal, it should go without saying that the ancient Sinhalese did not know this.

Grahayā, animate. By the same token, the planets were probably believed to be gods of some sort in ancient times, which places them in the animate category.

9. **Matá budáginī**.

10. **Ē minihātá thibáhai**.

11. **Eyātá mānsī**.

12. **Mamá kæthai**.

13. **Eyā vayásai/nāki**. The first word for old here is irregular, its adjective form is **vayasáká**.

14. **Gaha paráṇai.** More commonly, one might say **ē gaha hu^{n}gak kal thibuṇa**

Some adjectives are for animates or inanimates. Here, **paráṇá** is the opposite of **aluth**, "new." In English, "new" and "young" are different words, but they both have one opposite, "old." In Sinhala, though, there are two distinct words for "old" as well. This animate-inanimate gender distinction is very common in Sinhala.

15. **Kāmárá rasnei**.

16. **Matá rasnei**.

Superlatives

Hu^{n}gak is not the only word for "very;" in fact, there are a number of Sinhala words which have roughly the same meaning and usage.

One example is the word **hari**, which could have substituted for **hu^{n}gak** in the previous dialogue. These can be used to modify adjectives:

Hari rasne geḋárá - : The very hot house -

Ē geḋárá hari rásnei. That house is very hot. (using just **geḋárá** sounds unnatural).

The words **bohō** and **godak** can be used in the same way.

The **-má** suffix is the superlative, roughly equivalent to the English "-est".

Lokumá geḋárá- The biggest house-

Words with **-má** cannot be used in the **-i** form. To make simple sentences exactly like the ones we've already seen, we must use **thamai.**

Ē geḋárá thamai lokumá geḋárá. That house is the biggest house.

Thamai literally means indeed.

-má can modify **hari** as well, resulting in a word which means "extremely" or "tremendously":

Ē geḋárá harimá suḋḋai. The house is extremely clean.

Tikak means "little" or "few" and is the opposite of **hu^{n}gak** or **godak.**

Matá tikak mānsi. I'm a little tired.

All of these quantity words can be used independently:

Matá báth godak ḋenná. Give me a lot of rice.

Matá báth tikak ḋenná. Give me a little bit of rice.

Note that Sinhala verbs can inflect in many ways; one such form is the ***imperative***, which is used for giving commands.

The adjectives **vædiyá** or **vadā** mean "more than" and can be used for making comparisons:

Mē geḋárá ē geḋárátá vædiyá/vadā lokui. This house is bigger than that house.

The word **tharam** means "less than," and is used in the same way. **tharammá**, with the **-má** suffix, means "equal to."

Example Problems:

1. This book is much better than that one.
2. This school is quite new.
3. That's the messiest room in the house.
4. Give me your finest beer. (The word for beer is **bīrá**)
5. The house is too expensive for me.
6. That ring isn't good enough.

Answers:

1. **Mē pothá ē pothátá vædiyá/vadā hu^{n}gak ho^{n}ḋai**
2. **Mē iskōlē hu^{n}gak aluth**.
3. **Mēká thamai geḋárá thiyená hædimá kāmárē**
4. **Ho^{n}ḋámá bīrá matá ḋenná**
5. **Matá mē geḋárá ganaṅ vædī**
6. **Ē muḋḋá ho^{n}ḋá madī**.

Negation and Adjective Transformations

Nǣ means "not," and as we have seen, is also used to make the negative form for adjectives:

Sanīpái. (I am) well (in the sense of health).
Sanīpá nǣ. (I am) not well.
Sanīpá næthi kená- The sick person-

The **nǣ** form corresponds to the i-form in usage, and the **næthi** form is used like a plain adjective. Unlike the positive forms, this transformation applies to all adjectives, regardless of what kind of sound they end in.

Many adjectives can be given opposite meanings by the addition of the prefix **a-**.

Ḷamáyātá asanīpái. The child is not well.
Asanīpá kená- The not-well person-

Some adjectives can be converted into nouns by adding **-yā.**

Mōdá. Stupid
Mōdai. (Someone's) stupid.
Mōdáyā. Idiot

This transformation is more common for negative nouns than positive ones; a bad person is a **narákáyā**, but a good person is a **ho^{n}ḋá kenek** (you could say **naráká kenek**). This is just a generalization; the word for heroic is **vīrá**, and the word for hero is **vīráyā**. As this is not a regular transformation, it is not worth memorizing which words change in this way. It is useful to remember, however, if one encounters a new word that resembles an adjective.

Example problems:

1.It's not cold

2. The villain is unhappy (villainous = **ḋuṣhtyá**, happy = **santhōsá**)

3. The sick child still isn't awake. (The word for still asleep is **thāmá niḋi**)

4. I'm not stupid.

5. That crazy fool isn't scared.

6. This isn't easy.

7. He's not older than me.

1.**Sīthálá næ**.

2.**Ḋuṣhtyātá santhōsá næ**. Alternatively, you could say **Ḋuṣhtyātá ḋukai**, or most commonly **Ḋuṣhtyātá ḋuken innē**

3. **Sanipá næthi ḷamáyá thāmá niḋi**. **Asanīpá ḷamáyá** could be used instead.

4. **Mamá mōdá næ**. (if it were "I'm not that stupid," the word **echchárá** would be added after **mamá**)

5. **Ē pissu mōdáyā bayá nǣ**.

6. **Mēká lēsi nǣ**.

7. **Eyā matá vadā vædimahal nǣ**. Of course, the subject of this Sinhala sentence could also be a woman.

Verbal Adjectives and Adverbs

Any present tense verb can be converted in to an adjective by removing the final **vā**. For instance, the colloquial word meaning "intelligent" is formed using a verb meaning "be" or "being:"

Minihātá molē thiyenávā. The man is smart (lit. The man has brains)

Molē thiyená minihātá- The smart man-

The big difference between verbal adjectives and the normal kind is that they do not use i-forms. Instead, they just use the present tense of the verb. These forms are quite regular.

Adverbs, on the other hand, are frequently irregular. We have already seen that the adverbial form of **ho^{n}ḋá** is **ho^{n}ḋin**. It actually has another such form, **ho^{n}ḋátá**. In some cases, the adverb can be formed thusly:

Særá - "stern"

Særeṅ - "sternly"

But for "fast":
Hayyeṅ yaná - fast-moving
Hayyeṅ - quickly

(**Yaná** is the adjectival form of **yanávā**, "go, going").

And for "stupidly":

Mōdá - stupid
Mōdá vidihátá - stupidly

And:

Lassáná - "beautiful"
Lassánátá - "beautifully"

Effectively, there are four different situations in Sinhala with respect to adverbs:

Some adjectives form their adverb counterparts with the addition of **-tá**, and some are made into adjectives by replacing the final vowel with **-en**. The majority of adjectives can use both. A few use **-in** rather than **-en**. **En**/**in** endings behave differently if the adjective ends in **u** or **i**; in that case, the vowel is not replaced. Instead, **-ven** or **-yen**, respectively, is added to the end of the word.

Some adjectives have no distinct adverb form, and must be made into **viḋihátá** compounds to modify verbs (**viḋihá** or **viḋiyá**, pl. **viḋi** is a noun meaning "way" or "manner"). Though this can theoretically be done with any adjective, the result may not make sense.

Some adverbs have no corresponding adjective. These cannot be used directly on a noun; instead, they have to be coupled with the adjectival form of a verb.

Unfortunately, you can't tell what the adjective form will be if you know the adverb. For instance, the adverb **hayyen** looks like it ought to have a counterpart **hayyá**. But the second word is a noun meaning "strength," not "fast".

Adverbs are commonly used when describing the recent past:

Mamá badáginnen hitiyā. I was hungry. (**badáginnen** is the spoken form of the regular **-en** form **badáginiyen**. The latter is more "proper" but not used when speaking)

Hitiyā is the past tense form of **innávā**, a verb meaning "be," or in some contexts, "be present". It is used for animates, the inanimate counterpart is **thiyenávā**, past tense **thibuṇā**.

When referring to things in the more distant past, the word **issárá**, "earlier" is used, along with the i-form:

Eyā issárá mahathai. He used to be fat

Matá badágini vei. I will be hungry.

Vei is the future form of **venávā**, which means "become." Note that the probable form of the verb is used with the **matá** here, and that the adverbial form is not used.

When referring to things at specific point in time, a sentence will begin with a word indicating the time, such as **aḋá**, "today", **īyē**, "yesterday", **hetá**, "tomorrow", or **thavá**, "still", "yet."

Examples:

1. I was sleepy.
2. The book used to be expensive.
3. The sunset will be beautiful soon. (the word for sunset, literally setting sun, is **irá bahiná eká**)
4. The rice was tasty
5. That house was cleaner yesterday.

1. **Mamá niḋimathe(ṅ) hitiyā**. **Niḋimathá**'s adverb form may be optionally pronounced without a final **n**.
2. **Ē pothá issárá hari ganaṅ**
3. **Irá bahiná eká thavá tikakin lassáná vei**.

4. **Bath rahatá thibuṇā**. This sentence refers to an event in the recent past, so the inanimate counterpart of **hitiyā**, **thibuṇā** must be used.

5. **Īyē mē geḋárá mītá vædiyá / vadā suḋḋátá thibuṇā**

Example Problems:

1. She is eating quickly.
2. That was beautifully done.
3. I did poorly.
4. He talks quite strangely. (the word for "talk" is **kath^{h}ā karánávā**)
5. I glared at them angrily. (At them = **ē gollō ḋihá**)

1. **Eyā ikmánátá kanávā.** Hayyen could be used, but **ikmánátá** is more natural, **ikmánin** is a little formal
2. **Ēká hari lasánátá kerā/keruvā/káḷā**
3. **Mamá narákátá keruvā.**
4. **Eyā amuthu viḋihátá kath^{h}ā karánávā**
5. **Mamá ē gollō ḋihá** (in that direction) **tharáheṅ bæluvā**.

Summary and Supplementary Information

Adjectives can take the following forms:

	Example	Meaning
Plain	**Ho^{n}ḋá**	Good-
i-form	**Ho^{n}ḋai**	(Something) is good.
Negative	**Ho^{n}ḋá næthi**	Not good-
Negative i-form	**Ho^{n}ḋá nǣ**	(Something) is not good.

	Example	Meaning
Adverbial	**Ho^{n}ḋin/Ho^{n}ḋátá**	Well

Sinhala adjectives appear before the nouns they modify. Any adjective can be made negative in this form by adding **næthi** after it.

Adjectives at the end of sentences are declarations. Adjectives that end in vowels receive a final **-i** when used this way; other adjectives are unchanged. The negative version of this form is made by removing the **-i** if it was added, and then following the word with **nǣ**.

Adverbs are generally formed by adding **-en** or **-tá** to an adjective. Certain adjectives may add **-in** instead of **-en**, and others may lack one or both forms. These irregularities must be memorized.

Verbs:

1st person future	**Mama kárannam**	I'll do it.
1st person plural future	**Api kárámu**	Let's do it.
2nd person future (command)	**Oyā karanná**	You will do it.
2nd person future (prediction)	**Oyā kárai**	You'll (probably) do it.
3rd person future	**Eyā Karai**	He/she will (probably) do it.

The future tense is the only place where Sinhala verbs care about person and number. Even then, the separation is not absolute. You would say **matá thibáha vei**, and **vennam** would not be interchangeable with **vei** there.

Compare the above table to that of the present tense:

1st/2nd/3rd person non-past	**Mamá/Api/Oyā/ Ogollō/Eyā/Egollō káránávā**	I/we/you/you all/he/ she/they do it.

Nouns:

Sinhala nouns are divided into two classes: animate and inanimate. Animals, humans, spirits, and in general, sentient beings are animate. Everything else is considered inanimate.

	Animate	Meaning	Inanimate	Meaning
Nominative	**Ḷamáyā**	The child	**thē eká**	The tea
Dative	**Ḷamáyātá**	To/for the child	**thē ekátá**	To/for the tea

Nouns have various case forms. The two we have seen so far are identical, but this, as it turns out, is a coincidence.

For nouns, the plural is always provided if it exists; this is because memorizing them is the simplest way to go.

	Present	Past
Be, being (animate)	**Innávā**	**Hitiyā**
Be, being (inanimate)	**Thiyenávā**	**Thibuṇā**
Come, coming	**Enávā**	**Āvā**
Go, going	**Yanávā**	**Giyā**

	Present	Past
Take, taking	Gannávā	Gaththā
Give, giving	Ḋenávā	Ḋunnā
Become, becoming	**venávā**	vuṇā

What is the relationship between the present tense and the past? Well, for ***regular*** verbs, there is a way to derive the past tense form from the present, but of the the above verbs, only **venávā** forms the past tense regularly. For the other ***irregular*** verbs, the past forms just have to be memorized. Incidentally, the verbs listed above are some of the most common and important Sinhala verbs.

1-14: Translate the following sentences into Sinhala.

1. I'm not afraid.
2. He was less afraid than me.
3. That table is clean. (the word for table is **mēsē**)
4. That man is a little odd.
5. The tree isn't very old.
6. That child is the dumbest.
7. I'm very happy.
8. I'm extremely angry.
9. Give me warm tea.
10. The fresh/new rice is much more tasty than the old rice. (The dative form of **bath** is **bathválátá**)
11. That dirty dog is running fast. (The word for "dirty" here is **killitu**)

12. Quickly give me food. (A word for "quickly" is **tuk gallá**)

13. That woman was thin. (The word for "woman" is **gǣni**; "thin" is **kettu**)

14. That child quietly went to sleep. (A word for "quietly" is **saḋḋáyak næthuvá**)

15. I'm lonely. (the word for lonely is **pāḷu**)

15-28: Translate the following sentences into English:

16. **Matá hári rásnei.**

17. **Hædi kamará suḋḋá káránná.**

18. **Ē minissū harimá kæthai.**

19.**Matá badágini nǣ.**

20. **Godak ḷamai narákai.**

21. **Aluth geḋárak matá ḋenná.**

22. **Matá tikak thibáhai.**

23. **Oyāgē geḋárá hu^{n}gak lassánai.**

24.**Mē ḷamáyātá mahansi, ē vagemá niḋimathai**.

25. **Ará hayyeṅ aviḋiná miniha tharáheṅ wage**.

26. **Mama værádī.**

27. **Ēká kilitui.**

28. **Matá budagini næththi nisā kævē nǣ**.

29. **Ará kotá minihā hiyen æviḋinávā**.

30. **Ēká ḋigá maḋī**

Dialogue 2: Going out to eat

A group of friends deciding to go to a restaurant and trying to decide which one to go to. In Sri Lanka restaurants are called "hotels".

A: **Api īyē giyá hōtálētá yamuḋá**? Shall we go to the hotel that we went to yesterday?

B: **Etháná samáhará kǣmá raha vuṇātá vædiyá kǣmá jāthi thibuṇē nǣ**. Although the food was tasty at that place, they didn't have a lot of variety.

C: **Hæbæi ēká hu^{n}gak la^{n}gai. Apitá ikmánátá gihiṅ enná puḷuvan**. However it is very close. We can make the trip (literally, go and come) relatively quickly.

A: **Ou la^{n}gámá thiyená ho^{n}ḋámá hōtálē ēká thamai**. Yes, the best nearby hotel is that one.

B: **Etháná hari saḋḋai. Apitá ho^{n}ḋátá kath^{h}ā kárannávath bæri vei**. It's very noisy there. We also won't be able to talk easily.

C: **Ehenaṅ giyá sumāne giyá hōtálētá yamuḋá**? **Etháná kǣmath hari rahai**. Then shall we go to the hotel we went to last week? The food there is also very tasty.

B: **tikak ḋurai thamai, hæbæi ho^{n}ḋá katá ḋaná kǣmath thiyenávā, ne**? **Ehenaṅ api yamuḋá ē hōtálētá**. It's a little far, but it has good spicy food. Then shall we go to that hotel.

Others: **Hā, yamu**. Yes, let's go.

Using the above dialogue as a guide, translate the following sentences into Sinhala:

31. It's very far.
32. The food there isn't tasty.
33. The food there is very tasty, but it's very far away.

3
NON-PAST VERBS

3.1 Dialogue 3: Asking for Directions

In the following dialogue, A is in an unfamiliar neighborhood, looking for a friend's house, and asks a stranger, B, for directions.

A: **Podi uḋavvak káranná puḷuvanḋá?** Could you do me a small favor?

This is a standard expression when soliciting help from a stranger.

B: **Monāḋá ōne?** What (do you) need?

Another response might be **hā**, "yes", or **mokaḋḋá uḋavvá,** "what (sort of) favor?"

A: **Mē geḋárátá yaná hæti ḋannávāḋá?** Do you know how to go to this house?

After asking this, A could show B a piece of paper with the address. Alternatively **mē** address **eká**, "this address", or **mē thaná**, "this place," could be used instead of **mē geḋárátá**. Instead of **-yaná hæti ḋannávāḋá,** one could also say **-yaná pārá kiyanná puḷuvanḋá**, "can you say which road go (on)-"

B: **Thavá poddak isseráhatá ævidálā handiyeṅ vamátá hærenná.** After walking a little further ahead, turn left at the intersection (In Sri Lankan English, the term "junction" is much more common than the word "intersection").

If A was not going by foot, B might use **gihillā**, "having gone," instead of **aviḋálā**, "having walked," in this context "after walking."

A: **Bohomá isthūthi.** Thank you very much.

The initial **i** is colloquial; the formal expression would be **bohomá sthūthi**. In an urban area, "Thank you" might be used instead. There is no equivalent to the phrase "you're welcome", in this scenario, B might just smile in response.

We have already seen the "dictionary form" of verbs, which generally ends in **-návā**. Only one verb in the dialogue above (**ḋannávā**, "know") is actually in this form, however. **Gihillā** and **ævidálā** are forms that will be covered in the next chapter. **Puḷuvan**, "can" and **ōne**, "want/need," are ***auxiliaries***, the one type of verb that does not end in **návā** in the dictionary form. **Yanávā**, "go," is in its adjectival form, while **kiyánávā**, "say", and **hærenávā**, "turn," are found in their ***infinitive*** forms: **kiyanná** and **hærenná**.

3.2 The Plain Form and the Infinitive

Sinhala verbs are highly inflected, with a number of transformations which can change the meaning of the word. Unlike most other Indo-European languages, though, there is generally no subject-verb agreement; whereas English has "I do" versus "he does," Sinhala has one word for both cases. Let's look at the word **káránávā**.

Káránávā. "do, doing"

This is the form cited in dictionaries, and probably the most commonly used one. It can be used in several ways:

Mamá vædá káránávā. (I'm) doing work/ I'm working.
Api aḋá ēká káránávā. We're going to do it today.
Mamá káránávā. I do it.

In the first sentence, the action is occurring at that moment. In the second, it's happening in the future. In the third, it is taking place regularly, though not necessarily at the moment. The plain form is ambiguous with respect to time, although it is more often used to refer to the present.

The ***root*** of the verb is the part formed by subtracting **-návā** from the present tense form. The root can be used to build all of the present and future tense verb forms. The ***stem vowel*** is part of the root. It is the the last vowel before **-návā**. It is used for constructing past tense forms.

Now, the root for **káránávā** is **kárá**. It can be used to make the infinitive like so:

Káranná. "to do"

This form is identical to the imperative, discussed earlier. But it has another, non-imperative usage. Compare:

Ēká káranná. "Do it."
Ēká káranná ōnē. "(I) want to do it."

Note that the stem vowel shifted to **a**. This *only* happens when the stem vowel is **á**, the other vowels stay unchanged.

The command form may be accompanied by a short utterance, **ko**:

Inná ko: Stay there, please.

This form is more commonly used by women.

In the first example, **káranná** is followed by a ***modal,*** a special kind of verb which will be discussed later. Without an modal, this verb form is used to give commands in a relatively polite way. In informal speech, the variant form **kárándá** may be used. There are other forms derived from the infinitive. One is the ***emphatic***:

Kárannē. "do, doing"

This form is used when the speaker wants to add emphasis to their statement, and also when asking questions:

Ēká ehemá kárannē æi? "Why are you doing it that way?"

Examples:
1.Go to school!
2. I really want to eat.
3. He needs some water.
4. I eat meat.

5. That dog is barking loudly. (The word for "barking" is **buránávā**)

6. Take your medicine.

Answers:

1. Iskōlētá yanná.

2. Matá kanná ōnē. Ōnē can refer to both wants and needs. This may seem confusing, but in practice, the meaning is clear in context. Still, there are words that will allow you to explicitly distinguish between the two. Also note the case of the subject. The subject of **ōnē** is generally in the dative case, with one major exception. The earlier example of **ēká kárannē ōnē**, is *not* an example of such an exception; **ēká** is the object, and so is not dative.

3. Eyātá vathurá ōnē.

4. Mamá mas kanávā.

5. **Ará ballā hiyen buránávā.** Oddly, **saḋḋen** can't be used here.

6. **Beheth ganná**.

3.2 Talking About the Future

The dictionary form of the vast majority of Sinhala verbs, although generally associated with the present, can also be used in a way that corresponds to the future tense.

Ou, mamá party **ekátá yanávā.** Yes, I'm going to the party.

There are also ways to explicitly talk about future events. We have seen a future form of **enávā** also, in an idiomatic expression. More generally, one can say:

Mamá ennaṅ/ennam. I will come.

This first person future form is made by adding an **-m** (usually pronounced as **ṅ**) to the end of the infinitive of a verb. It is also called the ***promising*** form. The implication with this form is that you are talking about an action you intend to perform at a later time. For example:

Kárannam. "(subject) promises to do"

Oyā vædá kárákávāḋá? Are you working?
Ou mamá kárannam. Yes, I am going to work.

As before, **káránávā** is just as suitable as **kárannam** in the second sentence.

This form can only be used with first person pronouns like **mamá** "I" and **api** "we;" perhaps because of the limited value of promises made on behalf of others.

In English, verbs generally change based on the subject. This is called subject-verb agreement. For the most part, it does not occur in spoken Sinhala:

Mamá enávā. I come.

Oyā enávā. You come

Eyā enávā. He or she comes.

The sole exception is the future tense, where English does not do this:

Mamá ennaṅ / ennam. I will come (a promise).

Oyā enná / Oyā ei. You will come (a command / a prediction).

Eyā ei. He will come (a prediction).

The root is not used by itself. To make the non-first person future form, and **-i** is added to the root. This form carries with it a certain level of uncertainty, although this typically varies with context. For instance:

Oyā vædē káraiḋá kiyálā matá sækai. I'm suspicious whether you'll do the work.

Using **káránávāḋá** instead of **káraiḋá** would not be appropriate here, due to the probabilistic connotations of the former. It would be better suited for a sentence like this:

The two forms for "I will come" have the same meaning. The second form is technically more "correct," but in practice, the first form is much more common, though not universal.

A form used exclusively with api is the -mu form:

Kárámu. "let's do"

This form is used when talking to a group that you belong to:

Hariyátá kárámu. Let's do (it) right

All but 3 non-past verb forms in Sinhala are regular, meaning that all the forms can be derived from the dictionary form using a straightforward set of rules. The main problem lies in memorizing the rules to make each form.

Examples:

Translate the following into Sinhala.

1. I will buy food. ("buy" here is **kadeṅ arágannaṅ**)

2. Will he go to school?

3. I'll do this well. (The word for "this" here is **mēká**)

4. Let's go now.

Answers

1. **Mamá kæmá kadeṅ arágannaṅ**. **Arágańávā** means "take" or "taking;" specifying that it is "from the store" (**kadeṅ**) implies that the object was purchased, rather than gifted or stolen.

2. **Eyā iskōlētá yaidá**?

3. **Mamá mēká hondátá kárannam.** Why do we use **mēká** here instead of **mē**? **Mēká** literally means "this (inanimate) thing," in this context, probably some kind of job. **Mē** (and its counterparts like **ē**, "that") has to be accompanied by some kind of noun. **Mē vædak** could have substituted for **mēká** in the above sentence, for instance.

4. **Api dæṅ yamu**

3.3 Derivatives of the Plain Form

There are two forms that come from the plain present tense. The most common is perhaps the ***quotative***:

Kárānávalu. " (the speaker) was told (the subject) is doing"

This form is used when talking about hearsay, or just information that you aren't completely sure of:

Ēká narákátá kárānávalu. "(I) was told (he) is doing it poorly."

The **-lu** ending can be used on i-form adjectives as well, in which case it deletes any added i.

Kárānávanam. "if/when [subject] does" (conditional future)

This form is used to state some kind of future condition, followed by the consequences of that condition:

Oyā ho^{n}ḋátá káranávanam, mamá santhōsá venávā. "If you do well, I'll be happy." Alternatively, **santhōsai** could be used (in which case **matá** would replace **mamá**). In both cases, the use of **káranávanam** indicates that the sentence is referring to a possible future state of events.

Adding **-th** to the end of any word in Sinhala is equivalent of using the word "also":

Eyā ēká káránávath ekká thavá vædak káránávā. He's doing that (job) as well as some other work.

Eyāth ēká káránávā. He too is doing that.
Eyā ēkáth káránávā. He's also doing that.

The word for "with" is **ekká**, a postposition. It is frequently used with this form:

Mamá eya(th) ekká āvā. I came with him. In this example, **-th** is optional.

The ***adjectival*** form, described in the last chapter, is also derived from the plain form. This is made by simply removing the final **-vā**.

Examples:

1. **Eyā ehe giyālu**. I was told he went there.
2. **Meyā kaḷuvárātá bayálu**. I was told he was afraid of the dark.
3. **Ē vædá káranávanam ho^{n}ḋai**. If you do that work, it'll be good.
4. **Mamá ēká kárānávath ekkámá mēká peráluṇā**. As I was doing that, this thing fell. **Ekkámá** is **ekká + má**; it is used here to show that the thing fell at that very moment.

3.4 Forms from the Root

There are several forms which come from the root. The most prominent of these are the third person future, and the first person plural future, e.g. **kárai** and **kárámu**. There are a few other forms derived from the root that see some use.

In addition to the infinitive, there are other, ruder, imperative forms. Adding **-pan** to the root results in an informal command:

U^{m}ba ēka kárápan machaṅ Hey buddy, do this

This is not to be used in a formal situations, like school or work. An even ruder form is produced by adding **-piyā** to the root.

Kárápiyā - rude, used for talking down.

But the most common root form is probably the continuous form, which is made by doubling the root. For **káránávā** this would be **kárákárá**. It indicates that the action is ongoing, at least within the scope of the sentence. It is often used with **innákotá**, "while."

For instance:

Mamá vaththē vædá kárákárá innákotá vahinná pataṅ gaththā. While I was working in the garden (it) began to rain.

Examples

1. **Kaka innákotá eyā āvā.**
2. **Ikmánatá vædē kárápaṅ.**
3. **Kath^{h}ā kárákárá innē næthuvá vædē ikmánin kárápiyá.**
4. **Vathurá bibi kǣmá kanná epā.**

Answers:

1. While (I) was eating, he arrived. This is a doubling of the root of **kanávā**. Do not confuse with **kākkā**, "crow," or **kakka** "excrement." Generally, even irregular verbs have regular present tense forms. **Bonávā** is an exception; its continuous form is **bibi**.
2. Finish the work quickly.
3. Without sitting around talking, work quickly.
4. Don't eat while you're drinking.

3.5 Negative forms

We have already seen that the regular negative form is derived from the emphatic form:

Kárannē nǣ. “not doing” (negative)

Ēká kárannē nǣ. "(I'm) not doing that."(negative)

Like in English, this can be used in the sense of “I am not currently doing that,” or “I am not going to do that.”

An informal version of this form is **kárannǣ.**

Although **nǣ** is used to make the negative form of the verb, but a different word is used to make a negative command:

Kægahanná epā! don't yell!

This form uses the infinitive, rather than the emphatic form.The conditional form has a unique negative form also:

Kiyuvē næththaṅ- if (subject) didn't say-

The past tense of the verb is used. This form is used for past, present, and future conditional negatives.

All three of these can be paired with normal verbs and most modal verbs. We have already seen the present form, the first person future, non-first person future, and imperative (command) form. Another relevant form is the ***negative***:

1. I'm not coming.

2. Don't go there.

3. She doesn't live here.

4. I can't do that.

1. **Mamá ennē nǣ**.

2. **Ehe yanná epā.**

3. **Eyā mehe innē nǣ.**

4. **Matá ēká káranná bǣ.**

3.6 Modals

Modals are words which set the tone, or mode, of a sentence. English has a number of such verbs. Compare the following sentences:

"I do that."
"I like to do that"
"I want to do that."
"I need to do that."
"I can do that"
"I might do that"

The common theme above is that the original verb, "do," is converted to its infinitive form. Sinhala modals work the same way, Sinhala has three representative modals that cover all of these meanings. These are **kæmáthī**, **puḷuvan**, and **ōne**.

Mamá ēká káránávā. "I do that."

Mamá ēkátá káranná kæmáthī. "I like to do that"

Matá ēká káranná ōne. "I want/need to do that."

Mamá ēká káranná ōne. "I ought to do that."

Matá ēká káranná puḷuvan. "I can do that."

Mamá ēká káranná puḷuvan. "I might do that."

Notice that the **tá** ending is used differently with each modal. Some other, semi-overlapping modals are:

Karanná æthi. "might do"

Karanná æhækī. "be able to do"

Karanná avashyai. "required to do"

Karanná uvámánai. "required to do" (this word is less formal than **avashyai**)

These, unlike all other verbs, do not end in **-návā**. Rather than the root, as with the previous examples, the whole modal verb is inflected to make the previous constructions.

Kæmáthī behaves typically:

kæmáthī. "like"

kæmáthi nǣ. "not like"

kæmáthilu. "supposedly likes"

kæmáthinam. "if [subject] likes"

kæmáthi vei. "will like"

The shortening of **ī** to **i** occurs for all **i** final modals except **æthi**.

Modal verbs lack many of the forms which other verbs can assume. The forms shown above (except for those of **puḷuvan**) are all regular, and hence, no new verbs will be introduced with such lists.

Avashyai can be used to unambiguously express need, and **kæmáthī**, **vædiyá kæmáthī** (prefer), or **kæmáthīmá** can explicitly express degrees of desire. Note that use of **ōne** is more common and natural.

The adjectival forms are:

Avashyá

Uvámánā

Ōná

Æhæki

Kæmáthi

Puḷuvan

Æthi, when used as an adjective, means "enough."

Puḷuvan has an irregular negative form:

Puḷuvan: "can"
Bǣ. "cannot"
Bærilu. " supposedly cannot"
Bærinam. " if [subject] cannot"
Bæri vei. "possibly cannot"

Matá kǣ gahanná bǣ. I can't yell.

Puḷuvan can be used to mean "can" both in the sense of "being able to" and "being allowed to." Moreover, it can mean "might" when used with a first-person subject.

Ōne has an optional irregular pronunciation: **Ōnnǣ.** This is probably because its last syllable begins with [n], allowing it to undergo the same sandhi process as the regular verbs.

Regular auxiliaries behave like so:

Epā by itself is effectively negative modal, an alternate version of **ōne nǣ**.

Ōne nǣ. (I) don't want/need (it).
Epā. I don't want it
Ōne nælu. (Someone) supposedly doesn't want (it).
Ōne næththaṅ "if [subject] doesn't/will not/did not want/need (it)."

These negative forms can be used with plain verbs as well.

Hæ^{n}gennē nǣ. (I'm) not hiding.

Hæ^{n}genná epā. Don't hide.

Hæ^{n}gennē nælu. (Someone's) supposedly not hiding.

Hæ^{n}guṇē næththaṅ "if [subject] won't hide / will not hide / have not hidden"

The future forms of modal verbs are made as compounds with **vei**, the future form of **venavā**.

1. I can't eat this.
2. I like tea.
3. I'm not allowed to drink.
4. You may not come
5. She should work more.
6. He can help.
7. He should study more.

Answers:

1. **Matá mēká kanná bǣ**.
2. **Mamá thēválátá kæmáthi**.
3. **Matá bonná aithiyak nǣ / thahanam**. lit. I don't have the right. **bǣ** - i would not like\ i. = right, **thahanam** - not legal. **Nǣ matá ēká agunai. Gunai** - good for you. **Agunai** can range from unhealthy to an allergen. **Visai** - poisonous
4. **Oyā enná epā**.

5. **Eyā thavá vædá káranná ōne.**

6. **Eyātá uḋau káranná puḷuvan. Eyātá puḷuvan uḋau káranná. Puḷuvan** and **bǣ** can be used in a verb-second order.

7. **Eyā thavá padaṅ káranná ōne.**

Summary and Supplementary Information:

The main topic of this chapter is the myriad of forms that a verb in the base form can take. This list is not complete, but includes most of the standard forms that are associated with the present and future tenses. Although there are a lot of them, the inflections shown above are quite regular. Here is a list for the verb **ḋenávā.**

ḋenávā. "give, giving
ḋenná. "to give"
ḋennē. "[emphatic] give"
ḋennē næ: "not give"
ḋenávalu. "said to give"
ḋennam. "[subject] promises to give"
ḋenávanam. "when [subject] gives"
ḋei. "will give"
ḋemu. "let's give"
ḋenávath. "also give"

As you can see, this verb transforms exactly like the first. The "dictionary form," in this case, **ḋenávā**, consists of the ***root*** and the **-návā** ending. The root is part that actually inflects; it is used to make the various forms.

The shift between **a** and **á** in various forms is governed by a deeper principle. Generally, if the syllable is closed, that is if it ends in a consonant (as before a double consonant or at the end of a consonant final word) the sound will be **a**. If the syllable becomes open, it will regularly change to **á**, and vice-versa. There are various exceptions, discussed in the chapter on the Sinhalese alphabet, but the above rule is sufficient for dealing with the various inflections of verbs and nouns you will be dealing with.

In written Sinhala these two sounds are both regarded as a short "a" sound, and are not differentiated in the Sinhala script.

Although most Sinhala verbs are unconcerned with concepts like person and number, they have a massive number of forms, which need to be memorized. For regular verbs, however, only the dictionary form, ending in **-návā**, has to be learned.

Only a few verbs are irregular in these forms: **bonávā** has a continuative form of **bibi**, **innávā** has a future form of **i^{n}ḋī**, **gēnávā** has a future form of **genei**, and **ḋannávā** has no future form, with the compound word **ḋæná gannávā**'s future form, **ḋænágani** being used instead.

Exercises

Translate the following into Sinhala:

1. I'll drink it quickly.
2. Go to the store.
3. I want to go
4. Let's eat now.
5. I'll cook. (the word for "cook" is **uyánává**)
6. I want to drink a little water. ("A little water" is **vathurá tikak**)
7. Don't yell.
8. He's leaving soon/in a little bit. ("In a little bit" is **thavá tikákin**; this is the most natural way to say "soon" in this context").
9. (I was told) he was beaten.
10. Tomorrow she'll go to get a haircut. ("get a hair cut" is **kondē kapā gannávā**).
11. He's going to school soon.
12. I don't want to do that.
13. I might come later.
14. It might be true. (The word for "true" is **æththá**).

Translate the following into English:

15. **Matá ḋænáganná læbuṇē, eyā monávath biyuvē næ kiyálā.**
16. **Ē gollaṅ Gallátá yanávālu.**
17. **Eyāge aluth** computer **ekátá eyā kæmáthī.**
18. **Mamá ēká nemei kiyannē.**
19. **Oyātá káranná bærinaṅ, matá káranná vei.**
20. **Matá ē pothá ōne næ.**
21. **Matá ē pothá kiyávanná ōne næ.**
22. **Matá ḋæṅ kanná ōne.**

23. **Oyā i^{n}ḋá ganná kæmáthīḋá? I^{n}ḋá gannávā** means "sit down;" this is the irregular **ganná** form of **innávā**.

24. **Mamá** paper **eká liyanná yanávā**. There is a Sinhala word for "essay" as well, see chapter 12.

25. **Eyātá ēká thērei**. The word for "understand" is **thērenávā**.

26. **Hæ^{n}gená eká navaththanná. Navaththannā** means "stop."

27. **Ḋuvaná eká navaththanná epā**.

28. **Matá poth vagáyak ganná avashyai**.

29. **Matá ēká káranná æhæki**.

30. **Eyā thavá pādaṅ káranná ōne**.

31. **Eyā (kǣmá) kanná ōne**.

32. **Eyātá (kǣmá) kanná ōne**.

33. **Matá ēká ganná ōne nǣ**.

34. **Matá ēká ganná uvámána nǣ**.

35. **Matá pīnaná puḷuvan vei**.

37. **Mamá ævidinná yanávā**.

38. **Mamá ē gæná** internet **ekē kiyávánávā**. (**ē gæná**= about it/that," **ekē** here means "on the").

39. **Eyā bonnē vathurá vithárai. Vithárai** is a postposition meaning "only."

40. **Oyā ikmánátá ivárá káranná ōne. Ivárá káranná** means "to finish." Alternatively: **Oyā ikmánátá ivárá káranná uvámánai**.

41. **Vathurá navaththánávānam apitá yanná puḷuvan**.

42. **Eyā etháná i^{n}ḋi**.

Dialogue 4: Going to the beach

A: **Ḷamai læsthiḋá? Api thavá miniththu ḋahayákin yanná ōne**. Children, are you ready? We need to leave in about ten minutes.

(one of the boys starts shouting)

B: **Ammā**, **(apitá) væli sellaṅ kárāná ḋēval ganná/ gandá ōnē**. Mother, (we) need to take the things for playing in the sand. Here, **apitá** indicates that the playthings are for the speaker.

A: **Oyá kāmárē thiyennē arágená enná**. They're in that room. You can bring it yourself.

The child comes with the things

B: **Mamá gaththā**. I've got it.

A: **Ekak maḋi, oyá ḋennā sellam káranná gihāmá randu vei. Mallitath ekak arraṅ enná**. One is not enough. You two will start fighting when you start to play. Bring one for (your) the little brother also.

B: **Kō akkálā**? Where are the sisters?

C: **Apō hæmáḋāmá parakku venávā**. Oh, they're late as always (lit. everyday).

B: **vællātá yanávānaṅ ikmánátá enná. Api ḋæṅ yanávā**. If you're going to the beach, come soon. We're going right now.

Two sisters come running.

D: **Enávā, enávā**. (we're) coming, coming.

Using the above dialect as a guide, translate following sentences into Sinhala:

43. I need to bring the things (I) need for work.
44. We're eating right now.
45. (We're) going, (we're) going.
46. If you're coming to the restaurant, don't be late.

4
PAST TENSE VERBS

Dialogue 5: Preparing for Vesak

When celebrating Vesak, people light lanterns and hang them up.

A: **Malli gihillā Vesak** bucket **tiká gēnná**. Little brother, go and bring the Vesak lanterns.

Tika here is not an adjective, it is used to indicate a plural (as in "a few" or "a couple of").

Now here's a question: where's the word for "and" in the Sinhala sentence above?

B: **Maṅ ḋannē næ kohedá thiyennē kiyálā. Oyā gihillā gēnná**. I don't know where they are. You go and bring them.

Kiyálā is a word that means something like "having said (that)." It can be used to quote people precisely, but here it is just tacked on to the end of B's statement to add to the emphasis of the emphatic form. The second sentence again lacks the word for "and." Given that **oyā** means "you" and **gēnná** is the command form of **gēnávā**, "bring," we can guess that "and" must be bundled into **gihillā** somehow.

A: **Mamá ne paththu kárannē**. **Oyā gihillā ammāgen ahanná, ammā hoyálā ḋei**. I'm the one who's going to light them. You go and ask mother, she will find and give them to you.

Both **gihillā** and **hoyálā** are again used in such a way that "and" is bundled with their main meaning. Idiomatically, **hoyálā ḋenávā** means "find" in general, including cases where a person might identify the location of the object, but not actually retrieve it.

B runs, shouting: **Ammā ammā, vesak** "bucket" **matá hoyálā ḋenná kō**? Mother, mother, show me where the Vesak lanterns are kept.

C: **Mamá mē vædak. Akkātá gihillā hoyā ganná kiyanná**. I'm busy, tell your sister to go and find them.

B: **Ammā kiyuvā, akkālá hoyā ganná kiyálā**. Mother said for you to go and find them.

They go and get the buckets. They also need candles.

A: **Itipanḋám araṅ enná**. Go and bring candles. Lit. Get some candles and come.

B: **Mamá ginipettiyákuth genāvá**. I brought a box of matches also.

A: **Hā, mamá ḋæṅ eká eká paththu kárálā ḋennaṅ, oyā gihillā ellanná. Ellanná** means "to hang." I'll light them one by one and give them to you, you go and hang them.

B: **Hā hā mamá ḋannávā, paththu kárálā ḋenná ko**. Ok, ok, I know, light them and give them to me.

Notice that family members frequently address each other with their family titles. This very common in Sinhala.

The **-lā** form that appears throughout this dialogue is very common and useful. Here it is only used in two ways; the "and-adding" way and idiomatically with **kiyálā**. But this form, the ***perfect tense***, appears in all kinds of contexts.

4.2 The Perfect Tense

What, precisely, is the meaning of the perfect tense of a verb? Simply put, the perfect form indicates that the action described by the verb is completed ("perfectly" done) prior to the topic of the sentence. When coupled with future tense verbs, as in the previous dialogue, it indicates that the perfect tense verb will be done before the future tense one. For instance, in the above dialogue:

Mamá ḋæṅ eká eká paththu kárálā ḋennaṅ

This line tells us that, one by one, the candles will be lit, and then the speaker will give the buckets containing them to the listener. *Both* events take place in the future, but the one described by the perfect tense verb happens first.

In English, the future perfect of verbs is different in form than the present or past perfect, for example, the the corresponding forms of the verb "to do" are "will have done," "have done" and "had done." In Sinhala, however, all of these are expressed using the same perfect form, coupled with a verb in the appropriate tense.

Ēká hu^{n}gak kal mehe thibilā thiyenávā. It has been here for a long time.

When the perfect tense is coupled with a future verb, it describes an action that takes place in the future, but before the future tense verb. By contrast, the perfect tense coupled with a present tense verb refers to an action that was completed in the past, before the present. With a past tense verb, the perfect also refers to an action in the past, further back than that of the past tense verb.

The perfect tense can also be used by itself. There is not necessarily a difference between this usage and the plain past tense; i.e. **mamá kǣmá kālā**, "I have eaten" and **mamá kǣmá kǣvā**, "I ate" mean approximately the same thing. However, the latter implies that you ate some time ago whereas the former suggests you just ate. If you were talking about a substantial amount of time in the past, i.e. more than a few hours, you would have to use **kǣvā**. In Sinhala, it is more common to use the past tense, but the perfect is also understandable. However, sometimes the meanings may be more divergent. **Eyātá nindá giyā** means that the person being referred to went to sleep at some time in the past. But **eyātá nindá gihillā** implies that the person went to sleep and is still asleep. Because of usages like this, this form is often called the past participle.

The perfect tense is formed according to the following rules: The root of the verb is added to **-lā**. If the root ends in **-i** or **-a**, the corresponding vowel in the perfect is **á** (Except, of course, after **h**, since **á** is not found after **h** in Sinhala words). For i-stems an additional change occurs: any **a** becomes **æ**. For example **maninávā**, "measure" becomes **mænálā**, **illánávā**, "ask" becomes **illálā**). The **-e** in **e** roots changes to **i** in the perfect (for example **hīrenávā**, "to be scratched" becomes **hīrilā**).

Compared to the process for forming the past tense of verbs, which takes up most of this chapter, the perfect is formed very simply. Nonetheless, there are a few irregular perfect forms:

Present	Perfect
Venávā	Velā
Yanávā	Gihillā
Ḋenávā	Ḋīlā
Innávā	I^{n}ḋálā
thiyenávā	Thibilā
Bonávā	Bīlā
Gannávā	Arágená
Gēnávā	Genællā
Enávā	Ævillā
Ḋannávā	-
Pēnávā	Penilā
Gilinávā	Gillā
Manináwa	Manálā
Væráḋinávā	væráḋilā

The perfect can be used to form an adjective, but the precise form varies based on the vowel before **návā**. For verbs with present forms ending in **-a/ánávā** and **-inávā**, the **-lā** of the past participle is replaced by **-pu**.

Innávā. be (animate)
I^{n}ḋálā. been
I^{n}ḋápu. having been

For verbs with **-enávā**, the **-lā** of the past participle is replaced by **-chcha**:

Thiyenávā. Be (inanimate)
Thibilā. Been
Thibichcha. Having been (adj)

These replacements are quite regular, but there are some common exceptions, such as the participles ending in -**llā (gihillā - giyápu, ævillā - āpu, genællā - genāpu,)**. Also note the e-stem verb **ḋenávā**:

ḋenávā. Give
ḋīlā -. Having given
ḋīpu. Having given (adj)

Examples:

1. What is the difference between the following three sentences?

Mal pipilā pará venávā.
Mal pipilā pará vuṇā.
Mal pipilā pará vei.

2. What does **Surathtá gihillā ḋenná** mean?

1. Each sentence is talking about flowers blooming and subsequently wilting. In the first, the flowers have bloomed, and are starting to wilt. In the second, the flowers have already wilted after blooming. In the third, they have neither bloomed nor wilted yet. If **Mal pipilā** is

used by itself, the implication is that the flowers have bloomed and are still blooming.

2. The literal translation would be "go and give it to Surath". A more idiomatic translation would be "Bring it to Surath". Curiously, perfect constructions like this are more common in Sinhala than just using **gēnná**, especially when bringing an object to a specific person or location.

4.3 E-stems

The past tense hasn't been mentioned yet, and that is because it is not regular across all verbs. Moreover, even the verbs with regular past tenses are not as straightforward as in English, where all such verbs end in -ed. Instead, most of them resemble the "strong verbs," like "run," with a past tense of "ran."

In Sinhala, verbs can be sorted into three broad categories, based on the vowel preceding the **-návā**. The simplest such verbs are the **e**-stem verbs. These end in **-enávā**; to form the past tense, **-enávā** is replaced by **-uṇā**. For example:

Matá eká thērenávā. I understand that.
Matá eká thēruṇā. I understood that.

Easy, right? Well, don't get used to it.

Even the e-stem verbs have a few complications, namely, a few irregular verbs associated with them. **Ḋenávā**, for instance, has a past tense form of **dunnā**, and **pēnávā** has a past tense form of **penuṇā**. **Venávā**, though it forms the past tense regularly, (**vuṇā**), is also considered irregular because of its perfect form. In fact, *all* single syllable verbs with thematic vowels other than **ā** are irregular. Longer verbs can be irregular too; the most important example is the e-stem **thiyenávā**, with a past tense of **thibuṇā**.

4.4 Umlaut and I-stems

In order to explain how the past tenses of other verbs are formed, we need to discuss a process called ***umlaut***. Aside from e-stems, auxiliaries, and highly irregular verbs, all Sinhala verbs use umlaut to some extent to form the past tense.

Umlaut changes vowels according to the following rules:

If the vowel is...	It becomes...
i or u	i
e, á, or o	e
æ or a	æ

Length is preserved in this process, that is, **u** and **ū** become **i** and **ī**, respectively, **o** and **ō** become **e** and **ē**, respectively, and **a** and **ā** become **æ** and **ǣ**, respectively. The vowel **á** is not found in its long form in verbs.

There are five major types of regular verbs, each with a different umlaut rule. But there is no need to memorize the class a verb belongs to, because it can be determined by looking at the end of the root, the part of the verb before **-návā**.

The i-stem verbs are probably the most straightforward, after the e-stems.

There are two classes of i-stem verbs, each with a different process for forming the past tense, depending on the consonant before **-inávā**. If it is one of the two consonants which cannot double, that is, **r** or **ḷ**, the past tense is formed by removing **-návā**, and adding **-yā**. Otherwise, the consonant before **-inávā** is doubled (recall from section 2.1 that for a pre-nasal, "doubling" replaces the prenasal with the corresponding full nasal and full stop). Next, **-inávā** is removed, the first vowel is umlauted, and **ā** is added.

There are a couple of irregular i-stems which behave like e-stems, namely **varáḋinávā**, "err," past tense **væráḋuṇā** (compare **væráḋenávā**, which has the same meaning). There is also **hitinávā**, which has a past tense of **hitiyā**.

4.5 A-stem verbs and a summary of forming the Past Tense

A-stems can be sorted in three classes:

If the stem vowel is **ā**, remove **ānávā** and add **ǣvā**. This class of verbs consists only of single-syllable roots.

If a verb ends in in **-vánávā**, the past tense is formed by removing **-vánávā**, fronting all the vowels in the remnant, and adding **-vvā**. For longer verbs of this type, in addition to the regular perfect, there is an alternate, highly colloquial form, in which the medial **-ává-** becomes **ō**: **gaḷávánávā** "removing," for example, becomes **gaḷōlā** "having removed." Most verbs of this class share certain other behaviors, and are discussed further in section 10.7.

If the vowel is **á** or **a**, and the consonant preceding it is not **v**, the process begins by removing the final **-anávā**. The root vowels are fronted, *except* if the sound before the last consonant is **u** or **á**; these will remain unchanged unless both the pre stem and the preceding vowel is u. Finally, **-uvā** is added to the end of the umlauted root.

Each of these classes have a few irregular verbs associated with them. The verb **kanávā** behaves like an **ā** stem(past tense **kǣvā**), except, of course, that its present forms have a short vowel. **Ḋānávā**, "put," has a completely irregular past tense of **ḋæmmā**. Of the v-stems, a few do not umlaut completely. The a-stems, on the other hand, have two verbs which front completely, unlike what is predicted by the rules (in some dialects, this may be the norm, rather than the exception).

Stem Vowel	Root Ending	Verb Class	Present Example	Past Example	Meaning
A	ā	Ā stem	**gānávā**	**gævā**	Rub
	vá	V stem	**kiyávánávā**	**kiyevvā**	read
	a or á	A stem	**gahanávā**	**gæhuvā**	hit
I	**ri or ḷi**	R stem	**arinávā**	**æriyā**	Open
	i	I stem	**ḋakinávā**	**ḋækkā**	see
E	**e**	E stem	**kæpenávā**	**kæpuṇā**	Be cut
-	**(no návā)**	Modal	**ōne**	**ōne vuṇā**	want/ need

Examples:

The following verbs are regular according to the above rules. Determine their past tense forms.

1. **Maḋinávā** (polish)
2. **Ba^{n}ḋinávā** (tie up)
3. **Pihinávā** (wipe)
4. **Samaránávā** (remember)
5. **Ugullánávā** (uproot)
6. **Vaḋāránávā** (formal) speak)

7. **Pihitenává** (be established)

8. **Sæthápenává** (repose)

9. **Ravánává** (stare)

Solutions

1. **Mæḋḋā**. In Sinhala, this word can also mean "brushed" in a specific context: **Mamá ḋath mæḋḋā** means "I brushed my teeth".

2. **Bænḋā**. Remember this is the result of doubling a pre-nasal.

3. **Pissā.** Recall that **h** cannot double, and in situations where it must, it is replaced by **ss**.

4. **Sæmæruvā**. A penultimate **a** will be fronted, unlike an **á** in the same place.

5. **Igilluvā**. The second **u** of **ugullánává** is not the penultimate sound in the root, thanks to the double **ll**. Thus, it is affected by the umlaut.

6. **Væḋæruvā**. See example 4.

7.**Pihituṇā**. Note that the vast majority of e-stem verbs are pre-umlauted...

8. **Sæthápuṇā**. ...but the occasional one that isn't doesn't front its vowels when forming the past.

9. **Rævvā**

4.6 Forms Derived from the Past

The past tense form can be used to regularly make a conditional form:

Giyoth - "if [subject] goes -"

This **-oth** form is used to make conditional statements, like the **-vanam**. The meaning is similar to the latter, but using it suggests that the potential event is more likely to occur.

It can also be used to produce an adjectival form:

Giyá - "having gone -"

This particular word is prolifically used in an idiomatic way: **Giyá auruḋḋá**, literally, the year that has gone by, means "last year." Using these words in a straightforward way is quite common as well.

Matá badágini vuṇá nisā mamá kǣmá kǣvā

E-stem verbs have an alternate adjectival form, made by replacing the final **ā** by **u**, eg. **vuṇu, penuṇu, pipuṇu, hæruṇu, thibuṇu. Ḋenávā** is irregular in that it doesn't have such a form. Generally, these forms are more formal than the **á** final versions.

These transformations are highly regular, they are valid for verbs regardless of their regularity or class:

Innávā. Be (animate)
Hitiyā. Was

Hitiyoth. If [someone] was
Hitiyá. Was (adjective)

Thiyenávā. Be (inanimate)
Thibuṇā. Was
Thibuṇoth. If [something] was
Thibuṇá. Was (adj)

These adjectives behave like the base forms of normal adjectives. They do not have corresponding i forms; the plain verb is used instead.

Hayyen giyá balla. The dog-that-went-fast -
Balla hayyen giyā. The dog was going fast.

Past tense forms do not have an infinitive, but they do have an emphatic form, made by replacing the final **ā** with **ē**. This is used like the emphatic present, both to emphasize the word and to ask questions.

Verbs can also be converted to nouns using the past tense, but these forms are irregular. A common theme is the addition of **-má**, sometime **-imá**.

1. **Matá aethi venná salli thibuṇoth ē pothá ganná puḷuvan**. If I have enough money, I will be able to buy that book.
2. **Vuṇá ḋēval gæná kanágātui**. Alt. **vuṇu**. (I'm) sad about the things that happened. (The word for "about" is

gæná, a postposition)

4.7 Irregular Verbs

We have already discussed the mildly irregular verbs, which, in general, would be regular verbs if not for a few simple changes.

The highly irregular verbs, on the other hand, have no significant patterns. **Yanávā** and **innávā** are two such verbs.

Along with **innávā**, **gannávā**, "take," and **ḋannávā**, "know" could be classed together as n-stem verbs, they have only one big thing in common: their infinitives are formed just by removing **-vā**, i.e. **Ehē inná** "stay there!". Otherwise, as seen on the table below, they behave quite differently. They even have some irregularities outside the past tense: **gannávā** has a future form of **ganī**, but **innávā**'s is **i**^{n}**ḋī**, and **ḋannávā** must use the compound word **ḋænáganī** to express the same meaning.

There is only one commonly used o-stem verb: **bonávā**, "drink." Although **enávā** and **gēnávā** could be considered e-stems, their past forms are totally irregular also.

The only way to learn the irregular verbs is to memorize them; this is probably the second-most difficult hurdle towards learning Sinhala as a second language. A table of irregular verbs follows.

Meaning	Present	Past	Past Participle
Become	venávā	vuṇā	velā
Eat	Kanávā	Kæva	Kālā
Drink	Bonávā	Bīvā	Bīlā
Take (from)	Gannávā	Gaththā	Aragená
Take (to)	Geniyánávā	Genichchā	Geniyálā/ genihillā
Be	Innávā	hitiyā	i^{n}ḋálā
Bring	Gēnávā	Genāvā	Genællā
Exist/Have	thiyenávā	thibuṇā	thibilā
Keep	thiyánávā	thibbā	thiyálā
Go	Yanávā	Giyā	Gihillā
Come	Enávā	Avā	Ævilla
Give	Ḋenávā	Ḋunnā	Ḋīlā
Know	Ḋannávā	-	-
Mildy hurt	Ḋanávā, Ḋanánávā	Ḋævā, Ḋævvā, Ḋanuvā	- no common perfect
Put	ḋānávā	ḋæmmā	ḋālā
Be visible	Pēnávā	Penuṇā	Penilā
Swallow	Gilinávā	Gillā	Gillā

Some verbs have optional irregular forms. **Káránávā**, for instance, has a regular past tense of **keruvā**, but also two irregular forms, **kárā**, and **káḷā**, both of which mean the same thing. Like wise, **geniyánávā** has an optional irregular perfect form **genihillā** in addition to its regular perfect form **geniyálā**.

Examples:

1. **Surath udátá genichchá eká hoyā ganná**.
2. **Ēká geniyálā/genihillā api yaluvekutá ḋunnā**.
3. **Eyā** chocolate **bath vagē gillā**.

Answers:

1. Find the one that Surath took upstairs.
2. We took it and gave it to a friend
3. She was gulping down chocolate as if it were rice.

"Eating something like rice" is an idiomatic expression, meaning to eat it quickly or greedily.

Summary and Supplemental information

Many Sinhala verbs are compound verbs, consisting of a noun followed by a verb:

Vædá káránávā. work (work-do)

Bō venávā. propagate (much-become)

Uththárá ḋenávā. answer (answer-give)

The noun added is *not* subject to the sound change rules for forming the past tense. In most cases, this is straightforward, since the noun and the verb are written and spoken as separate words. But this is not always the case.

Igenágannáva, "learn"" is spoken as a single word, but it is a **gannáva** compound, which means that the past tense "learnt" is **igenágaththā**. (It is written as two words)

Many English words are converted into Sinhala verbs in this way (see Chapter 12).

Summary and Supplemental Information

In the context of Sinhala, umlaut is a sound change which causes vowels to be fronted. Sinhala vowels can be described by two parameters, height and frontness.

	Front	Central	Back
High	i		u
Mid	e	á	o
Low	æ		a

Table 4.3 Sinhala vowels

The Sinhala umlaut, then, is simply described by moving a vowel on this chart to the leftmost column, while keeping it in the same row.

Many of the apparent irregularities in past tense formation are the result of historical changes. For instance, the list of "e-like" i-stems were, at some point, e-stems; in some cases, the regular e-stem counterpart is still in use today. The **-iyā** type i-stems are a different case; at one time, all i-stem verbs formed their past tense in that way. However, the **i** of this ending tended to disappear, leaving a consonant cluster of the form **Xy**, which was then simplified to **XX**. The consonants that could not double, of course, did not take part in this process. Why does **hitinávā** still form this old "regular" past tense? The consonants **t**, **d**, **ṇ** in general show some resistance to doubling, though not as strongly as **ḷ** or **r**, in fact, outside of some i-stems, they are mostly found doubled in loanwords.

The mildly irregular a-stems, on the other hand, seem to be simple deviancies in various dialects; other books show verbs that are irregular in this book being regular, or vice versa. As such, memorizing this category is of questionable utility.

Many of the highly irregular verbs have past tenses formed by conflation; their past tenses are actually the regular past forms of other verbs. **Osávánávā**'s past form is that of **ussánávā**, for instance.

4.8 Exercises

1-10: Given the present form of the following regular verbs, provide their past, past participle, and past participle adjective forms.

1.**vætenávā** (fall)

2.**buranávā** (bark)

3.**orovanávā** (stare)

4.**thērenávā** (understand)

5.**paninávā** (jump)

6.**nægitinávā** (get up)

7. **i^{m}binávā** (kiss)

8. **kavánávā** (feed)

9. **arinávā** (open)

10. **nānávā** (bathe)

11-13: The past and past participle forms of the word **kiyánávā** (say) are used very often in Sinhala.

11. What are these forms?

12. Naturally, the past form is used when precisely quoting someone (**-lu** is used when reporting hearsay). Assuming the person being quoted has already been brought up in the discussion, how would you say "He didn't say that"?

13. When actually relaying an exact quote, the past participle is used like the English word "that". How would you say "He said that he wants to learn"?

14-20: Translate the following sentences into Sinhala. Only the regular verbs will need to be converted into past forms:

14. I wasn't crying.

15. She answered while drinking tea.

16. We still needed to walk a long way

17. That flower bloomed.

18. We went to sleep after being scolded.

19. I watched TV

20. They were listening to the radio.

21-30: Translate the following sentences into Sinhala.

21. I cleaned the house.

22. I brought the book and gave it to them.

23. I painted this picture.

24. They weren't able to answer the question.

25. She walked down the street and turned to the right.

26. He didn't brush his teeth before he went to bed.

27. I'm going to the store before I go to school.

28. Don't swim after eating.

29. I was there.

30. That tree has grown quickly.

31-40: Translate the following sentences, which may or may not contain irregular verbs, into English:

31. **Ē gollō ḋiha** (at them) **tharáheṅ bæluvā**

32. **Mamá kadētá giyā**.

33. **Api āvē næ.**

34. **Bath kālā, vathurá bīlā, ḷamáyātá ninḋá giyā**. **ninḋá giya** is not deliberate, reqs **tá, niḋā gannávā** doesn't

35. **Ayyā baisikálē hæḋuvā**.

36. **Hu^{n}gak tharáha gihiṅ hitapu miniha eyātá ho^{n}ḋátámá gæhuvā**.

37. **Ee ḷamáyā mahansi velā vædá káranná kæmáthī.**

38. **Mamá santhōsen hitiyā**.

39. (**Api**) **Ēkátá geválā thiyennē**.

40. (**Api**) **Ēkátá gevvā**.

41-50: Translate the following sentences into Sinhala:

41. I wasn't always like this.

42. Beautifully done.

43. There used to be a huge crowd.

44. I put down the book here and left.

45. The man I saw didn't run.

46. When I told him it was a bad idea, he became upset.

47. The man that was fishing went home.

48. I wanted to drink tea

49. Mother cooked rice.

50.The work I couldn't do was difficult.

51-52: The easiest highly irregular verb to memorize is surely **ḋannávā**, which simply has no past or past participle forms. How, then, might one translate the following English sentences?

51. I knew that

52. I used to know that.

53-60: Can you guess the meaning of the following past-tense derived nouns?

53. **kǣmá**

54. **bīmá**

55. **ḋænumá**

Dialogue 6: Telling a story

A: **Mathákáḋá Laṅkāvátá sunāmi eká āpu velāvá**? Do you remember the time the tsunami hit Sri Lanka?

B: **Apō ou. Api hitiye Hikkáduvē muhuḋá la^{n}gá hōtálēká.** Of course I remember. We were staying in a hotel in Hikkaduwe that was near the sea.

C: **Ithiṅ ō gollan mokáḋá kárē**? So what did you guys do?

B: **Sunami eká enákotá api ḋeveni thattuvátá næggā. E vuṇātá tiká velāvak yanákotá, ḋeveni thattuvátath vathurá āvā**. When the tsunami came, we went to the second floor. After a while, water reached the second floor. In Sinhala using "climb" is natural for going up. Bæssa for the reverse.

Ē vuṇātá is an idiomatic expression meaning "however": the **ē** can be replaced with something that opposes the second part.

D: **Ō gollantá bayá hithennæthi nēḋá**? h. Short for **Hithennē næthi. Hithenávā** is a verb meaning "feeling," or unconsciously thinking. It is the passive counterpart of **hithánávā**

B: **Ou, podi ḷamai kīpáḋenek a^{n}danná pataṅ gaththā. Loku ayátath bayá hithuṇā**. Yes, several little kids started crying. Even the adults were scared.

D: **Ethákotá monávāḋá kárē**? Then what did you do?

B: **Ho^{n}ḋá vellāvátá vædiyá vathurá āvē næ, api mēsával udátá nægálā, bēruṇā**. Luckily, there wasn't a lot of water, so we got to safety by standing on furniture.

56. What are two alternative ways of saying "then what did you do?"

57. **Bēruṇā** means "saved" or "rescued" (in this context, of course, the saved themselves). What is the present tense?

Translate the following into Sinhala

58. I also felt scared.

59. Do you remember the time we went to Sri Lanka?

Dialogue 7: Rain check

A: **Puthā, gamának yannáḋá haḋannē**? Son, are you getting ready to go out? **Gamáná** means a trip but can be very short "outing" or long "journey or in-between.

B: **Ou, matá taumē káranná vædá vageyak thiyenávā**. Yes, I have a few errands to run in the town.

A: **Ē vuṇātá, væssá hari thaḋai ne**? But its raining very hard.

B: **væssá pāyánákaṅ hitiyoth ḋavas gānak inná vei**. If I wait for the rain to cease, I'll have to wait for days.

Here, **innávā** is used to mean "waiting" rather than "being."

A: **Ithin mē mōsam kālētá ohomá thamai. Uḋēkátá kárāganná bæri vædakḋá**? This is the way it is during the monsoon. Is this something you can't do during the morning hours.

B: **Samáhará vædá uḋētá káranná puḷuvan vuṇātá hæmá ḋēmá káranná bǣ**. I can do some of it during the morning, but not everything.

A: **Ehenaṅ, væssá tikak adu venákam i^{n}ḋálā yanná**. Then wait till the rain lets up and go.

The **kam / kaṅ** form of a verb is a "time form." It indicates that what follows occurs at the same time as the **kaṅ**-verb.

60. If the rain lets up, she'll be able to leave.

61. Won't you be able to go tomorrow?

62. **Væssá pāyánákaṅ** means "when the rain stops." However, the word **pāyánávā** means something more like "clear up," rather than "stop." In light of this, what might **avvá pāyánákaṅ matá uḋaukáranná puḷuvan** mean?

Dialogue 8: Going out to play

A: **Yāluvō ekká sellaṅ káranná giyātá kamak nǣ, ho^{n}ḋá ḷamáyek vage, tiká velāvákin geḋárá ævillā, pādam káranná ōne**. : It's ok to go and play with your friends, but like a good child, you have to come home in a little while and study.

Kamak nǣ is another way of saying "it's not a problem." This sentence contains many elements that we have not yet dealt with.

B: **Ou ou mamá ikmánátá / ikmánin ennaṅ.** Yeah, yeah, I'll come soon.

A: **Ḋæn mathákai ne, geḋárá āváhamá pāḋaṅ káranná poronḋu vuṇā**. **Ho^{n}ḋátá pādam károth thamai vib^{h}āge** "pass" **venná puḷuvan**. Now don't forget, you promised to study when you come home. If you study well, you will be able to pass the exam.

B: **Hari hari**. Right, right.

B runs off.

A:**Hiyen ḋuvanná epā**. **Pārē kar enávā**. Don't run fast, there are cars coming on the road.

Translate the following into English:

63. I didn't run.

64. I studied well.

65. I can't work quickly.

66. Although I studied poorly, I passed. (A relevant way of saying "didn't do" is **nokáránávā**)

5
ANIMATE NOUNS

Dialogue 9: Placing Blame

An adult, A, hears a ruckus, and come across two kids, B and C, beating the tar out of each other.

A: **U^{m}bálā, mokáḋá raṇdu kárannē**? Why are you brats fighting? Literally, What's this fight (about), you lot?

B: **Eyā matá gæhuvā.** He hit me. Note that the person who was hit is marked with **-tá**.

C: **Næ næ eyai matá issálá gæhuvē.** No, no, he hit me first! The **-i** ending on **eyā** is used for emphasis.

A: **Eká æththáḋá?** (Is) that true?

B: **Eyā matá vihiḷu kárā. Ekai mamá gæhuvē.** He played a joke on me. That's why I hit (him). The target of a joke is also marked with **-tá** in Sinhala.

A: **Podi ḋevalválátá gahaganná ōne nǣ.** You don't need to go and hit (people) over small things. When **gannávā** is used in compound verbs, it means the person will perform the action himself.

Pæththákátá velā thamunge vædak kárágganná. Mind your own business and get back to your work.

When B fesses up to throwing the first punch, he doesn't state who he hit, because in context it is obvious. If he had, however, it might have gone like this:

Ethákotá eyātá mamá gæhuvā. Therefore I hit him.

Notice how the **-tá** ending is applied to the word for "he," in this sentence, unlike in the previous statements. This ending tells the listener who was hit; the person doing the hitting is not marked with it. It turns out there are a number of these ***case*** endings in Sinhala, each with different usages. Changing a noun from one case to another is called ***declension***.

Even the same case can have a different ending on different nouns, depending on whether it is animate or inanimate, singular or plural, and definite (the person) or indefinite (a person). For example, the singular definite form of the dative case is just **-tá**, but in the dialogue, we see the word **ḋevalválátá**, "about/over things," the dative form of the inanimate plural word **ḋeval**, "things."

At this point, you may be considering learning another language. But these aspects are not as torturous as they are in languages such as Latin or Sanskrit, because the case and gender rules are fairly simple. There are few irregular words like **mamá**, but other than those, there is little beyond the endings themselves to memorize. Let's look at the declension of the word **yakā**. The actual number of cases Sinhala has is a matter of debate; For animate nouns we will note five major cases:

Yakā. the demon (nominative)
Yakāvá. the demon (accusative)
Yakātá. to the demon (dative)
Yakāge: the demon's (genitive)
Yakāgen. from the demon (ablative)

As well three minor ones:

Yakā(ge) **athin**/ **yakā lavvá.** by the demon's hand/ by using the demon (instrumental)

Yakāla^{n}gá/ Yakāgāvá. near or with the demon (locative)

Yakō: you demon (vocative)

This chapter will focus on animate nouns and their behaviors; it turns out inanimate nouns decline rather differently.

5.2 Direct Objects

In our dialogue, the person doing the hitting, the ***subject***, is unmarked, while the person being hit, the ***object***, is is marked by **-tá**. However, this is not the only ending that can mark the object in Sinhala:

> **Yakā ḋeviyāvá maranávā.** The demon kills the god.
> **Yakāvá ḋeviyā maranávā.** The god kills the demon.
> **Ḋeviyā yakāvá maranávā.** The god kills the demon.
> **Ḋeviyāvá yakā maranávā.** The demon kills the god.

Here, the **-vá** ending tells us who's being killed; the noun without the ending is the subject, in this case, the one doing the killing. In English this information is given using word order, and switching the order of the words changes the meaning.

What determines whether **-vá**, the ***accusative*** ending, or -**tá**, the dative ending, is used? It appears to be the meaning of the verb; for instance, the following verbs all use **-vá.**

Mamá eyāvá arágená āvā. I brought him and came. This construction is used for animate objects, person being brought is marked with **vá**.

Ḷamáyāvá udá visi keruvā. I threw the child.
Eyā māvá thallu keruvā. She pushed me.

What do all of the **-vá**-using examples we've seen have in common? A lot of them involve moving the object, except for **maránávā** (unless you count moving from this life!). The common theme is that they are actions that affect the whole of the marked person. Some verbs can use both endings to mark an object, with each ending corresponding to a different meaning:

Ḷamáyāvá æ^{n}ḋuvā. (I) dressed the child

This implies that the child was completely dressed by the speaker. If **-ta** is used instead, the implication is that you just put an item of clothing or two on the child; the direct object would be the place the clothing was put on. When talking about dressing a person as a whole, use **-vá**; otherwise, use **tá**

Ḷamáyātá athá æ^{n}ḋuvā. Literally: I dressed (the child's) arm/hand for the child. In practice, this implies that that someone helped the child put on the sleeve of an outfit. Here **athá** is the ***direct*** object, (and as an inanimate, doesn't take the **vá** ending), while **ḷamáyā** is the ***indirect*** object (which, in this context in English, is represented by the preposition "for").

The **-vá** ending is also used to mark the subjects of passive verbs:

Yakāvá pēnávā. The demon is visible.

Examples:

Translate the following sentences into Sinhala:

1. The mother took the child to school.
2. We know one person who is here. (the sentence should begin with **metháná inná**; one person is **ekkenek**)
3. We chose a child for a competition. (for a competition = **thará^{n}gáyákátá**, chose = **thōrágaththā**)
4. Bring the baby. The word for baby is **babā**.

Answers:

1. **Ammā ḷamáyāvá iskole**(**tá**) **genichchā**. Recall that **geniyánávā** is used when taking objects to someplace.
2. **Metháná inná ekkenekvá api ḋannávā**.
3. **Api thará^{n}gáyákátá lamáyakvá thōrágaththā**. **Thōrágaththā** is the ganná form of **thōránávā**. The latter can mean both "choose" and "explain", but the former only means "choose".
4. **Babāvá arágená enná**.

5.3 Transitive, Intransitive, Active, and Passive Verbs

Verbs like **maránávā**, **gahanávā**, and **a^{n}ḋánávā** are ***transitive***: they have a subject and object. They are also ***active***, meaning that they are done by the will of the subject. Some verbs, however, are ***intransitive***, meaning that they have no direct object. For instance, **niḋā gannávā**, "sleep", can obviously take a subject, the person who went to sleep, but not a direct object. There might, however, be indirect objects, like the bed that was slept on, etc. Still other verbs, like **pēnávā**, (be visible), are ***passive***, meaning that the will of the subject is not a factor.

For active verbs, as we've seen, the subject is unmarked, and the direct object is marked with **-vá** or **-tá**, depending on the meaning. But if you have an active, *intransitive* verb, there cannot be a direct object, and as such, the **-vá** ending will *never* be used. The **-tá** ending, or another, might still be used, however; in fact, for both transitive and intransitive verbs, ***indirect objects*** are most often marked with **tá**. This occurs in situations corresponding generally with the English indirect prepositions "to" and "for."

Yakā ḋeviyatá ḷamáyāvá ḋunnā. The demon gave the child to the god.

Passive verbs, however, behave differently; strictly speaking, they do not take subjects. In practice, they take direct objects which basically behave as subjects, which are marked with **-vá.**

Yakāvá matá pēnávā. The demon is visible to me.

The **-tá** ending is is also used in contexts not corresponding to the English word "to," as we have seen:

Ḷamáyātá bádáginī."The child is hungry."

This usage has no English analogy, and must be memorized.

Examples:

Are the following verbs active or passive? Can you guess whether they are transitive or intransitive?

1. **Pāgánávā** "trample"
2. **Pǣgenávā** "be trampled"
3. **Gilenávā** ("drown")
4. **Pāvichchi káránávā** "using"
5. **Randu káránávā** "quarreling" fight **gaha gannávā** - to fight physically

Translate the following sentences into Sinhala:

6. She pushed me.
7. I wanted to see them
8. They beat him.
9. He died in bed.
10. I hoped you would come.

1. **Mamá bimá hitiyá ku^{m}biyāvá pāgálā mæruvā**. Active, transitive.

2. **Mage athin ku^{m}biyavá pægilā mæruvā**. Invol. Killing the ant. Passive, transitive

3. **Eyā giluṇā**. Active, intransitive

4. Active, transitive

5. **Mamá malli ekká randu keruvā**. **Randuvá** means fight, but it is only used for humans. That bear is fighting that leopard. **E valáhā diviyā ekká porá kanávā, porá kǣvā**. Fighting for animals. **Me ballo ḋennā porá kanávā**. Active, intransitive. Both fighters are considered participants.

6. **Eyā māvá thallu keruvā**. **māvá** required!

7. **Matá eyālāvá balanná ōne vuṇā**

8. There are several possible translations. **Ēyālā ohutá gæhuvā**. It sounds strange to say **eyā** and **eyālā** while referring to two different parties. **Ē minissu**, "those people," is most natural, even literary. **ohu** is more natural than using **eyā**. **Eyālā aráyātá gæhuvā**. **Ū** and its derivatives could also used: **Uṅ arūtá gæhuvā**.

9. **Eyā mæruṇē niḋágáná innákotá**. One semi-useful pattern is that e-stems that are active are generally intransitive).

10. **Oyā ei kiyálā mamá balāgená hitiyā**. The **gená** form indicates that an action is taking place at that point in time, like the English -ing ending.

5.4 The Ablative and Genitive Cases

Some indirect objects may take the ***ablative*** case. The animate ablative case is used in a straightforward manner, corresponding to most situations where English would use the word "from." For animates, it is formed by adding **-gen.**

Eyāgen matá liyumak avā. I got a letter from him.

It is also used in situations where information is passing from one person to another:

Akkā eyāgen prashnáyak æhuvā. Big sister asked him a question.

In general, it is used when receiving something, usually information or an item, *from* someone.

Mamá eyāgen salli horakaṅ keruvā. I stole money from him.

The ***genitive*** case, which is used to express possession, is more straightforward. For animates, it corresponds about exactly to the English genitive ending "'s". It is formed by adding **-ge**:

Roshange badu harima barai - Roshan's stuff is very heavy.

Examples:

Translate the following sentences into Sinhala:

1. My answer to her question was incorrect.
2. I got an answer from him
3. I borrowed a pen from her.
4. A letter from him arrived.

1. **Eyāge prashnētá mamá ḋunná uththáráyá væráḋī.**
2. **Matá eyāgen uththáráyak læbuṇā**
3. **Mamá eyāgen pǣnak illá gathā**.
4. **Eyāgen liyumak āvā**.

5.6 The Marginal Cases

The following inflections are for various reasons, sometimes not regarded as full cases at all.

The ***instrumental*** case exists as a simple ending for inanimates (in most instances equivalent with the ablative case), but for animates a similar meaning can only be obtained using postpositions. One such form is produced adding the word **athin** to either the nominative or genitive case:

Mallige athin pi^{n}gāná kaduṇā. The younger brother was responsible for breaking the plate.

This case is used to indicate that the action occurred as a result of the marked object's actions. **Athin** is used with passive verbs, not active ones:

Kāge athinḋá mēká kæduṇē? Who broke this?
Kauḋá mēká kæḋuvē? Who broke this?

By the same token, if you were inquiring who was responsible for someone's death, you might use **mæruṇē** with **kāge athin**, or **mæruvē** with **kauḋá**.

Kagáhari athin kæduṇa. - somebody broke this.

For inanimates, this case is merged with the ablative.

The ***locative case*** is used to indicate that something is physically near the marked object:

Mā la^{n}gá mage sākkuvē māláyak thiyenávā - i have a necklace with me/in my pocket.

This case can be used in the literal sense, but it is very commonly used to indicate that the speaker possesses something on their person. For inanimates, it is identical to the genitive case.

Mamá **māláyak ænḋā / ḋāgaththa -ḋāganávā** - put on

The ***vocative case*** is an archaic form that converts a noun into a second-person pronoun:

Yakō. you demon

Theoretically, you would use this to address a demon. In practice, it is a very rude word for "you." This case is only used literally in a few contexts in modern speech, but it sees wider use in various idiomatic words, like the one above. A non-native speaker could easily get away with simply using the nominative case, but there are certain limited circumstances where the vocative is commonly used by native speakers. For inanimates, and for practical purposes, most animates, this case is merged with the nominative.

The vocative case has a second form, commonly used with words for family members. It consists of replacing the final vowel with **-e**, or adding **-ye** to words ending in **i**.

Example Problems:
Translate the following sentences:

1. I have the book on me.
2.I didn't break this.
3. Good sir / gentleman, could you give me some money? (a word for sir or gentleman is **mahatháyā**, money here would be **salli tikak**)
4. I shattered the glass.
5. Mother, look at this.

6. Child, come outside (the word for outside here should be **eḷiyátá**)

7.His dog is staying near him.

8. I was the one who painted this. (the word for this here is **mēká**)

Answers:

1. **Ē pothá maṅgāvá/la^{n}gá thiyenávā.** If holding some elses book, saying you have it too, might use mē

2. **Mēká ma(ge) athin kædunē næ.** Or: **Mamá mēká kæḋuvē næ.**

3. **Mahaththáyo, matá salli tikak ḋenná puḷuvanḋá?**

4. **Mage athin vīḋuruvá binḋuṇā. Athin** implies that it wasn't intentional.

5. **Amme me balanná**

6. **Ḷamáyō cḷiyátá enná.**

7. **Eyāge ballá eyala^{n}gámá innávā.** Without **-má**, his dog is with him.

8. **Mamá thamai/mamai mē pinthurē ænḋē**

5.7 The Indefinite Form

The dictionary form of words is ***definite***, that is, **yaka** means "the demon" as opposed to "a demon". The latter would be **yakek**, which is declined as follows:

Yakek. a demon

Yakekvá. a demon (accusative)

Yakektá. to a demon (dative)

Yakekge: a demon's (genitive)

Yakekgen. from a demon (ablative)

Yakek athin. by a demon (instrumental)

Yakek la^{n}gá. near a demon (locative)

For the clusters (i.e. **kv**, **kt**, **kg**) only, **u** can be inserted (Adding a **u** for the accusative, and adding **u** after the nominative is a literary form. For the other cases, the **u** version is used both when speaking and writing).

5.8 Plurals

So far, we have danced around the issue of how plurals are formed. The reason for this is that it is possibly the most difficult aspect of learning Sinhala as a second language. While there are different "classes" like with verbs, animate noun classes cannot be determined from their base form. The plural form is declined like the others:

Yakālā: the demons

Yakālavá. the demons (accusative)

Yakālatá. to the demons (dative)

Yakālage: the demons" (genitive)

Yakālagen. from the demons (ablative)

Yakālāthin. by the demons (instrumental) separate words?

Yakālala^{n}gá. near the demons (locative)

Yakku(**n**). you demons (vocative)

Most plurals have lost the distinct vocative forms they once had; native speakers today just use nominative.

There is no definiteness distinction for plurals, like in English.

There are three major kinds of animate plurals: those ending in **lā**, those ending in **o** or **ō**, and those ending in **u** or **ū**. La-type plurals decline as above, but the others behave differently. U-type plurals insert **n** before their endings, and o-type plurals replace their final **o** with **an**, and are then suffixed with the normal endings.

For instance, **æthā**, "tusker," has a plural **æththu**(**n**), the genitive form is **æththunge**. **Ballā**, "dog," on the other hand, has a plural of **ballō**/**ballan**, and its genitive form is **ballange**. The **-an**/**-un** ending is a little more formal for the nominative case, and is used in complete sentences.

A small number of animate nouns form plurals by subtraction:

For example **harak**, "cows," gives **harákā**

It is not possible to determine the plural of a noun unambiguously from its singular form; accordingly, the plurals for all nouns that have them are provided in this book. However there are some general trends:

Malli, pl. **mallilā**. **Bappā**, pl. **bappálā**. **Puthā**, pl. **puthālā**. **Yakā**, pl. **yakālā**. Note that last two also have earlier plural forms of **puththu** and **yakku**, respectively.

Loanwords referring to people tend form the plural by adding **-lā**, and replacing a preceding **-ā** with **-á**. This includes the commonly used words for family members. Lately, the **-lā** ending seems to be replacing older endings in common speech, with the result that some words have two plurals.

Words that end in **-yā** or **-vā** usually form their plurals by replacing the final **-ā** with **-o**. Some, however, form their plurals by removing the final **ā**, in which case the final consonant (**y** or **v**) becomes **i** or **u**, or is deleted before another **i** or **u**.

Words that end in other consonants followed by **ā** may either form o or u-type plurals; there is no reliable way to tell. U type plurals are usually formed by doubling the preceding consonant if possible. A small proportion of these also form plurals by subtraction of **ā**.

Determining the singular from the plural is easier for animates:

For plurals ending in **-lā** , the singular is formed by removing **-lā**, and usually replacing any newly final **-á** with -**ā**. (Exceptions: **ḋuválā**, sg. **ḋuvá**; **ḋostháráIā**, sg. **ḋostḣárá**)

Plurals ending in **-u** form the singular by undoubling the previous consonant if it's doubled (as with doubling, **ss** corresponds with **h** and the half-nasals with full nasal-stop combinations), and replacing **-u** with **ā**.

Plurals ending in consonants form the singular by adding a final **-ā**. Plurals ending in **-i** add **-yā**; plurals ending in **-au** form the singular by replacing the final **u** with **vā**.

O-type plurals form the singular by replacing **ō** with **ā**.

For animates, almost all singular forms can be determined from the plural; unfortunately, even these have exceptions, while the situation for inanimate nouns is more difficult.

As mentioned previously, **-u** plurals may be pronounced more formally as **-un**, and **-o** endings as **-an**.

5.9 Summary and Supplemental Information

Animate nouns are those which were traditionally regarded as "sentient beings." They have a number of cases. The major ones are:

The ***nominative***, the case for the subject of the sentence,

The ***accusative***, the case specifying the direct object,

The ***dative***, the case specifying the indirect object,

The ***genitive***, which indicates possession, and

The ***ablative***, a case used to mark an object being moved away from, or someone from whom something was obtained.

Some minor cases are:

The ***vocative***, which is used for addressing people under certain situations.

The ***instrumental***, which for inanimates is equivalent to the ablative, but for animates requires certain postpositions.

The ***locative***, which for inanimates is equivalent to the genitive, but for animates requires certain postpositions.

Examples:

Case name	Definite Example	Indefinite Example	Plural Example
Nominative	Ammā	Ammek	Ammálā
Accusative	Ammāvá	Ammekvá	Ammálāvá
Dative	Ammātá	Ammektá	Ammálātá
Gentitive	Ammāge	Ammekge	Ammálāge
Ablative	Ammāgen	Ammekgen	Ammálāgen

Case name	Definite Example	Indefinite Example	Plural Example
[with a postposition]	Ammā la^{n}gá	Ammek athin	Ammálā gāvá
Vocative	Ammō	-	-
Familial vocative	Amme	-	-

Aside from the **-lā** type plurals shown above, there are o-type, u-type, and subtractive plurals.

	Singular nominative	Plural nominative	Plural genitive
O-type	ḋeviyā	ḋeviyō / ḋeviyan	ḋeviyange
U-type	horā	horu / horun	horunge
Subtractive	ḷamáyā	ḷamai	ḷamainge
Respectful	ḋeviyā	ḋeviváru	Ḋevivárunge

Note the presence of an **n** before the case endings for these plurals. If a subtractive plural ends in a consonant e.g. **harak**, a **u** is inserted where necessary: “to the bulls” is **harákuntá**. This effectively makes words like **harak** into u-type words.

There is actually a reasonably dependable, albeit insanely difficult way to determine whether a given Sinhala word is an o-type or a u-type; just refer to its Sanskrit cognate. If the pre-final syllable is heavy (if it has a long vowel (including e or o, which can only be long in Sanskrit) , has a post-vowel consonant cluster, or both) the word will be a u-type, otherwise, it will be an o-type. All you need is an extensive knowledge of Sanskrit and of historical Sinhala sound changes! (Actual Sanskrit words *in* Sinhala are typically o-types as far as animates go (see chapter 12).

5.10 Exercises

As you can see, sentences differing only in the inflection of one noun can have very different meanings. For instance:

Gūnáratná akkavá beheth ḋīlā sanīpá kerevvā.
Gunaratne gave (me) medicine and made (me) well. In context, this is fine, but if its not clear, **matá** and **māvá** have to be used.

This sentence is straightforward enough. **Beheth** is "medicine", and **sanīpá kerevvā** is a compound verb, meaning "making well." With this information in hand, deduce the meaning of the following sentences:

1. **Gūnáratnává akkā beheth ḋīlā sanīpá kerevvā.**
2. **Gūnáratnátá akkā beheth ḋīlā sanīpá kerevvā.**
3. **Gūnáratnáge beheth ḋīlā akkavá sanīpá kerevvā.**
4. **Gūnáratnágen beheth arágená akkavá sanīpá kerevvā.**

5. **Gūnáratná lavvá beheth ḋīlā akkavá sanīpá kerevvā.**

6. **Gūnáratnála^{n}gá thibuṇá beheth ḋīlā akkavá sanīpá kerevvā.**

Translate the following sentences into English.

7. **Mamá b-ekká kathá kárānákotá cvá hambuṇā.** (**hambenávā, hambá venávā** more formal)

8. **Matá eyāvá ahamben hambuṇā. Ahamben hambuṇā** = run into.

9. **Eyālāgen liyumak hambá vuṇain passē, mamá eyālāvá balanná giyā. Vuṇain** is a verb form used with **passē**, "after."

10. **Mamá eyāgen salli illá gathē næ. Illá gannávā** means "borrow."

11. **Mamá eyāgen prasháyak æhuvē næ.**

12. **Mamá eyāvá** "station" **eká la^{n}gá bæssuvā**

13. **Mamá innē handiyá la^{n}gá.**

14. **Maṅ gāvá ē** "recipe" **eká næ.**

15. **Kauḋá biththiyá ænḋē? A^{n}ḋinávā** means "draw."

16. **Eyāge athin mæruṇāḋá?**

17. **Kāge athinḋá mē vīḋuruvá binḋuṇē? Bi^{n}ḋenávā** means "to be shattered," and can be used for glass or ornaments. It is not quite the same as **kædenávā. Kædenávā** can be used for glass, ornaments, or many other kinds of objects, whereas **bi^{n}ḋenávā** can't be interchanged with **kædenávā** in other contexts.

18. **Kāge athinḋá mē kæmá hæluṇē?**

19. **Pi^{n}gan hōḋannná mamá eyāgen uḋau / uḋavvak illuvā.**

20. **Mamá eyātá pothak ḋunnā.**

21. **Mamá eyātá paḷáveni thæná ḋunnā.** "First place" = **paḷáveni thæná**

22. **Api ali balanná giyā. Alinvá** would not be said here, it is too formal.

23. **Ḋiviyā apigāvátámá āvā.**

24. **Va^{n}ḋurō apē kæmá ganná hæḋuvā. Haḋánávā** means "try" here; it can also men "build" or "fix."

25. **Ḋiviyā va^{n}ḋurāvá gaha udátá eḷevva.**

26. **va^{n}ḋurā kǣ gagahā, ḋiviyāgen bērilā giyā.**

27. **Ḋiviyā va^{n}ḋurāvá athá ærálā, vená deyak balannā giyā.**

28. **Pūsā ballāvá hiruvā.**

29. **Ballā pūsavá vikuvā / hæpuvā.**

30. **Mamá eyātá salli tikak ḋunnā.**

31. **Mamá maḋuruvāvá mæruvā.**

32. **Mamá eyātá** ice cream **gēnná kiyuvā**

33. **Mamá ḷamaintá panthiyátá enná kiyuvā.**

34. **Ḷamai panthiyátá yanná.**

35. **Ḷamáyō mē vædē hariyátá káranná.]**

36. **Pirimi ḷamáyá (kollā) gænu ḷamáyātá (kellátá)bōlē visi keruvā.**

37. **A Bvá Cgen æḋágená giyā. æḋágená yanávā** - drag

38. **Mamá oyātá bīmá ekak araṅ ḋennaṅ. Arraṅ ḋenná** means "buy me (a drink)."

39. **Ḷamáyāvá hembath velā thiyennē. Hembath** means "exhausted."

Dialogue 10: At the Zoo

A: **Ammē ammē matá ali balanná ōne**. Mother, mother, I want to see the elephants.

B: **Ali nætumá thiyennē havas velā, api ē velāvátá aliyo balámu**. The elephant dance is in the evening, so we can watch them at that time.

C: **Api ehenaṅ kurullō balanná yamuḋá**? Then shall we go and see the birds?

B: **Hā api kurullō balanná yamu**.

They go to see the birds.

C: **Apō girau jāthi kīyak innávāḋá**? Oh, look how many types of parrots there are.

A: **Kurullō balálā æthi velā, api vaⁿḋuro balanná yaṅ**. I'm tired of watching the birds, lets go see the monkeys.

B: **Balanná, ará vaⁿḋurā kūduvē elilā inná hæti**. See how that monkey is hanging on the cage.

A: **Anná balanná ará vaⁿḋuru pætiyā mallitá athá vanánávā**. Look, that little monkey is waving at malli. Anná - a way of saying look.

C: **Naṅgitá mahansi vage, mamá naṅgivá ussá gannáḋá**? Little sister, you're looking tired. Shall I carry you? Except for little kids and those too sick or infirm to move well on their own, **vadā ganná**, which has the same meaning, would be used instead.

A: **Næ næ, matá mahansi nǣ.** No no I'm not tired.

She starts walking fast.

B: **Na^{n}gige athin allá ganná**. (Somebody) hold her hand.

A: **Hari rasnei, api ais krīm kamuḋá**? Its very hot, shall we have some ice cream?

D: **Ammāgen ahanná**. Ask mother.

B: **Hā**, ice cream **ganná yamu**. Ok, lets go and have some ice cream.

This dialogue introduces the colloquial words for "younger brother" and "younger sister." Like the corresponding words for elder siblings, they can also be used non-literally in two contexts: 1) by a parent to a child with an older sibling 2) by someone older to someone younger (but not much younger).

40. Carry the parrot.
41. Sister, I want to go home.
42. There are many kinds of monkeys.

Dialogue 11: Introducing Someone

A friend of yours is visiting you at home. The two are talking, the mother comes out and is introduced to the friend.

A: **Ammā, mē mage yāḷuvā Nelum**. **Nelum, mē mage ammā**. Mother, this is my friend Nelum. Nelum, this my mother.

B: **Ā halo** aunty.

C: **Halo Nelum**. **Nelum hu^{n}gak kal i^{n}ḋálā apē ḋuvává ḋannávāḋá**? Hello Nelum. Have you known our daughter for a long time?

A: **Ou**. Campus **kālē i^{n}ḋálā**. Yes, since our campus days.

C: **Nelumge geval koheḋá**? Where are you from? Lit. Where is your house?

B: **Mamá Nuvárá**. I'm from Kandy.

C: **Ehenam mē ḷamáyā ḋaval kæmátá inná**. Then, child, stay for lunch. Normal to address much younger person as such.

B: **Ho^{n}ḋai** Aunty. Ok.

C: **Ehenaṅ oyá ḋennā kath^{h}ā kárá kárá inná ko**. **Mamá kæmá læsthi kárannam**. Then you two have a chat, I'll prepare lunch.

B: **Anē oyāge ammā hari ho^{n}ḋá pātai**. Your mother seems like a nice person.

When addressing a significantly older person, Sinhala speakers will refer to them as "uncle" or "aunty." The Sinhala equivalents, **māmā** and **næ^{n}ḋā**, are used as well. By contrast, **ayyā** and **akkā**, which may be used to refer to an older person of the same generation, are not commonly translated into English, even in urban environments.

43. I've known my friend since we were in school.
44. Where is the parrot's cage?
45. I asked him about that.

6
INANIMATE NOUNS

Dialogue 12: Planning a Trip

Api Nuvárá yanná hithánávā (**tá** would be incorrect) **monávāḋá balanná honḋá thæṅ?** We're thinking of going to Kandy, what places should we go and look (at)?
Ḋaḷáḋā māligāvá (temple of tooth), **Nuvárá vævá. Nuvárá yanávānaṅ, Pēráḋeniyá mál waththátath yanná. Nuvárá Eḷiyátath yanavāḋá**? The temple of the tooth, the Kandy lake. If (we're) going to Kandy, we should also go to the Peradeniya gardens. Should we go to Nuwara Eliya as well?

For inanimates, the dative **-tá** ending is used commonly to mark destinations, yet in the above two lines, the word **Nuvárá** is unmarked. For most words, including other -in type nouns, **-tá** would not be incorrect, for non -ins, its more common to include it. **Nuvárá** and **Kolá^{m}bá** do not require **-tá**, but other places do. This is in contrast to **vaththátath** (also (**-th**) to the garden) and **Nuvárá eḷiyátath** (also to Nuwara Eliya).

Monávāḋá ehe balanná thiyennē? What (is there) to see there?

Thē vaththákátá gihillā, thē koḷá haḋáná hæti balanná puḷuvan. If we go to the tea estates, we can see how the tea leaves are processed.

Hæti is a noun meaning "how," or "the way." Thus **haḋáná hæti** means the way they make it.

The indefinite form of **vaththá**, **vaththak,** has a dative form of **vaththákátá**.

Ē pæththá vædiyá rasne nǣ, hu^{n}gak lassáná pæthi thiyenávā. It's not that hot around that area, (and) there are many beautiful places there.

Thæn thunátámá giyoth / yanavānaṅ, ḋavas kīyak vithárá yaiḋá? If we go to all three places, how many days will (it) take? The **má** here implies all. **Vithárá** is a postposition meaning "about," or "around," in the sense of "approximately." Here it means the speaker is not looking for an exact answer.

Pæththá literally means "side," and can also be used in a figurative sense. Here it is simply used to refer to locations.

The plural of **pæththá**, is **pæthi**, but the plural of **thæná**, "place," is **thæn** (Sometimes shown here with the informal pronunciation **thæṅ**). Inanimate plurals are no more manageable than those of animates.

Ḋavas hathárak vithárá. Maybe four days.

Mokakḋá Nuvárá yanná ho^{n}ḋámá viḋiyá? What's the best way to go to Nuwara?

Kōchchiyeṅ yanná puḷuvaṅ, car **-ekákiṅ yannath puḷuvaṅ**. We could go by train or by car. - **kōchchiyá-** train,

As we know, the singular definite dative case is the same for animate and inanimate nouns, **-tá**. Likewise, the nominative is unmarked for both. But that is end of it. In fact, inanimates effectively have only four common cases: there is no difference between the nominative and the accusative, the genitive and the locative, or the ablative and the instrumental.

6.2 The Nominative-Accusative.

Sinhala nouns come in two genders. **Yaká** is an animate noun; the other variety are termed inanimate nouns. Remember that unlike languages such as German or Latin, Sinhala gender is natural, meaning that it can be determined by the meaning of the noun, and does not have to be memorized. Recall also that people, spirits, animals, and so-called sentient beings in general are said to be animate.

Everything else is considered inanimate. Thus **iskōláyá**, "the school," is inanimate.

Iskōláyá. the school (nominative and accusative)

Unlike animates, the form of the word when it is the subject of a sentence is identical to the form it takes when it is the direct object.

One important colloquialism is the tendency of inanimate nouns that end in **-áyá** to be pronounced with a final **-ē** instead. Hence, in practice, it is common to say **iskōlē** for "the school."

Examples:

1. **Mamá koḷáyak pæguvā.**
2. **Mamá ḋorá arinná yathurá pāvichi keruvā.**
3. **Kōchchiyá kanḋá udátá giyā.**

Answers:

1. I stepped on a leaf.
2. I used the key to open the door.
3. The train went up the hill.

6.3 The Dative Case

The inanimate dative is formed identically and used similarly to the animate version.

Iskōláyátá. To the school

It is very frequently used when giving directions, However, it is omitted in certain expressions, e.g. "I'm going home" **Mamá geḋárá yanávā**.

6.4 The Locative Case

This case is equivalent with the animate genitive:

Iskōláyē. In/of the school

It is used to show that something is present in or part of the marked noun.

Mage sākkuvē māláyak thiyenávā. I have a necklace in my pocket (**sākkuvá**, pl. **sākku** means "pocket").

Another complication is the existence of different types of inanimate nouns. A significant fraction end in **ē** to begin with; these do not change when in the locative case. Their formal forms, which end in **-áyá**, change regularly to **-áyē**. Another class of nouns presents a greater challenge. **Geḋárá**, "house," is a typical example. Its locative is also identical to the nominative; the problem, of course, is that it looks just like a regular noun. Inanimate nouns of this class must be memorized.

For a e-form inanimate like **iskōlē**, the locative is identical to the nominative.

Examples:

1-3. Translate the following into Sinhala.

1. I trampled the pieces of glass that were on the road. (pieces of glass = **vīḋuru katu**)
2. We saw him drown in the sea.
3. He died in bed. (The word for "bed" is **æ^{n}ḋá**)

What does the following sentence mean?

4. **Oyāge oḷuvē ho^{n}ḋátámá** "snow."

1. **Pārē thibuṇá vīḋuru katu matá pæguṇá**. I trampled the pieces of glass that were on the road. (pieces of glass = **vīḋuru katu**)
2. **Eyā muhuḋē gilenávā api ḋækkā**. We saw him drown in the sea.
3. **Eyā mæruṇe æ^{n}ḋē**. He died in bed.
4. There's a massive amount of snow on your head. While Sinhala has a word for snow (the Sanskrit loan **himá**), this is not used in spoken conversation.

6.5 The Ablative-Instrumental Case

This case is formed like the animate ablative:

Iskōláyen/Iskōlen: from/through the school (ablative and instrumental)

This case has a number of peculiarities associated with it. Most notably, although it can be commonly used like the animate ablative, as below...

Mamá Anuráḋʰápuren Ḋehiválátá giyā. I went from Anuradhapura to Dehiwala. Or, I went to Dehiwala by way of Anuradhapura

The same meaning is often communicated using a postposition:

Mamá Anuráḋʰápurē indaṅ Ḋehiválátá giyā. I went from Anuradhapura to Dehiwala.

Note that **geḋárá** behaves very irregularly:

Geḋárá. the house (nominative and accusative)
Remember that while this form is also used in the context of going to one's own home, the normal dative form is used otherwise. Compare
Geḋárá yanávā. (I'm) going home.

with

Mamá eyāge geḋárátá yanávā. I'm going to his house.

Geḋárátá. to the house (dative).
Geḋárá. of the house (genitive and locative)
Geḋárin: from the house (ablative and instrumental)

There are a small number of nouns that take this ending in their singular form. Like **geḋárá**, these ***-in-type***

words generally do not have a distinct genitive/locative form.

Some place names also take this ending:

Mamá kolo^{m}bin Ḋehiválátá giyā. I went from Colombo to Ḋehiwala. **Mamá kolo^{m}bá haráhā Ḋehiválátá giyā**. Through - literary

Place names which take -in in the ablative	Ablative form
Kolo^{m}bá	Kolo^{m}bin
Ḋehiválá	Ḋehiválin

Another form of **i^{n}ḋaṅ** ("from") is **i^{n}ḋálā**. The **-en/-in** endings here are used strictly in the instrumental sense. In most other contexts, it can be used to mean "from":

Kolo^{m}bin genāpu mālu kævā. I ate the fish that was brought from Colombo.

Another context where the **-en/-in** ending cannot be used to mean "from" is describing an interval of time:

Badāḋā i^{n}ḋála iskoletá yanáva: I'll be going to school from Wednesday (onwards).

Kāge uḋavvenḋá ēká oyā therum gaththē - With whose help did you understand it?

Examples:

Translate the following into English.

1. **Nuvárá i^{n}ḋaṅ Kolo^{m}bátá mamá kōchchiyē hitiyē.**
2. **Mamá kaden eláválu arágaththa.**
3. **Mamá eyāgen salli ḋīlā arágaththā.**
4. **Mamá kaden badu horákaṅ keruvā.**
5. **Ē geḋárá vahalá kædilā.** (**vahalá** means roof)

Answers:

1. I was on the train from Kandy to Colombo.
2. I got vegetables from the store.
3. I bought (something) from him.
4. I stole things from the shop.
5. The roof of that house is broken.

From the store, **arágaththā** is implied to mean buy, but not from a person, there **salli ḋīlā** must be added, otherwise ambiguity, could have taken by force.

6.6 The Indefinite Form

The indefinite form of inanimate nouns is formed with **-ak** instead of **-ek.**

Iskōláyak
Iskōláyákátá

Iskōláyáká

Iskōláyákin

Inanimate indefinite nouns decline the same way, regardless of their behavior in the definite form.

geḋárak. a house (nominative and accusative)

geḋárákátá. to a house (dative)

geḋáráká. of a house (genitive and locative)

geḋárákin: from a house (ablative and instrumental)

E-type nouns use their formal versions to form their indefinite forms:

vib^{h}āgē. the test

vib^{h}āgáyak. a test

Although the formal version may also be used:

vib^{h}āgáyá. the test

vib^{h}āgáyak. a test

6.7 Plurals and the Stem Form

Inanimate plurals are declined as follows:

geḋárával. the houses (nominative and accusative)

geḋárávalválátá. to the house (dative)

gedarávalválá. of the house (genitive and locative)

geḋárávalválin: from the house (ablative and instrumental)

Inanimate plurals have to be memorized also, though they present different challenges than animate nouns. For one thing, one subset of them behaves in a perfectly regular way.

That class consists of the **-eká** nouns, inanimate nouns which are mostly loanwords. For instance, the word for bus:

Bás eká. the bus
Bás ekak. a bus
Bás: the buses

Most inanimate plurals are formed by subtracting part of the ending. For instance:

Pothá. the book
Pothak. a book
Poth. books

If the noun ends in **-vá** or **-yá**, the whole ending is usually removed, instead of just the vowel.

The **-val** suffix is sometimes added when removing the last vowel would result in a single final consonant that is forbidden in Sinhala. The forbidden final consonants that trigger this are **r**, **ḷ**, **t**, **d**, **ṇ**, **ḋ**, **g**, and **b**. We have seen the example of **geḋárá**, which has the plural form **geḋárával.** The half-nasals are also forbidden word-finally, but they may also change into a single nasal instead: **a^{n}gá** ("horn") has two plurals **aṅ,** and **a^{n}gával.** The sound **h**, on the other hand, changes to **s** regularly.

Words of this type may also form plurals by replacing their final consonant with **-u** or **-i**. Words of this type usually replace the final **á** with **i** if the preceding vowel is a front vowel, and **u** otherwise though there are a fair number of exceptions. The word **pokuṇá**, "pond," for instance, has a plural of **pokuṇu**. *The plurals of nouns with pre-final forbidden consonants have to be memorized, because there is no way to be determine the plural from the singular.*

The above reference to "single" consonants is due to the fact there is another class of inanimate plurals, which end in a double consonant followed by **á**. These form plurals by ***undoubling***, that is, converting the double consonant into its singular counterpart, and usually replacing the final vowel with **u** or **i**. Words ending in full nasal-stop combinations followed by **á** will undouble to half-nasals, and words ending is **-ssá** will usually replace the **ss** with **h**. The final vowel is, usually **i** if the preceding vowel is a front vowel, and **u** otherwise. Some exceptions include **hoḋḋá**, "gravy," pl. **hoḋi**, and **æththá**, pl. **æththával.**

From the plural, on the other hand, it is sometimes the case the stems ending in **-u** or **-i** will double to form the singular; but it isn't guaranteed; some will add **-vá** or **-yá** respectively, others will just replace the final vowel with **á**.

Unlike animate plurals, all inanimate plurals decline the same way, regardless of their form.

Some inanimates have informal pronunciations that end in **e / ē** **mōlē** - place where you make rice into flour

The ***stem form*** of a noun is basically an adjective version of it. For instance the stem form of **amāruvá**, "difficulty" is **amāru**, "difficult." **Amāru**, however, can also mean "difficulties." It turns out that for subtractive type nouns, the plural form is also the stem. This is not true for all types of nouns. The stem of **pārá** is **pārá**, not **pārával.**

Given the singular and the plural, it is usually easy to determine the stem of an inanimate noun. Compare the two, letter by letter, counting digraphs (**th**, **ⁿg**) as single letters. If the two words are of different lengths, the shorter one is the stem. If the words are of the same length, the one which ends in **á** is *not* the stem. There are a few exceptions to this rule, such as **venásá** "difference", pl. **venaskam**, stem **venas**. Animate nouns have stems too, but determining them is much more complex, and they are rather less useful (see section 11.1).

6.8 Summary and Supplemental information

Inanimate nouns have four distinct cases:

The nominative-accusative, which is used both when the noun is a subject or the direct object of a sentence

The dative, which is used like the animate dative

The genitive-***locative***, which is used like the animate genitive, but also to indicate that something is in or on a noun

The ablative-***instrumental***, which is used like the animate ablative, but also to indicate that a noun is being used to carry out an action

E-type nouns have identical nominative and locative cases, both ending in **-ē**.

In-types have instrumental forms ending in **-in**.

Nom.-acc.	**vaththá**	**vaththak**	**vathu**
Dative	**vaththátá**	**vaththákátá**	**vathuválátá**
Genitive-locative	**vaththē**	**vaththáká**	**vathuválá**
Ablative-instrumental	**vaththen**	**vaththákin**	**vathuválin**

There are many kinds of inanimate plurals:

Plural Type	Plural Form	Singular Form	Meaning
Subtractive	**Poth**	**Pothá**	Book
	Aṅ	**A^{n}gá**	Horn
	Gas	**Gaha**	Tree

Plural Type	Plural Form	Singular Form	Meaning
Undoubling	Muḋu	Muḋḋá	Ring
	Pæthi	pæththá	Side
Subtractive -yá/-vá	Gedi	Gediyá	Fruit
	Boru	Boruvá	Lie
val	Pārával	Pārá	Road
Nu	Akuru	Akurá	Letter
Eká	Bas	Bas eká	Bus

All these types inflect by adding **-válátá**, **-válá**, or -**válin**, even the ones that already ending **-val.**

1-10: Translate to Sinhala:

1. Say it in Sinhala.
2. Stones were thrown at this house.
3. There's a flower in the garden
4.I work from home.
5. That's the man's pencil.
6. I read that in a book.
7. I came from Ḋehiwala.
8. I'm in Colombo.
9.I'll fix it with a hammer.
10. I'm the one who broke it.

11-45: Translate to English

11. **Mamá Anurāḋ^{h}ápuren Nuvárá Eḷiyátá giyā.**

12.**Mamá eyagen pænsálak illá gaththā.**

13. **Mamá** Boston **válin Kolo^{m}bátá giyā.**

14. **Mamá** New York **válin** Boston **valátá giyā.**

15. **Mamá Ḋehiválin nuvárátá giyā.**

16. **Mamá Maḋurasiyen Kolombotá giyā.**

17. **Api Kolombátá flight ekak gaththā.**

18. **Api athen kǣvā.**

19. **Mamá iskūruppu niyánen ēká hai keruvā** - tightened.

20. **Mamá bisikálē issáráha vaththē thibbā.**

21. **Mamá** exam/test **eká** pass **vuṇā.** Or **vib^{h}āgē** pass vuṇā.

22. **Mamá ē pituvá pothen irā gaththā. Irā gannávā** - tear out.

23. **Pænsálēkin mē koḷē liyanná epā.**

24. **Mamá ḋora æriyáhamá,** alarm **eká saḋḋá venávā.**

25. **Mamá hāl** bag **eká kussiyátá genāvā.**

26. **Mamá muhuḋē pīnuvā**

27. **Matá sippi katuvak vallēḋi hambuṇā.**

28. **Mamá kiyáthákin gás kæpuvā**

29. **Kurullō vagáyak ē gasválá innávā. Ē gasválá kurullō innávā.**

30. **Ē va^{n}ḋurā aththen aththátá paninávā. aththá** = branch (pl. **athu**)

31. **va^{n}ḋurō gahen bimátá paninávā.**

32. **Ē kadē velassaniṅ vahanávā. sāmānyen** - usually, but formal

33. **Api vællē i^{n}ḋá gená mahansi æriyā. Mahansi arinávā** means "rest."

34. **Paraná poth ain kárálā, aluth poth thiyanná/ḋānná ōne.**

35. **Kar ekákin ē pārávalválá yanná bǣ.**

36. **Kussiyen ho^{n}ḋá suva^{n}ḋak enávā.**

37. **Mamá kessel gediyá venuvátá / ḋīlá / næthuva a^{m}bá gediyá gaththā. Venuvátá** - instead of.

38. **Mage geḋárá kāmárá ḋekak thiyenávā.**

39. **Ē iskōlē panthi kāmárá hathárak thiyenávā.**

40. **Mamá pænen a^{n}ḋinná puruḋu vuṇā. Puruḋu venná** means "to practice."

41. **Mamá geḋárin gēnnaṅ.**

42. **Ēká biththiyē liyálā thiyenávā**

43. **Pūsā ballātá valigeṅ gæhuvā. Valigē / valigáyá** means "tail."

44. **Thavá tikákin bel eká gahanná ōne.**

45. **Mē pæththátá hærenná.**

Dialogue 13: In the Garden

A: **Kō mē ḷamáyā? Ḋuvē, ḋuvē!** Where is this child? Daughter, daughter!

B: **Mam mehe vaththē innē.** I'm here in the garden.

A: **vaththátá velā monávāḋá kárannē? Iskōlē yannath parakku vei.** What are you doing in the garden? you'll be late for school.

B: **Mamá mē mal tikak kadánávā iskōlētá geniyanná.** I'm picking some flowers to take to school.

A: **Ará vaththá pallehā thiyená rosá pa^{n}ḋuren mal tikak kadā ganná**. Pick some flowers from the rose bush that is at the bottom of the garden.

B: **Mē mal æthiḋá**? **æḋḋá** - informal version of **æthiḋá**. Showing the bouquet. Is this enough?

A: **Ará suḋu rosá malákuth kadā ganná**. **Thavá ḷamainuth mal gēnávāḋá**? Pick a white rose as well. Will any other kids be bringing any flowers?

B: **Ou**. **Anik ḷamainuth ē gollange vathuválin mal genei**. Kids will bring flowers from their gardens. Note that a formal version of the future form is **genevi**.

A: **Ha ha**, **ḋæṅ gētá yamu**, **æ^{n}ḋá ganná**. Ok, lets go in and get dressed.

46. There are no flowers in this garden.
47. The monkeys are in cages.
48. What are you doing in the store?

7
PRONOUNS

Dialogue 14: Hitching a Ride

A father is going to work and telling his son he can get a ride if he's on time.

A: **Puthā miniththu vissákin læsthi vuṇoth, māth ekká yanná puḷuvan**. Son if you can get ready in twenty minutes, you can go with me. **Māth ekká** is an irregular, more common version of **mamath ekká**.

B: **Thāththā kar ekenḋá yannē**? Father are you going by car?

A: **Ou, mamá aḋá kar eká araṅ yanná ōne**. Yes, today I have to take the car.

C: **Apō puthāvá araṅ yanná giyoth, oyātá parakku vei**. Oh, if you wait to take our son, you'll get late.

A: **Næ næ, aḋa matá** office **ekē echchárá vædak næhæ. Mamá kar eká haḋanná ḋīlā thamai** office **ekátá yannē**. No, no, I don't have much work at the office today. Anyway I'll first leave the car to be repaired and then go to the office.

C: **Ená sumāne mage kar ekath tayár māru káranná geniyanná vei**. Next week, my car will also have to be taken to change the tires.

A: **Mā la^{n}gá sīye nōttu ḋekai thiyenne. Oyā la^{n}gá thavá thiyánávānaṅ matá ḋenná**. I have only two hundred rupee notes with me. Give some notes if you have any.

The son arrives.

A: **Ā puthā læsthiḋá**? **Velāvath hari, api ehenaṅ yamu**. Oh, son are you ready? It's time to go, so let's leave.

B: **Thāththā apitá poth kadetath yanná puḷuvanḋá**? Father, can we also go to the bookstore?

A: **Ane ane, maṅlavvá vená vædath kárágganná haḋánávā nēḋá**. Oh, now you're getting me to do some other work? **manlavvá** is informal form of **mā lavvá**.

7.2 First Person Pronouns

Sinhala pronouns decline like regular animate nouns, for the most part. A major difference is that pronouns do not have a vocative form. The word for "I" is irregular. Its forms decline as if it were **ma** or **mā**. However, the nominative is **mamá**.

English	Sinhala
I	**Mamá**
Me	**Māvá**
To me	**Matá**
My	**Mage**
From me	**Magen**
By my hand	**Ma(ge) athin**
Near me	**Māla^{n}gá**

The word for "we" is **api.**

English	Sinhala
We	**Api**
Us	**Apivá**
To us	**Apitá**
Our	**Ape**
From us	**Apen**
By us	**Api athin**
Near us	**Api la^{n}gá**

Maṅ is an alternative first person pronoun. It is colloquial and informal.

English	Sinhala
I	**Maṅ**
Me	**Māvá**

English	Sinhala
To me	**Matá**
My	**Mage**
From me	**Mageṅ**
By my hand	**Maṅ athin**
By me	**Maṅ lavvá**
Near me	**Maṅgāvá**

-gāvá is an informal equivalent of **la^{n}gá**. It is more commonly used than **maṅla^{n}gá**. In contrast **māgāvā** is quite uncommon, with **māla^{n}gá** being the norm.

1. I have a pen on me. **Maṅ la^{n}gá pænak thiyenává**
2. He asked us yesterday. **Eyā īye apen æhuvā**.
3. Our house is very messy. **Apē geḋárá hari hædi**.
4. **Eyā maṅlavvá gē as káráganná hæḋuvā**. He tried to get me to tidy up the house.

7.3 Third Person Pronouns

Spoken Sinhala does not have a distinct word for "he" or "she", instead, it has the third person pronoun **eyā**.

English	Sinhala
He/she	**Eyā**
Him/her	**Eyāvá**
To him/her	**Eyātá**
His/hers	**Eyāge**
From him/her	**Eyāgen**
By his/her hand	**Eyā(ge) athin**
Near him/her	**Eyā la^{n}gá**

There are multiple words for "it." The pronoun **ēkā**, pl. **ēkun**, is used to refer to animals. It has a regular declension. **Eyā** can be used with animals, especially pets. This has the same effect as referring to animals as "he" or "she" in English.

Conversely, **ēkā**, as well as many other words that ostensibly refer to animals, can be used to refer to humans. Essentially, it is like referring to a person as an "it." In Sinhala, this is a normal, rude way to talk to or about people.

Note that **eyā** is still animate. If you are referring to an inanimate "it", like a building or a street, **ēká** is the inanimate equivalent:

English	Sinhala	Plural
It	ēká	ēvā
To it	ēkátá	ēvā(válá)tá
Its/in it	ēkē	ēvāválá

English	Sinhala	Plural
From/by/using it	**ēken**	**Evā(val)in evain**
In it	**ēkē**	**ēvāválá**

Since **ēká** is inanimate, it follows an inanimate declension pattern. Specifically, it follows the definite pattern. If you want to refer to a nonspecific it, you must use **ēkak** instead.

English	Sinhala
A thing	**Ēkak**
To a thing	**Ēkákátá**
A thing's	**Ēkáká**
From a thing	**Ēkákin**

Literary Sinhala does have other pronouns:

English	Sinhala	
He	**Ohu**	**Oun**
She	**æ/ æyá**	**Oun**
It (animate)	**ū**	**Un**

Ū sees some use in spoken Sinhala as a degrading way to refer to a person; in this way it is similar to **ēkā**. Also similar is the feminine pronoun **ēki**, pl. **ēkilā**. This is similarly impolite when used on people, but exclusively refers to female animates. There are some similar words:

Arū, pl. **arun**, which has roughly the same meaning, and **mū**, which means "this animal," pl. **mun**.

The word for "they" is formed by adding **-lā**, similar to the most common way of forming animate plurals.

English	Sinhala
They	**Eyālā, ē gollan**
Them	**Eyālāvá**
To them	**Eyālātá**
Their's	**Eyālāge**
From them	**Eyālāgen**
By their hand	**Eyālā athin**
Near them	**Eyālā la^{n}gá**

Ē gollō / an goes through the same transformations; it may actually be more common. It is less formal and non literary. The **gollan** form and its derivatives may also be pronounced with just one "l."

1. **Anná aru enávā api ḋuvámu**. Oh, he's coming, let's run.
2. **Ekūnge** "magazine" **eká ho^{n}ḋá thamai**. Their magazine is good indeed. Although the coarse pronoun is used, the overall effect is not derogatory.
3. **Ē ēgol(l)ange kar eká**. You could also say **eyālāge**. As with animate plurals, the o version is only used in the nominative.

4. **Ēvā pāvichchi káranná paráṇá vædī**. Those are too old to use.

7.4 Second Person Pronouns

Sinhala has a large number of second person pronouns, with varying levels of politeness. The most common and widely acceptable one is **oyā**.

English	Sinhala
You	**Oyā**
You (accusative)	**Oyāvá**
To you	**Oyātá**
Your	**Oyāge**
From you	**Oyāgen**
By your hand	**Oyā athin**
Near you	**Oyālangá**

To address multiple people, **oyālā** is used.

You all	**Oyālā**
You all (accusative)	**Oyālāvá**
To you all	**Oyālātá**
All of your	**Oyālāge**
From you all	**Oyālāgen**
By all of your hands	**Oyālā athin**
Near you all	**Oyālā la^{n}gá**

Ōgollan also more common. These forms have variant form **gollō**. The **gollō** forms are not usually found in writing, but the **lā** forms are.

Sinhala word for "you"	Plural	Politeness
Obávahanse	**Obávahanselā**	Most polite
Obáthumā	**Obáthumālā**	Extremely polite
Obá	**Obálā**	Very polite
Ohe	**Ohelā**	Archaic, quite polite
Numbá	**Numbálā**	Can be polite or impolite
Oyā	**Oyālā**	polite/neutral
Umbá	**Umbálā**	impolite
thō	**thōpi/thōpilā**	Very impolite
thōpá	**thōpálā**	Archaic, very impolite
Yakko	**Yakku/yakkun**	Extremely impolite

Thamusē - common, among men, referring to other men, rude to use on women.

The plural forms are made by adding **-la**, like before. An exception is **thō**, the plural of which is **thopilā**.

The concept of politeness deserves more discussion here. A non-native speaker would most likely only be expected to know the word **oyā**, and it is usable in both formal and informal situations.

In modern society, **obávahanse** is usually reserved for monks. **Obá** and **nu^{m}bá** are used in highly formal contexts, like business mētings and interviews.

U^{m}bá is impolite; it isn't suitable for usage in a formal environment, though it might be used in a teasing manner amongst family and friends. It may often be accompanied by the word **baṅ**. This word is not quite a word for "you," because even though it can be used by itself, it doesn't decline.

Thō is rude. It can be used in a teasing manner with close friends, but is otherwise reserved for heated verbal jousting. Think of it as the equivalent of peppering an English sentence with mild swears.

Thō is irregular. **Thotá** is more common than **thōtá**. **Thōva allaganī polisiyen**. The police will catch you. **Thogen** is the normal ablative, while **thōgen** is rare, if not unheard of.

You	thō
You (acc)	thōva
To you	thotá
Your	thoge
From you	thogen

Yakō is a fighting word. It can also be used for teasing with very close friends, but is generally used by people who are very angry or very drunk. Don't use it unless you're ready to rumble. Like other vocatives, and **baṅ**, it is not a fully fledged word for "you;" it is just a separate word that can be used to address people.

Thaman / thamun - myself / yourself.

Examples: Translate the following sentences into English:

1. **Thoge ammāvá mamá allágannávā**.
2. **Obáthumāvá hamu vuṇá eká gæná apitá santhōsai. Hamu** is a form of **hambá**.
3. **U^{m}bá koheḋá giye**?
4. **U^{m}ba æi parakku vuṇē**?
5. **U^{m}bá paráyek**. The word **paráyā** is offensive.
6. **U^{m}bá mokáḋá vuṇē**?
7.

Answers:

1. I will catch your mother.
2. We're happy to have met you.
3. Where did you go?
4. Why were you late?
5. You're a real bastard. **Paráyā** literally means "pariah," but is nowadays used as a general term of offense.
6. What happened to you?

7.5 The Interrogative Pronoun

The interrogative pronoun declines as follows:

Who?	Kauḋá
Whom?	Kāváḋá
To whom?	Kātáḋá
Whose?	Kāgeḋá
From whom?	Kāgenḋá
By whose hand?	Kā(ge) athinḋá
Near whom?	Kā la^{n}gáḋá

For inanimates, the word **mokak**, what, is commonly used. Its standard form **mokakḋá** is often pronounced as **mokaḋḋá**.

Mokaḋḋá me velā thiyenne? What has happened?

It declines like a normal inanimate indefinite word:

Mē lamáyā mokákátá ē gamáná giyāḋá ḋannē næ. I don't know why this child went on that trip.

Mokákátá here is the reason for going. Notice that in this inflected form, **-ḋá** attached to the verb at the end of the action **mokákátá** is referring to. The question particle may be omitted entirely in some cases:

Mokakinḋá mēká kæpuvē? With what was this cut?

This word is not to be confused with **mokáḋá**, which means "why":

Mokáḋá ohomá innē? Why are you staying like that?

A plural word for "what" is **monávāḋá** (which can also inflect with forms like **monávātá** or **monávath**)

Notice that when asking any question with a question word, verbs have to be in the emphatic form.

Examples:

Translate the following sentences into Sinhala:

1.Who broke the plate?
2. Who are you looking for?
3. Who wants to go home?
4. Whose books are these?
5. From whom did you receive that letter?
6. Who is responsible for breaking this plate?
7. Who's got fifty dollars on them?

Answers:

1. **Kauḋá pi^{n}gāná kaduvē**?
2. **Kāváḋá hoyannē**?
3. **Kātáḋá geḋárá yanná ōne**? Note that auxiliaries can be used without any change in form.
4. **Mē poth kāgeḋá**? Or **Kāgeḋe mē poth**?
5. **Kāgenḋá liyumá labuṇē**? or **Liyumá labuṇē kāgenḋá**?
6. **Kāge athinḋá pi^{n}gane kæduṇē**?
7. **Kā la^{n}gáḋá dollar panáhak thiyennē**? Alternatively **Kāge gāváḋá** dollar **panáhak thiyenne**?

7.6 Asking Questions

Questions can be formed in several ways. Any statement can be converted to a question by addition of the suffix **-ḋá**.

Oyā kanávā. You"re eating.
Oyā kanávāḋá. Are you eating?
Eyāgāvá pothá tiyánávā. He has the book.
Eyāgāvá pothá tiyánávāḋá. Doe he have the book?
Ḋeviyā yakāvá maruvā. The god killed the demon.
Ḋeviyā yakāvá maruvāḋá. Did the god kill the demon?
Sīthalai. it is cold
Sīthaláḋá. is it cold?

Note that for adjectives, **ḋá** replaces the **i** of the i-form, and that for these questions, the verb does not need to be emphatic.

Other kinds of questions can be asked using question words. Most of these must be accompanied by the **ḋá** particle:

Oyā mokákḋá káranne? What are you doing? (without understanding)

This word is used under specific circumstances, when you don't understand what the speaker is doing, like asking what someone solving a complex problem is on, or as a way of checking if someone is sane.

Moná is a more formal, general-purpose word for "what" or "which:"

Moná "show" **ekáḋá mēká?** Which show is this?

It has the same plural form as **mokáḋá**:

Oyā monávāḋá kanne? What are you eating?

The word for "how" can be used to ask about the condition of things. It is commonly used by itself in conversation:

Kohomáḋá. How(are you)?

This is effectively the Sinhala word for "hello," in this respect it is similar to asking "how's it going" in English.

There is a separate word for asking about quantities:

Kīyak salli ōneḋá. How much money do (you) need?

There isn't an actual word for "when", instead, you can ask:

Velāvá kīyáḋá. What time is it?

Another way to say it is:

Koi velāveḋá ēká vuṇē? When (at what time) did it happen?

7.7 Here and there

In English, when talking about places, one might say that it is *here*, or that it's over *there*, or if the location is unknown, one might ask *where* it is. In Sinhala, there are more possibilities:

Meaning	More Formal	Less Formal
Here	**methāná**	mehe
There, near addressee	**otháná**	ohe
There, away, but relatively close	**atháná**	arahe
There, close or far	**etháná**	ehe
Where	**kothánáḋá**	koheḋá

Mehe is a casual way to say "here". There are three comparable words for "there": **ohe** is used to refer to location near the person you're talking to. **Aráhe** is used to refer to something that isn't near the speaker or the listener, but that the speaker can indicate to the listener. **Ehe** is a generic word for "there," which can be used in the same context as **aráhe**, but also to refer to a location not visible to either person.

Examples:
Translate the following sentences into English.

1. **Mehe hari rasnei. Ehe hari sīthálai.**
2. **Oyā kohedá yanne**?
3. **Ohe hulaṅ særáḋá**?
4. **Mama ē pothá aráhe ḋækkā**.

.

Answers:

1. It's very hot here. It's very cold there.
2. Where are you going?
3. Is it very windy over there where you are?
4. I saw that book over there.

7.8 This and That

There are two general words for "this", based on the animacy of the subject. **Mēká** means "this thing," and can be used to refer to inanimates in general.

Meyā means "this one," and can be used for animates in general, although it is more often used to refer to people. **Mū** is a word which means "this animal?."

There isn't, however, just one word for "that;" instead, there are three, differentiated on the same basis as the words for "there":

Meaning	Sapient	Sapient plural	Animal	Animal plural	Inanimate	
Near speaker	**Meyā**	**Mēgollō**	**Mēkā**	**Mēkun**	**Mēká**	**Mēvā**
Near addressee	**Oyā**	**ōgollō**	**Ōkā**	**Ōkun**	**ōká**	**Ōvā**
Away, but relatively close	**Aráyā**	**Arágollō**	**Arákā**	**Arákun**	**Aráká**	**Arávā**
Away, close or far	**Eyā**	**ēgollō**	**Ēkā**	**Ekun**	**ēká**	**Ēvā**
Question form	**kauḋá***	**Koigollōḋá**	**Mokekḋá / Mokeḋḋá**	**Moná saththuḋá***	**kōkáḋá*/ mokaḋḋá**	**Monávāḋá**

*also **koi**[subject]**ḋá**

1. **Koi ekkenāḋá āve**?
2. **Oyā ōká visi káranná**.
3. **Aráyā koheḋá yannē**?
4. **Mokaḋḋá** A **karannē**? **Eyā niḋi**.
5. **Ē gollan yatin ennē**.

Answers:

1. Who came? This could alternatively be **kauḋá āve**?

2. Throw that thing (of yours / that you're holding / near you) away. If you were telling the person to throw something that you were pointing to, aráká would be used instead. **Ēká** could also be used in that context, or if you were talking about throwing

3. Where is that person over there going?

4. What's A doing. He's asleep. **Eyā** is the only choice here, **aráyā** is used for people not referred to in the conversation.
5. They come from below.

7.9 More Relative Terms

Meaning	Way	Quantity	Time	Side
This...	**Mehemá**	**Mechchara**	**Mē Pārá**	**Me pæthá**
That... (related to addressee)	**Ohomá**	**Ochchara**	**Oyá pārá**	**Oyá pæthá**
That.. (something nearby or already said)	**arámá**	**Achchara**	**Ará pārá**	**Ará pæthá**
That (all-purpose)	**ehemá**	**ēchchara**	**ēpārá**	**ē pæthá**
What	**kohomá..ḋá**	**Kochchara**	**Koi pārá**	**Koi pæthá**

Not all such terms in Sinhala have the full five-fold division shown above. For instance, the dative forms the inanimate pronouns have informal variants:

	Formal	Informal
To This	**Mēkátá**	**Mītá**
To That (assoc. with listener)	**Okátá**	**Oitá**

	Formal	Informal
To that (assoc. with third party)	Ēkátá, Arákátá	Ītá

Mītá and **ītá** can, moreover, be used in time statements; for instance:

Mītá passē mamá iskōlē yannē nǣ. From now on (literally, "after this") I won't be going to school.

In this context, **oitá** cannot be used, and the only two choices are simple equivalents of the English words "this [time]" and "that [time]."

Examples:

1. **Oitá vædiyá ho^{n}ḋai mehemá károth.**
2. **Eyātá achchárá ḋeyak káranná puḷuvan kiyálā mamá hithuvē nǣ.**
3. **Mehemá káranná kiyálā mamá eyātá kiyuvā.**
4. **Koi pæththátáḋá hærenná ōne?**
5. **Mamá ē pæththátá hæruṇā.**

Answers:

1. It's better to do it this way [compared to the way you're doing it].
2. I didn't think he could do something of that magnitude.
3. I told her to do it this way.

4. Which way should (we) turn?
5. I turned to that side.

7.10 The Generic Forms

The "generic" forms can prefix any inanimate, except for the special cases described above.

Generic Prefix	Example	Meaning of Example
Mē	**Mē Kālē**	This time
Oyá	**Oyá kālē**	That time
Ará	**Ará kālē**	That time
ē	**Ē kālē**	That time
Kō ?	**Koi kālē**	What time?

Indefinite Pronouns

Indefinite pronouns, like "someone", "anyone," or "no one" are formed rather irregularly in Sinhala. They are usually compounds of question words and certain other words. Some examples and generalizations are below.

Someone: "who" (**kauru**, **kāvá**, etc) + **hari**,

Something: **mokak hari**, sometimes: **samáhará velavátá**, some time: **koi velāve hari, kātáhari**,

Anytime: **ōná velāváká**, anything: **ōná ḋeyak** (you want), **monávā hari ḋeyak** no one: **kauruvath(má)** … **nǣ**, no where: **kohevath nǣ**, nothing: **monávath nǣ, kisi** … **nǣ**, never: **kavaḋāvath** (…) **nǣ** (lit. Not on any day), **ayeth** … **nǣ** never again,

Kisimá … **nǣ** is more generally a way of expressing negativity:

kisi(**má**) **viḋiyak nǣ** - there's absolutely no way to do it.

Any	**ōná** (anything (you) want), **monávā hari**
Some	**kauru, kāvá, mokak, koi**… + **hari**
None	Question word + **th** … **nǣ**

Words for "every" are more simple, they just use **Okkomá** "all," or **hæmá**, "every." Examples: **hæmá ḋenāmá, okkomálā.** "Everyone" **okkomá paththárávālá.** all of the papers, **hæmá paththárēkámá.** every paper. Notice that when used with generic nouns, **okkomá** uses the plural genitive/locative form, while **hæmá** uses the indefinite genitive/locative form.

1. **Mēká kātáhari ḋenná**. Give this to somebody. **Mēká illáná kenekutá ḋenná** - give this to someone who asks for it.
2. **Ēká gæná ḋanná kauruhari innávāḋá**? Is there anybody who knows about it?

3. **Kāváhari a^{n}dá gahanná puḷuvaṅḋá**? Can you call someone over?

4. **Mē kanthōruvē kauruth næ**. No one is at this office.

5. **Kāváhari gēnná.** bring someone

6. **Matá ēká hæmá velēmá varáḋinávā**. I always get it wrong.

7.11 Summary and Supplemental Information

Sinhala has quite a few pronouns. The following is a basic set:

	Singular	Plural
1st Person	Mamá	Api
2nd Person	Oyā	Ōgollō
3rd Person	Eyā	Ēgollō

There are quite a few other pronouns, especially in the second person. These range from forms which are respectful, like **obá**, to intensely disrespectful, like **thō**. Several have irregular case forms.

The English categories "this," "that," and "what" have counterparts in Sinhala. While "this" and "what" have exact counterparts in the prefixes **mē**/**me** and **koi**/**ko**, there are three different categories for "that:" **oyá**/**ō**, **ará**/**a**, and **ē**/**e**.

Most English question words have good Sinhala equivalents:

Who	kauḋá
What	mokaḋḋá, mokakḋá, monávāḋá
Where	Koheḋá
When	Koi vellāváḋá
Why	mokáḋá
How	kohomáḋá
Which	Koi-

The indefinite pronoun "some" is formed by combining the the above words (without **-ḋá**) with **hari**. "None" is expressed by replacing **-ḋá** with **-th**, and ending the sentence with **næ**.

7.12 Exercises

Translate into Sinhala:

1. What is this thing?

2. What is this thing made of?

3. (pointing) What is that thing over there?

4. There is no one to help me.

5-14. Translate these sentences into English, and guess the contexts in which they might be used.

5. **Mahaththáyō, matá uḋavvak káranná puḷuvanḋá**?

6. **Obá gæná mamá ahalā thiyenávā**.

7. **Obá matá a^{n}dá gæhuvāḋá**?

8. **Obávahanse pansálátáḋá vædámá kárannē**?

9. **U^{m}bá pādam kāránávāḋá**?

10. **Thō mēká gæná monávāḋá ḋannē**?

11. **U^{m}bá horákaṅ károth**, **mamá u^{m}bává allágannávā**.

12. **Mamá thotá ho^{n}ḋá ḋa^{n}duvámak ḋenávā.**

13. **Kauḋá yakō kǣ gahannē**?

14. **Gahannáḋá yakō ennē**?

Translate into Sinhala:

15. It seems like these people are doing something wrong.

16. Those two always do well on the tests.

17. Where did that guy come from?

18. There's never any good food here.

19. The food here is never any good.

20. I know a place where there's always something to do.

21. Sometimes this class is good.

22. Are they coming today?

23. What do you think of this restaurant?

24. Put this book with the rest.

25. These sentences aren't clear.

26. Give it to us.

27. He got the answer from us.

28. They chased us away.

29. Do you have those over there?

30. Do those grow over there where you are?

31. Is it raining where you are?

32. That chair (you're sitting in) looks very comfortable.

33. That chair (on display) looks very comfortable.

34. This chair (on display nearby) looks very comfortable.

35. That chair (that you saw earlier but isn't visible now) looks very comfortable.

36. That chair is better than this one.

37. No one can stop mē.

38. Sometimes she goes over there.

39. I always come here to eat.

40. These questions look a lot easier than the ones from last time. An adjective meaning "from last time" is **giyá pārá**.

41. Nobody was able to help me with those questions.

42. I'd rather be anywhere but here.

Translate the following into English

The following 3 exercises all refer to a single story, which the speaker heard recently.

43. **Ē kath^{h}āvá matá ḋænáganná hambuṇē īye**.

44. **Ēká ará issellā kiyapu kath^{h}āvátá vædiyá venas**.

45. **Oyá kath^{h}āvē hætiyátá mē prashnē hungak kal thibilā thiyenávā**.

46. **Æi aḋá atē kōchchiyá mē tharam parakku**?

47. **Kohomáḋá gē hoyā gaththē?á**

48. **Kohomáḋá oyá kæmá hæḋuvē**?

49. **Oitá vædiyá honḋai rathu pātá**.

50. **Poddak ohomá inná**.

51. **Mē viharē/pansálē kauruth næ**.

52. **Mē geḋárá kauruth næ**.

53. **Matá ehe yannath bæ**.

54. **Kauruhari bel eká gæhuvāḋá**.

Dialogue 15: Waiting on a Letter

Two people are talking.

A: **Ará mamá kiyápu liyumá āvāḋá**? Did that letter I was talking about arrive.

B: **Oyá kiyannē iyē āpu liyumá gæná venná æthi. Ēká pitá ratin āpu liyumak**. You might be talking about the letter that arrived yesterday. The letter came from a foreign country.

A: **Kō ē liyumá**? Where is that letter?

B: **Mē thiyennē**. Here it is.

Translate the following into Sinhala:

55. B came bringing the letter.

56. B hands over the letter.

57. I went to the store you were talking about.

Dialogue 16: Flower Shopping.

A: **Ē mal monávāḋá**? What kind of flowers are those?

B: **Ē Japan rosá**. Those are Japanese roses. (pointing to another kind of flower)

A: **Ará mal monávāḋá**? What kind of flowers are they?

B: **Ē ḋahas mal**. Those are marigolds. (Pointing to the marigolds)

A: **Oyá mal hu^{n}gak kal paváthinávāḋá**? Do those flowers stay fresh for a long time?

B: **Tiká ḋavasak**.

A: **Ehenam matá mē malválin ḋahayak ḋenná**. Then give me ten of those flowers.

58. Why does A use **oyá** to refer to the marigolds after previously using **ará**?

8
COMPLEX SENTENCES

Dialogue 17: Getting to School

A: **Æi oyā adá kar ekeṅ āvē**? Why did you come by car today?

Notice that **æi** typically comes at the start of sentence. Otherwise, this sentence has a typical word order: First, the subject, **oyā**, followed by a time word, **adá**, then an adverb/ instrumental noun, then a verb.

B: **Ayyath ē velāvemá pitá vuṇá nisā, mamá ayyā lavvá bassá gaththā**. I got a ride from my brother, because he was leaving at the same time.

Now the first part of this sentence has the same structure as the previous sentence: a subject, a time word, and a verb - but the verb is in the adjectival form, prefixing **nisā**. **Nisā** is a conjunction, meaning something like "because;" the whole thing in front of it is an adjectival clause.

The second part of the sentence has a similar structure. It too has the basic word order of subject-object-verb. A new word is **lavvá**, an instrumental postposition.

A: **Geḋárátá kochchárá ḋuráḋá**? How far is it to your home?

Note that i-form adjectives can be considered verbs for our purposes here.

B: **Hæthakmá ḋekak vithárá**. About two miles.

This sentence, on the other hand, is quite different from the ones we have just seen. It has a single noun, **hæthakmá**, "mile" (in the indefinite form with emphasis), followed by two postpositions, a number and **vithárá**, "about."

A: **Ḋavaltath ayyā eiḋá**? Will your brother come in the afternoon also?

B: **Hariyátámá kiyanná bǣ, hæbæi, ayyā āvē næththaṅ, mamá æviḋágená yanávā**. I can't be sure, but if he doesn't come, I'll walk.

A: **hæmáḋāmá uḋētá ayyā ekká enná puḷuvaṅ veiḋá**? Will you be able to come with your brother every morning?

B: **Ēká kiyanná bǣ, kar ekeṅ hari æviḋágená hari thamai ennē**. I can't be sure, I'll come to school either by car or walking.

A: **Æi bas ekak næḋḋá**? Why, isn't there a bus? (Here, "why" is a separate clause from the second question, which is why **ḋá** appears)

B: **Bas ekak thiyenavā, hæbæi ēká iskōlē gāvá navaththannē nǣ**. There is but it doesn't stop near the school. **Hæbæi** is another conjunction, but unlike **nisā**, it doesn't follow an adjective.

A: **Samáhará ḋavasválátá, Mā ekkath geḋárá yanna puḷuvaṅ**. On some days, you can go with me.

B: **Ā eká ho^{n}ḋai. Ḋavaltá hari rasnei**. Oh that's good, it's very hot in the afternoon.

8.2 Lists

When forming lists, the postposition of choice should appear behind each word on the list:

Mamá uyannai kiyávánnai kæmáthī. I like to cook and to read.

The most common way to say "and" is simply to suffix each word on the list with **-i**. Remember that **á**+**i** = **ai.**

Matá pænsálákui pǣnakui ōnē. I need a pencil and a pen.

Words that end in consonants are suffixed with **-ui** instead.

The i-suffix for nouns has an alternate meaning when it is used on only one noun in a sentence:

Ēká thamai æththá! -That is it indeed. **Ēkai æththá** would just mean "that is the truth," while **ēká æththá** just means "that is true."

Here, it simply emphasizes the word on which it is suffixed.

Hari is a similar word, meaning "or":

Pænsálak hari pǣnak hari ḋenná?

Hari should be included after each element.

A more formal way to say "and" is **hā**. **Saha** is still more formal.

Matá pænsálak saha pǣnak ōne.

For these, the "and" word only appears before the last element.

Examples:

1. **Matá pænsálákui pǣnákui māker ekákui ōne**.
2. **Matá pænsálak pǣnak hā mākáná kǣlak** (eraser) **ōne**.

3. **Mamá elōlui bathui kanná kæmáthī.** (The word **elōluvá** means "the vegetable").

Examples:

1. I want a pencil, pen and a marker. Note that **-i** appears after every item in the list.
2. I want a pencil, pen, and an eraser.
3. I like to eat vegetables and rice. Note that in the above example, both "rice" and "vegetables" were in their plural forms. Since **bath** ends in a consonant, it is suffixed with **-ui**, but **elōlu** ends in a vowel, so it just receives a **-i**.

8.3 Place Postpositions

Many place-related words are used as postpositions:

English	Sinhala	Instrumental form	Locative form
near	**la^{n}gá**	**la^{n}gin**	**la^{n}gá**
far	**ḋurá**	**ḋurin**	**ḋurá**
above, on top	**udá**	**udin**	**udá**
under, underneath	**yatá**	**yatin**	**yatá**
inside	**æthuḷá**	**æthuḷen,** less commonly **æthuḷin**	**æthuḷē**
outside	**eḷiyá**	**eḷiyen**	**eḷiyē**
through	**athárá**	**athárin**	**athárē**
above	**ihálá**	**ihálin**	**ihálá**

English	Sinhala	Instrumental form	Locative form
below	**pahalá**	**pahalin**	**pahalá**
below	**palleha**	**pallehain**	**palleha**

Mē pothá mēsē udá thiyanná. Keep this book on top of the table.

Unlike the other postpositions we have dealt with, however, these words inflect. Many of them are like **-in** type inanimate nouns:

Eḷiyátá giyā. (someone) went outside.

Ū udin yanávā. It's flying above us. **Ēká** would be for a plane.

La^{n}ge thiyenávā. (It) is nearby.

Æ^{n}ḋá yatá mamá bæluvē næ. I didn't look under the bed.

Api ḋennā athárē sambanḋáyak næ. There is no connection between the two of us. **Sambanḋáyak** means "connection," **ḋennā** means "the two of us." **Athárá** is irregular, even though it has an -in-type instrumental, it has an -e-type locative.

Kurullā gas athárin piyæ^{m}buvā. The bird flew through the trees.

With adjectives, there is usually no distinction between the **-tá** and **-in** endings, but this is not true of the ***place postpositions***.

Ḷamáyā gas yatin ḋivvā. The child ran under the trees (on the way to some other place)

Ḷamáyā gas yatátá ḋivvā. The child ran under the trees (here, the trees are the destination)

The **en**/in ending, which for these words is basically purely instrumental rather than ablative, is favored if there is no motion:

Ēká kadetá udáhin thiyennē. (It's) above the shop. If it was below, one would use **pahalin**, or **pallehaiṅ thiyennē** instead. **Udáhin** is an alternate version of **udin**.

But these words can also function very similarly to adjectives, in addition to their use as postpositions. They can be used as i-forms:

Bohomá ḋurai. (It's) very far.

They cannot directly modify nouns, however, and in this respect they behave like adverbs:

Æthuḷe inná ballátá thibáhai. The dog that's inside is thirsty.

Examples:

Translate the following sentences into Sinhala:

1. Who lives in that house under the bridge? (the word for bridge is **pālámá**)

2. He came from far away.

3. There's a huge crowd outside.

4. The nearby shops aren't that good.

Translate the following sentences in English:

5. **Eká hinḋā thamai mamá pallehatá yannē**.

6. **Saruṅgále udátá giyā**. **Saruṅgále** means "the kite."

7. **Kurullá mage la^{n}gin giyā**.

Answers:

1. **Ē pālámá yatá thiyená geḋárá kauḋá innē**?

2. **Eyā ḋurá i^{n}ḋálā āvē**. **Ḋurin hariyátá ḋækkē næ**. I couldn't see it properly from far away. **Ḋurin pēná viḋiyátá ēká podī**. It looks small from a distance. Note: the first sentence cannot be **ḋurin**.

3. **Loku sená^{n}gak innávā eḷiyē**. **Eḷiyē** could also mean "in front."

4. **La^{n}gá thiyená sāppu echchárá ho^{n}ḋá næ**.

5. It's indeed for that reason that I am going down. Unlike with "up," there are a number of words for "down." See also **pahalá balanná.** "to look down."\

6. The kite went up. Here **udá** is not just the direction of motion, but the destination. Thus, **udátá** is used.

7. The bird (flew) right by me

8.4 Clause conjunctions

A ***clause*** is a phrase that could stand as a sentence on its own, but might instead just be part of a larger construction. For instance, the following are single clause Sinhala sentences:

Matá mānsī. I'm tired.

Mamá niḋā ganná yanávā. I'm going to sleep.

These two sentences can be combined to yield a single sentence:

Matá mānsi nisā, mamá niḋā ganná yanávā. I'm tired, so I'm going to sleep.

Nisā means "so" or "because." The entire first clause can be replaced with **ē** (or another such word). The phrase **ē nisa** is effectively a word meaning "therefore." Another similar word is **ithin**, which means "then" or "since":

Matá mānsī; ithin mamá niḋā gaththā.

Notice that in the first sentence, **mānsi** is in its plain form, but in the second, it is in its i-form. The primary distinction, grammatically, between **nisā** and **ithin** is that the former follows an adjective, while latter must follow a complete sentence. At first glance, this might seem like a colossal difference, but, thanks to the existence of adjectival forms of verbs (and conversely, i-form adjectives), just about all sentences can be expressed using either word. **Hinḋā**, "because of" is a similar word; like **nisā**, it accepts an adjective predicate.

The following sentences all translate to "he ate a biscuit, so he's not that hungry:"

Eyā "biscuit" **kālā; ithin echchárá badáginnak næthuvá æthi**.

Eyā "biscuit" **kāpu hinḋā echchárá badáginnak næthuvá æthi**.

Eyā "biscuit" **kāpu nisā echchárá badáginnak næthuvá æthi**.

You could use **kǣvā** in the first example above, with no change in meaning. Another difference between **ithin** and **nisā/hinḋā** is that the other two can be used at the end of sentences:

Echchárá badáginnak næthuvá æthi "biscuit" **kāpu hinḋā**.

Echchárá badáginnak næthuvá æthi "biscuit" **kāpu nisā**.

An analogous sentence cannot be made with **ithin**; it does not conclude sentences.

Ithin has some idiomatic usages:

Ithin kiyanná. Then say it!

Ḋæṅ ithin æthi. Now it's enough.

There are some similar words with the opposite meaning. **Namuth** means "but":

Matá niḋimáthai namuth mamá niḋā gaththē næ.

Hæbæi is similar:

Matá mahansī hæbæi mamá niḋá gaththē næ.

Ē vuṇátá is also used in the same way. Verbs with **tá** can in general have this meaning:

Mamá æhuvātá eyā uththaráyak ḋunnē næ.
Although I asked him, he didn't answer.

A verb with **-th** can also be used this way.

Matá mahansī vuṇath mamá niḋiyá gaththē næ.
Although I felt tired, I didn't sleep.

Examples:

1-2: How would you express the following in Sinhala using **nisā**? **hinḋā**? **ithin**?

1. I ate well, so I'm not hungry.
2. We quarreled, so now we're not talking.

Translate the following into Sinhala using a. **Namuth** b. **hæbæi** c. **ē vuṇátá**

3. He went there but he didn't like it.

Translate the following into English

4. **Sená^{n}gá godak hitiyath eyā ehetá yanávā.**

Answers:

1. **Mamá ho^{n}ḋátá kǣvá nisā, matá budágini nǣ. Mamá ho^{n}ḋátá kǣvá hinḋā, matá budágini nǣ. Mamá ho^{n}ḋátá kǣvā; ithin matá budágini nǣ.**
2. **Api randu vuṇá nisā, ḋæṅ kath^{h}ā kárannē nǣ. Api randu vuṇá hinḋā, ḋæṅ kath^{h}ā kárannē nǣ. Api randu vuṇā; ithin ḋæṅ kath^{h}ā kárannē nǣ.**
3. **Eyā ehetá giyā; namuth ehetá kæmáthi vuṇe nǣ. Eyā ehetá giyā; hæbæi ehetá kæmáthi vuṇe nǣ. Eyā ehetá giyā; e vuṇātá ehetá kæmáthi vune nǣ.**
4. She goes there even though it is crowded. To express this using **namuth** or **hæbæi**, the sentence must be changed slightly: **Sená^{n}gá godak innávā namuth eyā ehetá yanávā.**

8.5 Interjections:

There are a number of random things people say in Sinhala. Adding these phrases to your speech will give it a more natural quality.

Interjection	Usage/Meaning
Ā	Hey, **ā kohomáḋá** hey, how are you
Ayyō	Oh dear (lit. oh brother)
Appachchiyō	Oh no (lit. oh father)
Anē	Please, how sad, now now
Ammō	Oh no (lit. oh mother)
Ko	A generic particle

There are three interjections that are related in meaning, which mean something like, "there!" or "oh!" These are **menná**, **onná**, and **anná**. These have the same kind of relationship as **mītá**, **oitá**, and **ītá**.

1. What's the difference between the following: **Onná, othāná balanná. Menná, methāná balanná. Anná athāná balanná/ anná, ethāná balanná.**

Answers:

1. Look over there, where you are. Come and look over here. Go and look over there.

8.6 Sentence Structure

We now have the pieces to deal with more sentences. Mind you, in Sinhala it is often acceptable to omit various parts of speech. For instance, the following is a full sentence in Sinhala:

Budáginī. (I'm) hungry.

The pronoun is inferred by context; people will assume the speaker is the one who's hungry. It is also acceptable to include the pronoun:

Matá budáginī. I am hungry.
Eyātá budáginī. He/she is hungry.

Note that the dative form is always used with this adjective, and that the word "to be" is not used. In general, Sinhala uses "to be" less than English. It also has two verbs for it: **innávā** and **thiyenávā**. The former is used for animate nouns, and the latter is used for inanimate nouns.

Mamá innávā. "I exist"/"I'm here"
Eka thiyenávā. "It exists"/"I have it"

Although they are probably the best translations for "to be," they clearly have different connotations. **Innávā** is used indicate that someone is present, and **thiyenávā** is also equivalent to the verb "have" (used by a speaker on an inanimate object to indicate that it belongs to them). What exactly these verbs mean in a given situation can only be determined by the context.

The typical word order in Sinhala is SOV, however, other orders are also possible. For instance:

Ē gǣni ḋuvánávā mamá ḋækkā. I saw that woman running

Mamá ḋækkā ē gǣni ḋuvánávā. I saw that woman running.

Examples:

Translate the following sentences into Sinhala in two different ways

1. I arrived yesterday
2. She helped me
3. I saw that woman.

Answers:

1. **Mamá īye āvā, Īye mamá āvā**
2. **Matá eyā uḋau keruvā, Eyā matá uḋau keruvā**
3. **Mamá ē gǣnivá ḋækkā, Ē gǣnivá mamá ḋækkā**.

In these latter two sentences, "woman" is accusative because it is the object of **ḋækkā**. This differs from the example in the above discussion, where the object was the woman running. Putting **mamá ḋækkā** before **Ē gǣnivá** would sound odd; it is more natural for the verb to end the sentence

8.7 Passive Verbs

With knowledge of the case system in hand, we can elaborate on the concept of ***passive*** verbs. Many verbs have passive counterparts, which are usually formed by replacing an **-i/a/ánávā** stem with **enávā**. For instance:

kapánávā. "cut"
kæpenávā. "be cut"

Mage athin bimá vatuṇā. matá bimá ḋānná vuṇā. Matá kapanná vuṇá. Involuntary actions are done with infinitive + **vuṇā**.

These verbs behave differently from their active counterparts:

Mamá ēyavá kapánávā. "I'm cutting him/her."

Māvá ēyatá kæpenávā. Literally, "I'm being cut by him/her" but it is, in practice, used idiomatically to mean "Him/her and I are well suited to each other."

The subject of a passive verb is always in the accusative case (unmarked for inanimates), the direct object (which for a passive verb is the person or thing actively doing something) takes the dative case.

Although many passive verbs differ from their regular counterparts only by an **-e-**, this is not universally the case:

Pēnávā. "be visible"
ḋakinávā. "see"

For that matter, e-stems may not always be precise counterparts to their active form, or passive verbs at all. For instance:

Gillinná epā! Don't swallow (it)!
Gillenná epā! Don't drown!

Examples:

What is the difference between the following two sentences?

1. **Mamá laṇuvá kapánávā**.
2. **Māvá laṇuvátá kæpenávā**.

Translate the following sentences:

3. **Kathuren mage athá kæpuṇā**

4. Mē æththange æ^{n}ḋuṅ themilā. Here are three useful bits of information: **Æththō** is a respectful way to refer to either one person or a group of people, **æ^{n}ḋuṅ** "clothes" is an informal pronunciation of **æ^{n}ḋum**, and the verb **themánávā** means "moisten" or "make wet."

Answers:

1. I'm cutting the string

2. The string is cutting me. Notice that the item performing the action is dative. This is because a passive verb takes no subject, and "me" is the direct object.

3. (I accidentally) cut my arm using scissors. The use of the instrumental case here is because the scissor was (presumably) being used to cut something else; and it was presumably because of this that the speaker inadvertently got cut. In the previous example, the tight string was not presumably not operated by anyone, at least, not for the purpose of cutting. Thus the string cut the speaker, but in this example, the speaker was accidentally cut by the scissors he or she was using.

4. This guy's clothes got wet. First, note that **themilā** is the perfect form of **themenávā**, the passive counterpart of **themánávā**. Thus, the sentence indicates that the person's clothes became wet, without specifying what caused this.

8.8 Causative Verbs

Most verbs also have a ***causative*** form. In Sinhala, "climbing" is **naginávā,** "rise"(inanimate) in that sense is **nægenávā**, **nægīmá** ,and "cause to climb", or "raise" is **naggá**(**vá**)**návā**.

(**Mamá**) **eyāvá taksiyátá naggávánávā/nægguvā**. I help/ed him board the taxi. Note the existence of an alternate form **naggávánávā** / **næggevvá**. These dual forms are quite common for causatives of i-stem verbs.

The above example could mean that the person was literally lifted into the taxi, but more metaphorically it indicates that the subject helped the person board; like holding the passenger's hand or making sure the passenger doesn't fall. That said, the verb can be used in a literal sense in some contexts:

Ḷamáyāvá gahatá naggánávā mamá dækkā. I saw the child being helped to climb the tree.

The general procedure for forming a causative verb is as follows: remove the stem (including the stem vowel), and add **-ávánávā**.

Unfortunately, the form of causative verbs cannot be reliably predicted from the active form of the verb. This is because the form resulting from the above rule can be affected by certain sound changes. The first such change is deletion of the initial **á**, resulting in forms like **ḋalvánávā** ("kindle"). The second possible change is a simplification of the consonant cluster into a double consonant, such as **bassánávā** ("cause to lower" or "to drop off," from earlier **basvánávā**, from **basinávā** / **bahinávā**, "lower." Note how the doubling rules discussed earlier still apply; an **h** doubled is always **ss**).

There is no reliable rule to predict this, but a-stem verbs seem to be least likely to undergo these sound changes, while i-stem verbs seem to be the most likely to do so. E-stem verbs seem to be in between, while v-stem verbs don't ever seem to, perhaps because most of them are causative already.

To add more confusion into the mix, there can be causatives of causatives; for instance, **bassavánávā**. These effectively have the same meaning as the plain causative form.

The causative form in Sinhala is often used to indicate that an action, usually some kind of task, must be done. It does not necessarily mean that the person being addressed must perform the action themselves, merely that it must be accomplished somehow. Thus, it is often used for transmitting instructions or orders.

If the action, on the other hand, has a person as its object, the implication is usually that the speaker is helping the object somehow. In the case of **bassanávā**, for instance, the target is being lowered, or in a more abstract sense, being dropped off somewhere.

Some causative verbs have diverged from this usage. For instance, the causative form of the verb **enávā**, "arrive" is **evánávā**,"cause to arrive," or "send." Likewise, **kiyánávā** "say" vs **kiyávánávā** "read," probably from "cause to be said (later, by reading after it had been written down)."

Examples:

Two common causative verbs are **yavánávā** and **evánávā**. These both mean "send," but are used in different contexts.

1. **Api mallitá pāsáláyak yavánávā**.
2. **Malli apitá liyumak evánávā kiyálā kiyuvā**.

What could the following causatives mean?

3. **Kavánávā**
4. **Kárávánávā**

Answers:

1. We sent a package to little brother. **Yavánávā** is used when the speaker is sending something.

2. Younger brother said that will send a letter to us. **Evánávā** is used when someone is sending something to the speaker. From the speaker's perspective, **yavánávā** causes the item being send to go, while **evánávā** causes an item to arrive.

3. "cause to eat" i.e. "feed." Sinhala also has a word for "cause to drink": **povánávā**. It is an aberrant irregularity, considering the plain form is **bonávā.**

4. "cause to do" that is, get someone to do the work.

8.9 Time Word Predicates

Time words can also be used as predicates. For example:

Bath kāpugamaṅ niḋimathá venávā. As soon as (I) eat rice, (I) become sleepy.

There are several verb transformations which are like this:

Form	Formation	Meaning	Example
-vanam	Present + nam	If it is done	Ēká káránávānam
-oth	past - ā + oth	If it is done	Ēká keruvoth
-kotá	present adjectival +kotá	While doing it	Ēká káránákotá
-gaman	Perfect adjectival + gaman	As soon as it's done	Ēká kárápugaman
-hamá	Past adjectival + hamá	After it's done	Ēká kárálhamá

Hamá tends to decay, with the **h** of **hamá** being deleted. Thus, rather than **káráhamá**, one would say **kárāmá**. Note the irregular form **gihāma**.

When the **hamá** form is used with a past adjective with a **u** or **i**, the pronunciation is changed: cf. **ḋækkáhamá** "After … seen," vs. **ipáḋuṇahamá** "After … born." A notable exception is **vuṇáhamá**.

Kárápu is common, but **kárágamaṅ** is not commonly used. In general, however, the **gamaṅ** form is equally likely to be used with the past adjectival form, so **vuṇugamaṅ**/ **vuṇágamaṅ** and **vechchágamaṅ** are equally common. The form has the same meaning, regardless. The other forms typically use the adjectival verb tense listed in the table above.

Mē væde ivárá vuṇāmá apitá yanná puḷuvan. When this job is done we can go.

Examples:

1. **Ē vadē káránákotá parissámeṅ káranná**.
2. **Mamá eyālātá uḋau kárāmá matá santhōsai.**
3. **Vadē kárápugaman geḋárá yanná puḷuvan**.
4. **Bath kāpugamaṅ niḋimathá venávā**.
5. **Hetá venákotá matá mahansī vei**.
6. What is the difference between the following sentences?
   a) **Ēká vechchágamaṅ mamá geḋárá giyā**
   b) **Ēká vechchágamaṅ mamá geḋárá yanávā**
   c) **Ēká vechchágamaṅ mamá geḋárá yannam**

Answers:

1. When you're doing it, do it careful.
2. When I help them I feel good.
3. Once I'm done I can go home. The same sentence could be constructed using **magē geḋárátá**, "to my house," but this sounds odd.
4. As soon as (I) eat rice, (I) become sleepy. Using **vuṇā** here instead makes it "I felt sleepy as soon as I ate rice."
5. I'll be tired by tomorrow.

6. a): As soon as it happened, I went home. b): As soon as that happens, I'm going home. c): As soon as that happens, I will go home. Note that the second example is, in some sense, in the future as well. It can also mean "I go home as soon as that happens" describing a general, regular occurrence.

8.10 Summary and Supplemental Information

Sinhala Word	Meaning
nisā	because
namuth	but
-i	and
hari	or
ithin	Then, since
vithárá	about
vithárai	only
issellā	before
passē	after
æthi	enough
ekká	with
hæbæi	but
indaṅ	from

Sinhala Word	Meaning
indalā	from

8.11 Exercises

1-19. Translate the following into Sinhala:

1. Now since it's over, let's start the next task.

2. If I don't fail, it'll be good.

3. I saw the child turn onto that road.

4. A lot of stars can be seen in the sky today. The word for sky is **ahasá**, pl. **ahas**, the word for star is **tharuvá**, pl. **tharu**, or **thārákāvá**, pl. **thārákā**.

5. Sunlight is shining (literally falling) through the clouds. **Valākuḷu**, **valākuḷá** = clouds. **Avvá** = sunshine / sunlight, uncountable.

6. The child ate all the rice because he was hungry.

7. He always arrives late for everything. It's his way to arrive late for everything.

8. He's a glutton, after all. **Ḋakshá** means "capable," and so a **ḋaksháyā** is a clever or skilled person. A **kanná ḋaksháyā** is a "pro eater," or a glutton.

9. So, what happened next?

10. I'm tired but I'll do it.

11. Brush your teeth before going to sleep.

12. We'll do that work later.

13. He's about ten years old.

14. Will this food be enough for them?

15. For vegetables we only have carrots at home. **elōḷuvá** - vegetable. **Elàváḷu, Elàváḷuvá** formal.

16. I'm the only one who knows that.

17. I told him to come at about five in the evening.

18. I also came with him.

19. The child is going to school with his mother.

20-42: Translate the following into English:

20. **Ḷamáyā putuvē i^{n}ḋaṅ innávā.**

21. **Thāththā ḷamáyāvá gaheṅ hemihitá bassávánávā.**

22. **Āchchī ḷamáyātá bath kavánávā.**

23. **Ammā babātá vathurá povánávā.**

24. **Ē kattiyá minissu lavvá tharáha kāráyantá gassávánávā.** **Kattiyá, katti** means group, groups. **Tharáha kāráyan,** "angry guys" is used figuratively here, meaning "enemies."

25. **Guruthumā lamain lavvá panthiyá as kárávágaththā.**

26. **Eyā polīs kāráyek lavvá horāvá allá gaththā.**

27. Ēká matá ḋæn thērenávā.

28. Matá ē salli mē māsē læbenávānaṅ ho^{n}ḋai.

29. Matá ē liyumá læbuṇā.

30. Iskōlētá hu^{n}gak ḋurá nisā, ævidágená yanná amārui.

31. Kolá^{m}bai Gāllai Nuvárai balanná ōne.

32. Kolá^{m}bá Gallá hā Nuvárá balanná ōne.

33. Kolá^{m}báta Galláta saha Nuváráta yanná ōne.

34. Matá pēnávā kōchchiyá ḋurá i^{n}ḋálamá enákotá.

35. Ē gæná kath^{h}ā kāranná mamá kæmáthi nǣ.

36. Ē gæná kath^{h}ā mamá ahalā thiyenávā.

37. Mamá enná issellā kauḋá mē vædá kárē?

38. Ḷamai panthiyatá enna issellā panthiyá athu gānná ōne.

39. Ekai mekai kiyuvahamá harimá honḋai.

40. Ou, matá pēnávā, ammā ḷamáyinvá nāvánávā.

41. Bas ekeṅ bahinnánaṅ, bell eká gahanná ōne. Ethákotá ī la^{n}gá "halt" ekē bas eká navaththai.

42. Mamá vædá kárānákotá ōká káranná bǣ.

43. Mata ethánātá yanná puḷuvaṅ vuṇa, hærámitiyá pāvichchi keruvá nisā.

Dialogue 18: Making a Grocery List

The lady of the house and the maid are talking about what to buy.

A: **Kamálā, geḋárá lūnu thiyenávāḋá**? Kamala, do we have onions at home?

B: **Tikak thiyenávā. Nōnā kadē(tá) yanávānam, apitá pol gedi kīpáyákuth ōne**. We have a few. Lady, If you're going to the market, we need some coconuts. The **-tá** here may be omitted. **Kadē yanávā** is also an idiom meaning "support," "carry water."

A: **Vená moná elōluḋá / eláváluḋá thiyennē**. What other vegetables do we have at home?

B: **Vædi ḋeyak nǣ. Alai govai thiyenávā**. Not much, we have potatoes and cabbage.

A: **Ā, Ehenam, mamá bōñchī gotukoḷai gēnnáṅ. Kamálā sīni bothálē hæḋuvāḋá**? Ok, then I'll bring beans and gotukola. Did you wash the sugar bottle?

B: **Kiri pitith ivárá venná la^{n}gai.** The milk powder is almost finished as well.

A: **Ā, ehenaṅ, mamá kiri piti tin ekákuth gēnnam**. Then I'll get a tin of milk powder.

44. If you're going to study, eat well.
45. I'm going to bring onions and a tin of milk powder.
46. The potatoes are almost finished as well.

Dialogue 19: Looking for Something

Somebody has misplaced something. Maybe a tennis ball.

A: **Ammā ammā, apē** tennis **bōle ḋækkādá**? Mother, mother have you seen our tennis ball?

B: **Mamánam ḋækkē nǣ, puthālā thiyápu thænáká æthi**? I haven't seen it, it must be wherever you kept it.

A: **Mamá hæmáthænámá bæluvā, udá kāmárávālath bæluvā**. I looked everywhere, even in all the upstairs rooms.

B: **Eḷiyē bæluvādá**? **vaththá palleha ogollan sellaṅ kárāná hariyē**? Did you look outside? at the far end (lit bottom) of the garden, where you normally play.

A: **Ou, vaththē hæmáthænámá bæluvā**. Yes, I looked everywhere in the garden.

C: **Monávādá me malli hæmáthænámá hoyannē**? What is malli looking for?

B: **Eyāge** tennis **bōle næthi kárágáná**. He has lost his tennis ball.

C: **Æi thāththā ēká ará mēsē udá lāchchuvē araṅ thibbā. Mallilā boleṅ gahagaththá nisā**. Father put it in the top drawer of the desk because the kids were hitting each other with it.

47. I went everywhere in that town.

48. We even looked in all the boxes.

Dialogue 20: Housework

This conversation takes place in a house between family members. **Mēká geḋáráká paulē kipádennek athárá vená kath^{h}āvak**.

A: **Ammā matá uḋau venná enávā kiyálā kivvā. Thāmath āvē næ. Ammāvá ḋækkāḋá**? Mother said that she'll come and help me. She's still not here. Did you see her?

B: **Ou, mamá enákotá dækkā ammā podi ayátá kavánávā. Ammātá enná thavá velā yai, oyātá thavá godak vædá thiyenávāḋá**? Yes, when I came here I saw her feeding the little ones. It'll take some time for her to come, do you still have a lot more to do?

A: **Ou, tharámak vædá thiyenávā, ammā uḋau venávā kiyápu nisā mamá vædiyeṅ vædá bārá gaththā**. Yes, quite a bit is still left, since mother said she would help, I took on a lot of work. **Bārá gannavā** = take responsibility.

B: **Ammā enákaṅ, ōnenam mamá uḋau kárannam**. I'll help you till mother comes if you want.

After a while, **tharámak vellāvákátá passē**,

A: **Ā ammā enávā**. Oh, mother is coming.

C: **Ḷamaintá kavanná gihillā matá hu^{n}gak parakku vuṇā**. I got very late by going to feed the children.

A: **Ammā, ḷamainvá narak káránávā**. **Ē gollantá thaniyeṅ kanná puḷuvan**. You're spoiling them, they can eat alone/by themselves.

B: **Podi ḷamai ammā lavvá kavā ganná kæmáthī**. Little kids like to be fed by their mother. k.g. fed by.

C: **Ā ekeṅ kamak nǣ, ḋæṅ monávādá káranná thiyennē**.
Oh it's fine, what do we still have left to do?

49. What are two other, equally valid ways of saying "Mother said that she'll come and help me," in Sinhala?

50. I'll fix it if you want.

51. She went to the store by herself.

9
NUMBERS

Dialogue 21: At the Farmer's Market

At a farmers market (**polá**), a person is selling all kinds of vegetables and fruit. A customer comes by and says:

A: **Matá a^{m}bá gedi pahak ḋenná**. Carrot **pansīyákuth ḋenná**. **Kesel averi dekákuth ḋenná**. Give me five mangoes, 500 grams of carrot and give me two bunches of bananas.

In Sinhala numbers (**nombárē**/**nombáráyá**, pl. **nombárá**) are typically listed after the item they enumerate. Thus **gedi pahak** means "five fruits."

Remember that **eká** type English loanwords like "carrot" form plurals by removing **eká**, with conversion to an English plural form being optional. The word for five hundred here is **pansiyákuth**, it is the result of **pansiyak** (five hundred of an object)+ **th** "also." When listing items like this, it is normal to add **th** to every quantity after the first. The word for "grams" is not used, it is assumed that the person is not looking to buy five hundred individual carrots. Previously, it was more common to indicate units, since there was a transition from the imperial system, when units like **rāththálá**, pl. **rāththal**, "pound" were still in use.

B: **Līks ganne næḋḋá**? **Mevā hari aluth**. Aren't you buying any leeks, they're very fresh.
A: **Ehenaṅ līks ḋesiyá panáhak ḋānná**. Put 250 grams of leeks (in the bag). Someone might add **-uth** here as well, but it is optional.

B: **Pol ganne næḋḋá**? Aren't you buying any coconuts?
A: **Pol gedi ḋekak ōne**. I need two coconuts
B: **thavá monávāḋá ōne**? What else do you need?
A: **Karápinchā mitiyak ḋānná**. **Aḋá amu miris næḋḋá**? Give me a bunch of curry leaves. Don't you have any green chilies today?

Indefinite quantities like **mitiyak** come after the words they refer to as well.

B: **Amu miris okkomá ivárá velā**. We're all out of green chilies.
C: **Ammā æpál gannē næḋḋá**? Mother aren't we buying any apples?
A: **Æpál hari ganaṅ**. Apples are expensive.

B: **Nōnātá adu kárálā ḋennaṅ. Mē æpál gedi thuná rupiyal thunsiyákátá ḋennaṅ**. I'll give a discount to you, lady. For these three apples, give me three hundred rupees.

When enumerated, the noun itself does not inflect; instead the numeral does. Notice that its form is identical to that of the inanimate indefinite dative. Also note that **thunsiyákátá**, "for..three hundred", refers to the price. Here the units are stated, but they could also assumed by both the speaker and the listener, in which case **rupiyal** might be omitted.

A: **Thavá rupiyal panáhak adu károth mamá gannaṅ**. If you reduce it by another fifty rupees, then I'll buy it.
B: **Ha ha, onná ḋæmmā** bag **ekátá**. Ok, I'm putting the apples into the bag.
A: **Okkomá baduválátá gānā kīyáḋá**? How much is it for all the items? **okkomá**, or both **okkoma** and **baduvala** could be omitted. The order of the remaining words could be inverted in any of these cases.
B: **Rupiyal ek ḋās atásiyá hæththá pahai**. One thousand eight hundred and seventy five rupees.
A: **Maṅ gāvá māru næ, ḋeḋāhe nōttuvak thamai thiyennē**. I don't have any change, only a two thousand rupee note.

Here the word **ḋeḋāhe**, "two thousand-," appears before **nōttuvak**. Why? Notice the difference in form; here **ḋeḋāhe** is basically an adjective, referring to the type of bill.

If you were enumerating the value of it (eg.) or saying you had 2000 notes (eg.), then it would be used as before.

B: **Prashneyak næ, maṅ gāvá māru salli thiyánávā**. Its alright, I have enough change.

The word for "change" is **māru salli**; it is frequently shortened to **māru**.

As you can see, in Sinhala numbers behave in a rather complex manner. They are basically postpositions, but also behave like nouns, and can be used like adjectives. Before we can worry about this, however, we must learn the basic Sinhala numbers.

9.2 1-99

The numbers from 0-12 are not formed as compounds with anything, and have to be memorized:

Sinhala	Meaning
binḋuvá	0
eká	1
ḋeká	2
thuná	3
hathará	4
paha	5

Sinhala	Meaning
hayá	6
hathá	7
atá	8
namáyá	9
ḋahayá	10
ekoḷáha	11
ḋoḷáha	12

The numbers from thirteen through nineteen are, except for 15, formed as compounds with **ḋaha**, with some having a more colloquial contracted form with **ḋā**:

Sinhala	Meaning
ḋahathuná	13
ḋahahathárá, ḋāhathárá	14
pahaḷová	15
ḋahasáyá, ḋāsáyá	16
ḋahahathá, ḋāhathá	17
ḋaha atá	18
ḋahanamáyá	19

The numbers from 20 to ninety are formed using the same principles, substituting a different word for **ḋaha**. Unlike the teens, there are no irregularities, though unlike the former, the words for "twenty," "thirty," and so on are usually slightly different than the stems used to make compounds.

Sinhala	Meaning
vissá	twenty
visi eká	Twenty-one
thihá	thirty
this eká	thirty-one
hatháḷihá	forty
Hathaḷis eká	forty-one
panáha	fifty
Panas eká	fifty-one
hætá	sixty
Hætá eká	sixty-one
hæththǣvá	seventy
Hæththæ eká	seventy-one
asūvá	eighty
Asū eká	eighty-one
anūvá	ninety
Anū eká	ninety-one

Examples:

Translate the following numbers into Sinhala

1. Twenty-two.
2. Ninety-five

3. Seventy-four.
4. Forty-six

Answers:
1. **Visi ḋeká**
2. **Anū paha**
3. **Hæththæ hathárá**
4. **Hatháḷis hayá**

To help with memorization here, notice that base forms that end in **vá** form compounds by removing it, and like wise base forms ending in **ha** form compounds by replacing the final **ha** with **s**.

9.3 100-10,000,000

The hundreds are formed by making compounds with **sīyá**.

One hundred and one **ek siyá eká**

Sinhala	Meaning
sīyá	hundred
Eká siyá eká	101
ḋesīyá	Two hundred
thunsīyá	Three hundred
hārásīyá	Four hundred
pansīyá	Five hundred
hayásīyá	Six hundred

Sinhala	Meaning
hathsīyá	Seven hundred
atásīyá	Eight hundred
namásīyá	Nine hundred

The thousands are formed identically to the hundreds, but with **ḋāha** instead of **sīyá**. The ten thousands, however, are formed in a manner similar to the numbers 11-100, and are essentially direct translations of their English names.

1000 and one: **Ek ḋahas eká**

Four thousand is **hārá ḋāha**, stem form **hārá ḋahas**. Aside from this, **hathárá** is used as its own stem.

Sinhala	Meaning
ḋāha	thousand
ḋeḋāha	Two thousand
ekoḷosḋāha	Eleven thousand
ḋoḷosḋāha	Twelve thousand
ḋahathunḋāha	Thirteen thousand
ḋahatháráḋāha	Fourteen thousand
pahaḷosḋaha	Fifteen thousand
ḋāsáyáḋāha	Sixteen thousand
ḋāhathḋāha	Seventeen thousand
ḋaha atá ḋāha	Eighteen thousand
ḋahanamáḋāha	Nineteen thousand

Sinhala	Meaning
visiḋāha	Twenty thousand
thisḋāha	Thirty thousand
hathalisḋāha	Forty thousand
panasḋāha	Fifty thousand
hætáḋāha	Sixty thousand
hæththáḋāha	Seventy thousand
asūḋāha	Eighty thousand
anūḋāha	Ninety thousand
lakshháyá/ siyá ḋahas	One hundred thousand

The numbers from two to nine are used with **lakshá**, the stem form of **laksháyá** to make numbers from two hundred thousand to ninc hundred thousand in analogy with **sīyá**. One million is **ḋasálaksháyá**; the numbers from 1.1 million to nine million can formed in the same manner as the numbers from eleven thousand to ninety thousand, but they can also be formed using **lakshá**. Ten million is **kōtiyá**. Its stem form is **kōti**. In modern times, the word **miliyáná**, "million," has become very common:

Koláᵐbá pæththeṅ geyak ganná rupiyal miliyáná thihakvath ōne. A house in Colombo costs at least thirty million rupees.

1. 791. **Hath siyá anū eká**
2. 55, 362 **Panas panḋahas thun siyá visi thuná**

3. 150,000 **Ek lakshá panas ḋahai**

4. 20,000,000 **Miliyáná vissak, lakshá ḋesīyak, kōti ḋekak**

5. 315. **Thun siyá pahaḷová**

9.4 Counting

When referring to people, a special set of words must be used. The word for "a single person" is **ekkenek**, and the word for "a pair of people" is **ḋennek**. Higher numbers are compounds with **ḋenek**. The latter behaves like a normal indefinite animate noun:

x people	Ḋenek
x people (accusative)	ḋenekvá
To x people	ḋenekutá
x people's	Ḋenekge
From x people	ḋenekugen

It is used as follows: Note that the commonly used word for "two people," unlike all the others, has a double **n**.

a group of x people	x =
Ekkenek	1

a group of x people	x =
Ḋennek/ḋeḋenek	2
thun ḋenek	3
Hathara ḋenek	4
Pas ḋenek	5
Hayá ḋenek	6
Hath ḋenek	7
Atá ḋenek	8
Namá ḋenek	9
Ḋaha ḋenek	10
Ekoḷos ḋenek	11
Ḋoḷos ḋenek	12
Ḋaha thun ḋenek	13
Ḋa(h)ahathárá ḋenek	14
Pahaḷos ḋenek	15
Ḋa(h)asáyá ḋenek	16
Ḋa(h)ahath ḋenek	17
Ḋahātá ḋenek	18
Ḋahanamá ḋenek	19
visi ḋenek	20
visi ek ḋenek	21
visi ḋeḋenek	22

Aside from the presence of **ḋenek**, the big difference here is that the stem forms of the words appear even for multiples of ten.

The larger numbers follow the pattern:

Siyá ḋenek	100 people
Eká siyá ek ḋenek	101 people
Eká siyá ḋaha ḋenek	110 people
Eká siyá ekoḷos ḋenek	111 people
Ḋesiyá ḋenek	200 people
Ḋesiyá hathális thun ḋenek	243 people
(Ek) Ḋahas ḋenek	1000
Ek ḋahas pansiyá anū hath ḋenek	1597 people
Ḋeḋahas ḋenek	2000
Thunḋahas ḋenek	3000
Hāráḋahas ḋenek	4000
Panḋahas ḋenek	5000
Hayáḋahas ḋenek	6000
Hathḋahas ḋenek	7000
Atá ḋahas ḋenek	8000
Namá ḋahas ḋenek	9000
Ḋahaḋāhas ḋenek	10000
siyá ḋahas ḋenek	100000

Siyá ḋahas ek ḋenek	100,001
Eká siyá ekoḷos ḋahas ḋenek	111,000

For large numbers of people, it is more natural to say **lakshájákátá væḋiyá minissu.** more than a hundred thousand people. **Ḋahas gānak sená^{n}gá hitiyá**. There were thousands of people.

For animates in general, use the indefinite singular for one, then this scheme for others, eg: **eká ballek, ballo ḋennek**, etc.

For inanimates, the singular is formed the same way:

Eká gahak

But higher numbers are formed by using the base numeral form, replacing the final **-á** for **-ak.**

Gas ḋekak
Gas thunak
Gas pahak

For the words **pārak**, "time", and **særáyak**, **pæththá**, "side", it is more common to use stems:

Eká pārak / særáyak
Ḋepārak / Ḋesæráyak

thun pārak
Hathárá pārak
Pas pārak

When prefixing, the above numbers are used rather than the pure ones. **Ḋenek** is used for animates, along with the plural of the noun. Inanimate objects use the inanimate form with plain numbers. Inanimate concepts like "time," or "side," use the format detector above.

Examples:
Translate the following:
1. **Ḷamai ḋennā nānná giyā**.
2. **Peráhærátá nættuvō pas ḋenek ōnē**.
3. **Iskōlē yanákotá pænsal ḋekak geniyanná**.
4. **Ammā kǣmá pāsal hathárak hæḋuvā**.

Answers:
1. The two children went to wash (themselves)
2. . Five dancers are needed for the Perahera.
3. Bring two pencils when you go to school.
4. Mother made four parcels of food.

9.5 Applications

There are several particular ways to express various numerical operations. The most common way to talk about addition, for example, is as follows:

Ekai ekai - one plus one (literally, one and one)
Ḋoḷáhai pahalávai visihathai. 12 + 15 = 27

A common way to ask an addition problem would be:

Ḋoḷáhatá pahalávak ekáthu keruvahamá kīyáḋá? What's is twelve plus fifteen? (Literally: How much is (there) when fifteen is added to twelve?) Note how one number is dative, and the other is indefinite.

Subtraction is stated in a similar way:

Thihen pahalávak adu kárāmá kīyáḋá? What's 30 minus 15? (Literally, how much is (left) when fifteen is taken away from thirty?) (**adu káránávā**, as seen in the earlier dialogue, also means "reduce." Note, however, that the quantity which is being reduced is in the instrumental case)

There are two common ways to talk about multiplication:

Thuná varak hayá kīyáḋá? What is three times six? Notice that in this construction, the first number is in its stem form, and the second is in the nominative-definite form.

Hayá thuneṅ vædi káráhamá kiyáḋá? Same as above (Literally, how much is it when six is multiplied by three?) (**vædi káránávā** more generally means "increasing" and is used as the opposite of **adu káránávā**)

Unlike the other basic math operations, division uses the word **beḋánávā**, which in other contexts means "distribute":

Hayá ḋeken beḋuvahamá kiyáḋá? What is six divided by 2?

Note that the terms given above are colloquial. Arithmetic in an academic context has its own particular vocabulary. **Ḋ^{h}aná** can be used to mean "plus" or "positive, while **riṇá** (spelled **r̥ṇá**, see ch. 13) is used to mean "minus," or "negative." These are the only ways to talk about positive or negative numbers.

Paha ḋ^{h}aná ḋeká samānai hathá is equivalent to **pahatá ḋekak ekáthu karāmá hathátá samānai**, or **pahai ḋekai hathai**. Both of the example sentences here mean "5 +2 = 7."

Samāná is an adjective meaning "equal." It can be used in other contexts:

Ē poth godával ḋeká samānai. The two piles of books are (of) equal (height)

The colloquial mathematical operations are most commonly used in situations involving money. Prices may be stated in a standalone fashion using the i-form of the numeral:

Ēká rupiyal siyai That's 100 rupees.

Rupiyal pahai sathá thihai 5 rupees and 30 cents.

Rupiyálá, pl. **rupiyal**, is the common word for "rupee," "cent" is **satháyá**, pl. **sathá**.

Examples: Translate the following:

1. **Ēká venáḋātá vadā rupiyal ḋekak adui**.
2. **Vissai vissai hathálihai**.
3. **Ēká aḋá dollar ekak adui**.
4. **Aḋá ēkē milá siyátá panáhakin adui**.

Answers:

1. It's two dollars off today. (lit. compared to other days)
2. Twenty plus twenty is forty.
3. It's a dollar less today.
4. It's 50% off today.

9.6 Summary and Supplemental Information

This chapter introduces numerals, which have several unique behaviors:

English Number	Sinhala	Stem Form
One	Eká	Ek-
Two	Ḋeká	Ḋe-
Three	Thuná	Thun-
Four	Hathárá	Hārá-
Five	Paha	Pas-
Six	Hayá	Hayá
Seven	Hathá	Hath-

English Number	Sinhala	Stem Form
Eight	Atá	Atá-
Nine	Namáyá	Namá
Ten	Ḋahayá	Ḋaha
Eleven	Ekoḷáha	Ekoḷos-
Twelve	Ḋoḷáha	Ḋoḷos-
Fifteen	Pahaḷová	Pahaḷos-
Twenty	Vissá	Visi-
Thirty	Thihá	This-
Fourty	Hathálihá	Hathális-
Fifty	Panáha	Panas-
Sixty	Hætá	Hætá
Seventy	Hæththǣvá	Hæththæ-
Eighty	Asūvá	Asū-
Ninety	Anūvá	Anū-
One Hundred	Sīyá	Siyá-
One Thousand	Ḋāha	Ḋahas

A single digit number is simple, but, except for the numbers with unique names given above, Sinhala numbers are constructed according to the following rule: the stem form of all the components of the numbers name is used except for the lowest one. So "thirty seven" is made with the stem form of thirty, **this**, and the base form of seven, **hathá**. Three hundred and seventy four, on the other hand, consists of the stem forms **thun**, "three," **siyá**, "hundred," **hæththæ**, “seventy,” and **hathárá**, “four.” Until one hundred thousand, Sinhala number names match English ones for this purpose. Traditionally, 100,000 was a special quantity, **laksháyá**, and ten million was **kotiyá**, but these see less use in modern times; the loanword **miliyáná** is increasingly common.

Inanimate objects are enumerated by using the plural form of the noun, followed by the desired number in its indefinite form. Animate nouns instead use the plural, followed by the stem form of the number, followed by **ḋenek**. In the case of “two” (*not* twenty-two, five hundred and two, etc) the word **ḋennek** is more common than the regular form **ḋeḋenek**.

The stem form of “seventy” has a slang version: **hæththá**. This is not to be confused with an identical word **hæththá**, pl. **hæthi**, which means something like “group,” “pack,” or “brood.” It is commonly used as an impolite way to refer to a group of people.

9.7 Exercises

Translate the following into English:

1. **Apitá pahaḷos ḋenekutá idá ōne**.
2. **Matá prashná hathárákátá uththárá liyanná bæri vuṇā**.
3. **Mamá pænsal hayak arágaththā**.
4. **Ē ḋennā hæmá velēmá ekátá innē**. **ekátá** - together
5. **Mē pothē pitu thun siyá anu ekak thiyenávā**.
6. **Matá siyeṅ lakuṇu asuvak læbuṇā**.
7. **Matá siyeṅ eká lakuṇak læbuṇā**.

8. **Eyātá sathiyē hæmá ḋavásátámá a^{n}duṅ thuná gānē thiyenávā**. **Gānē** means "each."
9. **Eyāge** address **eká nombárá vissá** Pieris **pārá, Ḋehiválá**.
10. **Eyāge geḋárá thiyennē Ḋehiválá** Pieris **pārē nombárá vissē**.
11. **Paṅ gedi thunak ganná**.
12. **Ē shá̄t ekē gāná rupiyal pansiyá panáhai**.
13. **Mē pothē gāná rupiyal hathsiyá anu namáyai**.
14. **Hathai atai ekáthu keruvahamá pahalávai.**
15. **Eká siyá ekoḷáhatá this ḋekak ekáthukáráhamá ekásiyá hathális thunai.**
16. **Thun varak namásiyá ḋeḋās hathsiyai**.
17. **Laksháyak binḋuveṅ vædi káráhamá, uththárē binḋuvai.**
18. **Pas varak binḋuvá binḋuvai.**
19. Laksháyai **laksháyai ekáthu keruvahamá lakshá ḋekai**.
20. **Siyá varak sīyá ḋaha ḋahai**.
21. **Ḋāhákin ekak adu káráhamá namá siyá anu namáyai**.
Translate the following into Sinhala:
22. 33 divided by three is 11.
23. 100,000 divided by 100,000 is one.
24. Zero divided by 6 is zero.
25. Don't divide by zero.
26. 100 divided by ten is ten.
27. 10,000 divided by 1000 is ten.
28. We lost three times before we won.
29. I have only one more chance to pass.
30. There are two sides to everything.
31. The school only has three teachers.

32. I saw six monkeys.
33. I have four rupees and fifty cents.
34. I need to read six more books.
35. We have two trains to choose from.
36. That costs 99 cents.
37. All three of my brothers came.
38. She has three daughters.
39. She has one son.
40. She has one daughter.
41. Both his grandfathers are still alive.
42. When you leave, I'll be lonely.
43. What are the differences between these two answers?

Dialogue 22: Packing.

Someone is going to live in a dorm, and packing things to take:

A: Hostel **ekátá ōná badu laisthuvak liyā gaththānaṅ ho^{n}ḋai**.

B: **thavá ḋavas thiyánávā ne**.

A: **Ḋæṅ liyámu ethákotá adu padu ganná velā thiyei**. Uniform **kiyak ōne veiḋá**? **Adu padu** = things that you don't have, an expression, informal.

B: **Geniyaná ōná badu laisthuvak hostel ekeṅ matá evvā**.

A: **Ehenan ēká arágená matá kiyávanná**.

B: Uniform **pahai. Mēs kuttaṅ atai. tai(s) ḋekai**. Exercise **poth ḋahayai. Pātá pænsal pettiyak. Sabaṅ kætá hayak. Panāvak. Sapaththu kuttam ḋekak. Gaum pahak**.

A: **Echcháráḋá**?

B: **Ou, thavá podi podi ḋeval thiyánávā, menná laisthuvá**.

A: **Ā mamá meká balálā, thavá ōná ḋeval thiyánávānaṅ, laisthuvátá ekáthu kárannam**.

44. Translate the above dialogue into English

Dialogue 23: Math Practice.

45. A Sinhala version of this dialogue can be found in the answer key. Before looking at it, try to translate the dialogue below.

A: Son, have you finished studying your times tables?

B: Yes, I'm done.

A: I'll ask you a few multiplication problems, let's see if you've gotten the hang of it. Twelve times eight?

B: Ninety-six.

A: Seven times nine.

B: Fifty six.

A: No, fifty six is wrong.

B: Oh, wait a minute… Sixty three.

A: Four times eleven.

B: Forty four.

A: 6 times three.

B: Twenty four.

A: That's wrong, you haven't studied properly. Go back and study again.

10
TIME

Dialogue 24: Asking for the Time

Two people are planning to go on a trip and are going take the train.

A: **Api Senásurāḋā kīyátáḋá yannē**? What time are we leaving on Saturday?

B: **Næ Senásurāḋā nevei, api Sikurāḋā yamu**. No, not on Saturday, let's go on Friday. **Nevei** is an alternate, less formal pronunciation of **nemei**. Sinhala day names are compounds using **-ḋā**.

A: **Sikurāḋā vædá kárāná ḋavásak ne**? Friday is a weekday though? Meanwhile, the actual common word for day is **ḋavásá**, pl. **ḋavas**. A alternate, formal word is **ḋináyá**, pl. **ḋiná / ḋinával** which could also mean "date"

B: **Næ Sikurāḋā Poyá nisā, nivādu ḋavásak**. No, since Friday is a Poya day, it's a holiday. Notice that there is no need to use any kind of word meaning “to be” when stating the time.

A: **Ā, hathveniḋātá yamu kiyálāḋá kiyannē**? **Mamá hithuvē pahaḷos veniḋā yanávā kiyálā**. Oh, are you saying we’re going on the seventh? I was thinking of the fifteenth.

B: **Ou, hathvenidā gihillā, sumānekin vithárá emu**. Yes, let's go on the seventh and come back in about a week.

A: **Hathvenidā uḋēmá yamuḋá**? Let's go early in the morning on the seventh.

B: **Paḷáveni kōchchiyá thiyennē hathárai panáhatá**. The earliest train is at 4:50.

A: **Apō ēká vēlassáná vædi**. **Geḋárin thunáhamārátá pitá venná vei**. Oh, that's too early. We'll have to leave home at three thirty.

B: **Ehenaṅ**, **hayai kālē**/ **hayai pahalávei kōchchiyá gamuḋá**. Then shall we take the six fifteen train?

A: **Ou ēká ho^{n}ḋai, apitá pahatá vithárá geḋárin pitá venná puḷuvan**. **Nuvárá yanákotá kīyátá vithárá veiḋá**? Yes, that's good, we can leave home at about five. What time will it be when we reach Kandy.

B: **Ekoḷáha pahu vei**. It'll be after 11.

10.2 Telling time

There are a couple words for time . **Kālē**, formally **kāláyá**, can refer to a specific point in time, or more generally, to some sort of time period. **Velāvá** can be used similarly, and is also the most common word used for describing a particular time of the day.

Velāvá atai. It's eight o'clock.

The i-form is used both for the hour number and the minute number:

velāvá atai panas hathai. It's eight fifty-seven.

It is common to use special expressions for certain times:

Velāvá atáhamārai. It's eight thirty.

One could also have simply said **atai thihai**, but the former expression is more common. Likewise:

Velāvá atai kālai. It's a quarter past eight/ It's eight fifteen.

Velāvá atai hathálispahai. The time is eight forty five.

These expressions, show that the time after the hour specified. Contrast them with:

Velāvá thunátá kālai. It's a quarter to three/ It's 2:45.

In this expression "to three" is translated with **thuná** in the dative case, rather that the i-form.

In Sri Lanka, the AM / PM system predominates, but in the spoken language, the words for "AM" or "PM" are not used. In situations where this could make things ambiguous, the words for morning, afternoon, evening, and night are used instead.

Word for time of day	Sinhala word
morning	uḋē
noon/afternoon	ḋaval
evening	havásá
night	rǣ

These are used before the numerical time, with the latter in the dative form:

Ḋaval thunátá. 3 pm.

There isn't a formal boundary between the afternoon and evening, either could be used above. 1:00 PM is firmly in **ḋaval** territory, however.

Examples: Translate the following into Sinhala:

1.It's one o'clock.

2. He arrived at 12:17 pm.

3. Finish by 9:30!

4. It's 4:28

5. It's 5 to 11.

Answers:

1. **Velāvá ekai.**
2. **Eyā ḋoḷáhai ḋāháthátá āvā.**
3. **Namáyá hamārátá ivárá káranná.**
4. **Velāvá hathárai vissi atai.**
5. **Velāvá ekoḷáhatá pahai.**

Here are some common words having to do with time:

English	Sinhala
day	ḋavásá
month	māse
year	auruḋḋá

10.3 The Days of the Week

The days of week are compounds formed with **-ḋā**.

English	Sinhala
Sunday	Iriḋā
Monday	Sa^{n}ḋuḋā
Tuesday	A^{n}gaharuvāḋā
Wednesday	Baḋāḋā

English	Sinhala
Thursday	Brahaspathinḋā
Friday	Sikurāḋā
Saturday	Senásurāḋā

These can be used as singular or plural with identical base forms to convey the appropriate meaning.

To say something occurred during a specific interval of time, the words **i^{n}ḋála** and **venakal** are used:

Baḋāḋā i^{n}ḋála sikurāḋā venákal væda kárai. I'll be working from Wednesday to Friday?

These words are sometimes pronounced **i^{n}daṅ** and **venakaṅ**.

Examples: Translate the following into Sinhala:

1.The exam will be at one o'clock on Sunday.

2. I'll be busy from Monday till thursday.

3. Let's meet at 3 pm on Wednesday.

4. I wake up at 10:00 on Saturdays.

5. On Fridays, The restaurant is open from 3 in the afternoon to 2 in the morning.

Answers:

1. **Vib^{h}āge thiyenne Iriḋā ekátá**. Just like with other time words, the numerical time here appears in the dative case to convey that it happens *on* Sunday.

2. **Matá Sa^{n}ḋudā i^{n}ḋaṅ Brahaspáthindā venákaṅ hu^{n}gak vædá thiyenávā.**

3. **Baḋāḋā thunátá hambávemu.** "PM" isn't specified because it's obvious.

4. **Mamá Senásurāḋātá nægitinnē ḋahayátá.**

5. **Sikurāḋátá hōtále ḋaval thunē i^{n}ḋaṅ uḋē ḋeká venákaṅ ærálā thiyenávā.**

10.4 Months and Holidays

The standard months can be coupled with the word **māse** (month), or used by themselves. They are based off of the Dutch month names, and filtered through 17th-century Sinhala pronunciation, so there are some deviations from the English naming scheme.

English	Sinhala
January	Janávāri māse
February	Pebárávāri māse
March	Mārthu māse
April	Aprēl māse
May	Mæi māse
June	Jūni māse
July	Jūli māse
August	Agōsthu māse
September	Sæpthæmbár māse
October	Okthōbár māse

English	Sinhala
November	Novæmbár māse
December	Ḋesæmbár māse

Months are collective nouns as well:

Mamá ipáḋuṇe Januvārivālá. I was born in January.

The traditional Sinhala calendar is used to determine the start of the Sinhala new year, and other holidays in Sri Lanka. It is a lunar calendar, with the start of each month, the Poya day, marked by a full moon.

Month Name	Starts at the full moon in...
Vesak	May
Poson	June
Æsálá	July
Nikiṇi	August
Binárá	September
vap	October
Il	November
U^{n}ḋuvap	December
Ḋuruthu	January
Navam	February
Mæḋin	March
Bak	April

Mæḋin but **mæḋḋen** - both mean the same thing

The ordinal numbers, i.e. "1st," "2nd," etc are formed by adding the number's stem form to **veni**. To express a date, as in the first of a month, **-ḋā** would be added. Hence "second" would be **ḋeváni**, third would be **thunveni**. The word for first is irregular: it is **paḷáveni**, or more formally **paḷámu**.

1. The school year begins in the first week of January. **Aluth pāsæl/iskōlá auruḋḋá pataṅ gannē Janávāri mulá sathiyē**. m.s. = **mulá**- begininng **s.** - week. **agá** - end.
2. My vacation is from the first of June until the seventh of July. **Mage nivādu kāláyá Junī paḷávenidā i^{n}ḋaṅ Julī hathvenidā venákaṅ**.
3. On Vesak day we go to see the thoran. **Vesakḋātá thoran balanná yanávā**. **Pandol** - thoran, these are lighted decorations. p. We go to the temple on Vesak poya day. **Pansal yanávā** - going to (some) temple, **palli yanávā** going to (some) church
4. **Poson ḋā api pansal yanávā**. **Pansal yanávā** is an idiomatic way of saying **pansal(átá) yanávā**.

10.5 Years, Dates, and Seasons

Here are some other words for units of time:

Year	auruḋḋá	auruḋu
Minute	miniththuva	miniththu

Second	Formal: **thathpáráyá**, less formal: **thappáráyá**, Least formal: **thappárē**	Formal: **thathpárá**, informal: **thappárá**

Dates are stated as follows:

Adá Sæptember doḷos venidā. Today is the twelfth of September.

Eká vunē dedas dāhathē Sæptæmbur visi venidā. It happened on September 20th, 2017.

Most places in Sri Lanka have two seasons, one rainy, and one dry. However, there are two rainy seasons, each affecting a different part of the island. The word **kāláyá**, "time period," is used to refer to seasons.

Sinhala Season Name	English Translation	Approximate Duration
nirithá digá mōsámá	Southwestern Monsoon	May-September
	Inter-Monsoon Period	October-November
īsāná digá mōsámá	Northeastern Monsoon	October-January
	Dry season	December-April

While there are only a few months where there is no monsoon anywhere on the island; each region has a long stretch during which it experiences mild weather. This period is called **viyáḷi kāláyá**, "the dry season," while the rest of the the year is called **væhi kāláyá**, "the rainy season." The southwestern portion of Sri Lanka tends to get more rainfall in general, and is consequently referred to as **theth kalāpáyá**, "the wet zone," while the northeast is called **viyáḷi kalāpáyá** "the dry zone."

Sinhala has other words used when referring to the weather of other countries, although English names may simply be substituted as well.

English Season Name	Sinhala Translation
Winter	Sīthá kāláyá
Spring	Vasanthá kāláyá or Vasantháyá
Summer	Grīshmá kāláyá or Gimhāná kāláyá
Fall	Sarath kāláyá or Rithu kāláyá

There isn't much variety to the weather in Sri Lanka; the typical question is whether it will rain, and if so, for how long. Other questions include wether it will be particularly hot, (it will never be cold, but some days are hotter than others), or weather it will be windy.

1. **Me ḋavás anthimá sīthai.** These days are very cold

2. It will be spring soon. **Vasanthá kāláyá la^{n}gai.** Lit spring is near. An expatriate might just say "Spring"
3. I wrote this book in 2017. **Mamá mē pothá liyuvē ḋeḋās ḋāhaththē**.
4. That day was November tenth, 1999. **Ē ḋavásá ek ḋās namásiyá anū namáyē Novæmbár ḋahavenidā**.

10.6 Summary:

Numerals use several inflected forms to refer to various times:

I-form	Specifying hours and minutes	**velāvá pahai**	It's 5 o'clock
tá-form	Specifying relative times with respect to other times or events	**uḋē ekoḷohatá**	11 in the morning
Ē-form	Used with years, to show that something occurred in that year	**Mēká vunē ek ḋās namásiyá anū hayē(ḋi)/ [auruḋḋē]**	This happened (in) [the year] 1996

Times are expressed using the i-forms of numerals: **velāvá pahai** means "five o'clock." The **tá** form is used when talking about relative times (10 to 2) or specifying the time (11 in the morning). The **ē** form is used when specifying the year.

First	Paḷáveni
Second	Ḋeveni
Third	thun veni
Fourth	Hathárá veni

The ordinal numbers in Sinhala are formed using the stem form of a numeral + **veni**. The irregular word for "first" is **paḷáveni** or **paḷámu**. Although the standard word for "day" is **ḋavásá**, "the first day" (of a month) would be **paḷáveniḋā**; "the second" would be **ḋeveniḋā**.

10.6 Exercises:

Dialogue 25: Asking about the Weather

In the following dialogue, A asks B about the weather.

A: **Aḋá hu^{n}gak rasneḋá, næththaṅ vahinávāḋá**? There is a formal way to ask about weather: **kohomáḋá ḋēságunē**? But it is not really used.

B: **Apō, muḷu ḋavásámá vahinávā**

A: **Hiyen vahinávāḋá?**

B: **Hiyen nemei podá væssá. Podá væssá** = drizzle.

A: **Hetath vahinávāḋá**?

B: **Næ hetá vahinnē nǣ, hæbæi hari/thaḋá hulaṅ**

A: **Ehenaṅ hetá vædiyá rasne næthuvá æthi.**

1. Translate the above dialogue.

2-20: Translate the following sentences from Sinhala to English

2. **Mage mītimá thiyennē uḋē namáyátá.**

3. **Ek ḋahas namá siyá hætá namáyē** Neil Armstrong **ha^{n}ḋátá giyā.**

4. **Mage upandináyá Mārthu pahaḷosvenidā**

5. **Iskōlá auruḋdá ivárá vennē Ḋesæmbár māsē.**

6.. **Ī la^{n}gá sumāná thunē matá nivādu.** (**ḋālā thiyennē**)

7. **Ī la^{n}gá sumāná thuná mamá nivādu ḋālā thiyenē.**

8. **Mamá uḋē namáya hamārá indaṅ havásá hayai hathalis paha venákaṅ hæmáḋāmá vædá káránávā.**

9. **Mamá muḷu væhi kāláyámá vædá káránávā.**

10. **Nirithá ḋigá mosam kāláyá Mai indaṅ Sæptembar venákaṅ.**

11. **Mamá iskōlē gihillā geḋárá enákotá ḋeká vithárá venávā.**

12. **Sumānē anthimátá mamá sāppu yanávā.**

13. **Giyá sumānē mamá mevā arágaththē. Mamá mēvā giyá sumānē arágaththē.**

14. **Maṅ lankavátá pitath vuṇē giyá māsē. giyá** - says that you came here last month. **Pitá venávā** = depart.

15. **Ená auruḋḋē mamá vishvá viḋyāláyátá yanávā.**

16. **Matá upāḋiyá læbuṇē giyá auruḋḋē.**

17. **Iyē ræ, mamá niḋiyá ganná giyē ḋoḷáhai pahatá.**

18. **Matá práthipalá læbuṇē īyē.**

19. **Eyā enávā kiyálā thiyennē hetá havásá hathárai ḋahayátá.**

20. **Lankāvá niḋáhas ratak vunē ekḋahas namásiyá hathális atē Pebárávāri hathárá veniḋā.**

21-40. Translate the following sentences from English to Sinhala.

21. The second world war ended on September 2, 1945. "World war" would be **lōká yuḋḋʰáyá.**

22. I was born on March 23rd 2003.

23. Anuradhapura became the capital of Sri Lanka in the fourth century BC.

24. They arrived at the last minute.

25. This town was founded in the fifteen hundreds.

26. I started this job five years ago.

27. I will be in college for 2 more months.

28. The library closes at 8, but you should be ready to leave at 7:50.

29. My vacation will last from June 14th to July seventh.

30. This essay is due in six days.

31. By the time I had gotten to the 31st problem, it was midnight.

32. As the weeks went by, it became easier.

33. Stay here for the next ten minutes.

34. Solve as many problems as you can in the next hour and 25 minutes.

35. At 8:30 we'll stop.

36. It will be over in seconds.

37. It will take a few hours to recharge.

38. We've been traveling for several months. **Thissē** - for

39. We are supposed to be there by 12:07.

40. We'll probably get there by 12:15.

41. I left home at 7 in the morning.

42. He will turn seven this year. He turned seven. This is one of the few contexts where **labánávā**, the un-umlauted version of **læbenávā** is used.

The following dialogues take place in academic environments. Note some of the highly formal word choices.

Dialogue 26: History

In a school, a teacher is preparing the students to enter a history contest. On this day, she's checking their knowledge.

A: **Ā balámu, ḷamainge aithihāsiká ḋanumá kohomáḋá kiyálā**? **Mamá loká ithihāsáyē væḋágath siḋḋ^{h}i gæná prashná kárannai yanne. Prashnáválátá uththáráyá ḋanná ḷamai athá ussanná. Paḷáveni prashnē. siḋḋ^{h}i** meaning incidents, **siḋḋ^{h}iyá** incident. **væḋágath** - important
A: **Sri Laṅkāvátá niḋáhasá læbuṇu ḋináyá kaváḋāḋá**?

Several children raise their hands. The teacher points to one child and says

A: **Ā oyá ḷamáyā uththáre kiyanná balanná**.

B: **Ek ḋās namásiyá hathális atē Pebárávāri hathárá veniḋā**.

A: **Hari**. **Ī la^{n}gá prashnē**. Bastille **ḋináyá siḋu vuṇē kaváḋāḋá**?

She calls on another kid.

B: **Ek ḋās hath siyá hætá namáyē Julī ḋāhathárá veniḋā**.

A: **Næ ēká værádī. Thavá kauruhari kiyanná balanná.**

C: **Ek ḋās hath siyá asū namáyē Julī ḋāhathárá venidā.**

A: **Hari, Ī la^{n}gá prashnē. Langkāvá Brithānyá aḋ^{h}irājyátá givisumákin yatath vuṇu ḋináyá kaváḋāḋá?**

B: **Ek ḋās atá siyá pahalá vei. Mai ḋahavenidā.**

A: **Næ ēká værádī. Vená kenek uththárē ḋannáváḋá?**

C: **Ek ḋās atá siyá pahalá vei, Novembár pas venidā.**

A: **Næ e uththáreth værádī. Vená uththárá thiyenáváḋá?**

D: **Ek ḋās atá siyá pahalá vei, Agōsthu ḋahavenidā.**

A: **Okkomálāmá** (everybody) **hari auruḋḋá kivvath, ḋinē væræḋḋuvā. Hari ḋináyá Marthu ḋevenidā. Ḷamainge ḋænumá thāmá madī. Geḋárá gihiṅ thavá pādam káranná. Api hetá āpahu hamu vemu. Væræḋḋuvā** is the past form of **varaḋḋánávā**, which is the causative of **varáḋinávā.- Oyā matath ēká varaḋḋánávā.** You're making me get it wrong as well. **Væræḋḋak karanavā.**

43. Translate the above dialogue.

Dialogue 27: Test Results

A: **Vib^{h}āgē ho^{n}ḋámá lakuṇu gaththē, Saman. Samantá vædimá lakuṇu ganná puḷuvan vuṇē, eyā honḋátá pādam kárāpu nisā. Ho^{n}ḋá ḷamai vage anik ayath thavá pādaṅ**

károth vædi lakuṇu ganná puḷuvan. Saman kochchárá velā mē vib^{h}āgētá pādaṅ keruvāḋá.

B: **Pæyak vithárá.**

A: **Pæyákátá vadā pādaṅ kárápu ḷamai athá ussanná.**

No one raises their hand.

A: **Miniththu hathális pahak pādaṅ kárápu ḷamai ath ussanná.**

One person raises their hand.

A: **Pēnávā nēḋá, padaṅ káráná hætiyátá thamai lakuṇu hambá vennē. Mē lamáyátá thamai ḋeveniyátá ho^{n}ḋámá lakuṇu thiyennē. Miniththu thihak padaṅ karapu ayá ath ussanná.**

Several people raise their hands.

A: **Oyá ḷamai ītá vadā padaṅ káranná ōne. Ḋæṅ eḷiyátá gihillā sellaṅ káranná hæbæi ho^{n}ḋá ḷamai vage, miniththu pahalávákin panthiyátá enná ōne.**

44. Translate the above dialogue.

11
VOCABULARY

11.1 Animals and Animate Stems

The word for animal is **sathā** (pl **saththu**).Here are some common animal names:

Mosquito	maḋuruvā	maḋuruvō
Ant	kuᵐbiyā	kuᵐbi
Fly	mæssā	mæssō
Fish	māluvā	māluvō
rooster	kukuḷā	kukullu
hen	kikili	kikiliyō
bat	vaulā	vaulō
Pig	ūrā	ūrō

Female pig	īrī	īrīyō
bull	gonā	Gonnu
cow	eḷáḋená	eḷáḋennu
bull	harákā	harak
Water buffalo	Mī harakā	mī harak
dog	ballā	ballō
female dog	bællī	bælliyō
camel	otuvā	otuvō
mammal	shīrápai	
elephant	aliyā	aliyō
Female elephant	keṇerá	-
tusker	æthā	æththu
Female tusker	æthinnā	æthinniyō
goat	eḷuvā	eḷuvō
bird	kurullā	kurullō
sheep/lamb	batáluvá	batáluvo

As mentioned in section 6.7, all nouns have stem form, which serves as an adjectival version of the noun. For inanimate nouns, the stem is also commonly used as the plural, and less often as the singular form of the noun. For animate nouns, the situation is different. Only a few words use the stem form, and the usefulness of that form in general is limited.

For animates ending in **-yā** or **-vā**, with plurals ending in **ō / an**, the stem is obtained by removing **-yā** or **-vā**. Finding the stem for other words is more complex, and requires a brief discussion of so-called final permitted consonants.

In normal Sinhala words, only certain consonants may occur at the end of words, namely **k**, **ṅ**, **th**, **n**, **p**, **m**, **l**, and **s**. (also, **v** and **y**, though this book represents these as **u** and **i** at the end of words). All other consonants, as well as doubled versions of the above consonants are not ordinarily present at the end of words. Why does this matter?

For u-type animate plurals the stem is formed by removing **-ā** from the singular form *except* if this would result in a forbidden consonant at the end of a stem. If the final consonant is **h**, it changes to **s**, otherwise, a final **á** is added to make the stem.

For o-type plurals other than those that end in **yā** or -**vā**, the stem is again produced by removing the final vowel, with the same exception as before. However, is that for o-type stems with forbidden endings, the final vowel may be **u** or **i**. If the pre-final vowel is front, the final vowel of the stem will be **i**, otherwise, it will be **u**. Words with pre-final consonant clusters in the singular form have these simplified: doubled consonants become singular, and full nasal-stop clusters become half-nasals.

Additionally, there are some irregularities. One is the result of sounds like **ḷ**. Although historically a forbidden consonant, in modern times it has merged with **l**, which is allowed at the end of words. Thus there are cases like **kukuḷā**, pl. **kukullu**. It is a u-type plural, but the plural form uses a the allowed "l," while the singular does not. It turns out that the proper stem is **kukul**. Another such irregularity is **kurullā**, pl. **kurullō**; the true stem is **kuruḷu**. Of course, these examples are only irregular as far as their spelling is concerned.

A number of **-yā** or **-vā** type may be exceptions to these rules. The stem of **muvā**, "deer," is **muvá**, even though it has a regular plural of **muvō**.

Examples:

The Sinhala names of various meat products is usually formed using the stem form of the animal the meat came from, followed by the word **mas**, "flesh." Using the list above, deduce the Sinhala words for the following foods:

1. Beef

2. Pork

3. Chicken

4. Goat meat

Answers:

1. **Harak mas**

2. **Ūrā** is an o-type plural, and has a final-forbidden pre-final consonant. Therefore the stem is **ūru**.

3. **Kukul mas**

4. **Eḷu mas**

11.2 Plants

The word for "plant" is **pæláyá**. In Sinhala, most plants are itemized using certain words as bases:

English	Sinhala	Plural
Plant	pæláyá	pælá
Tree	gaha	gas
Flower	malá	mal
Fruit (as in a fruiting body)	gediyá	gedi
A long, narrow seed-containing plant part	karálá	karal

These are all independent nouns, but they also be combined with certain stems: **gotukoḷá - mitiyá** may be optional if you are going to pick some versus going to the store

English	Sinhala	Suffix
Lotus	nellum	- mál
A lotus-like plant	Mā nel	- mál
Rice plant	goyam	- pælá
grass	thaṇákoḷá	- gas
banana	kesel	- gedi

English	Sinhala	Suffix
yam/potato	alá	-gedi
Sweet potato	bathálá	- gedi
orange	ḋodamá	ḋodam/- gedi
cabbage	gova	- gedi
Lady fingers	baṇdakkā	- karála
beans	bōñchi	- karála
pumpkin	vattakkā	- gedi
cucumber	pipiñña	- gedi
mango	a^{m}bá	- gedi

In order to talk about countable plants, the name of the plant must be combined with an appropriate descriptor. **Gedi** means "fruit," but is used with both fruit and vegetables. It is used to refer to a discrete item rather than the concept of a fruit. Instead, **paláthurá**, pl. **paláthuru**, is used for fruits, **eḷáváluvá** (informally **eḷōluvá**) for vegetables. **Mal** is used with flowers.

The stem alone is used to talk about dishes: e.g. **gotukoḷá sambōlē**, "gotukola sambol."

Batháláyā - fat person (insult)

11.3 Anatomy

English	Singular	Plural
head	**oḷuvá**	**oḷu**
neck	**bellá**	**beli** - also name of a fruit
arm	**athá**	**ath**
stomach	**badá**	**badával**
leg	**kakulá**	**kakul**
knee	**ḋanissá**	**ḋanissával**

11.4 Clothing

The word for clothes is **æ^{n}ḋum** or **reḋi**. Here are the names of some common articles of clothing:

shirt	**shā́t eká**	**shā́t**
hat	**thoppiyá**	**thoppi**
pants	**kalisámá**	**kalisam**
shoe	**sapáththuvá**	**sapáththu**
sock	**mēs eká**	**mēs**
underwear	**yatá æ^{n}ḋumá**	**yatá æ^{n}ḋum**
belt/string	**patiyá**	**pati**
bra	**thanápatiyá**	**thanápati**
tie	**tai eká**	**tai**
jeans	**denim kalisámá**	**denim kalisam**
shorts	**kotá kalisámá**	**kotá kalisam**

sarong	saráma	saram
slipper	sereppuvá	sereppu
undershirt	bæniyámá	bæniyam
ring	muḋḋá	muḋu
earring	karābuvá	karābu
necklace	māláyá	mālá
(eye)glasses	(æs) kannādiyá	(æs) kannādi
contact lense	sparsha kācháyá	sparsha kāchá

11.5 Colors

The word for "color" is **pātá**(**yá**). Here are the names of the colors themselves

Blue	nil
Red	rathu
White	suḋu
black	kaḷu
green	koḷá
orange	thæ^{m}bili
purple	ḋam
brown	ḋu^{m}buru
grey	aḷu

pink	rōsá
Light (relative)	la-
Dark (relative)	thaḋá-

English color names can also be used. All color names must be used in conjunction with the word **pātá** in the i-form, but this conjunction is optional in the plain form, which can also be used as an adjective meaning "colored.":

> **Matá nil pātá shāt eká ōne**: I want the blue shirt.
> **Sapaththu kaḷu pātai.** The shoes are black.

11.6 Chores

A chore is simply **vædá** "work,"or **vædak** "a job."

sweep	athu gānávā
tidy up	as káránávā
decorating	sarásánávā
repair	haḋánávā
polish	maḋinávā
Brushing teeth	ḋath maḋinávā.
scrubbing	athullánávā
wash	hōḋánávā
fold	navánávā
compress, tighten	thaḋá káránávā

11.7 Cooking

Here are some common vocabulary words associated with cooking:

cook	uyánávā
boil	thambánávā
fry	baḋinávā
roast	rōs(t) káránávā

cook mallung	malávánávā
steam	humāláyen thambánávā
get burnt	kará venávā/káránávā

spoon	hænḋá	hæ^{n}ḋi
knife	pihiyá	pihi
fork	gǣráppuvá	gǣráppu
bowl/dish	ḋīsiyá	ḋīsi
plate	pi^{n}gāná	pi^{n}gān

11.8: Food and Drink

The word for food is **kæmá**.

fruit	gedi
meat	más
chicken	kukul más
goat meat	eḷu más
beef	Harak más
pork	ūru más
fish	mālu
dry fish	karáválá

maldive fish	u^{m}bálákadá
chick peas	kadálá
lentils	parippu
gravy	hoḋḋá, st. hoḋi
curry	kariyá
rice	bath
bread	pān
water	vathurá
drink	bīmá
beer	bīrá
arak	arakku
moonshine	kasippu

A peculiarity of Sinhala is that words for food and drink are typically collective nouns; by themselves, they would be used only under limited circumstances, for instance:

Mamá pānválátá kæmáthī. I like bread.

Most of the time, the stem form of these words is coupled with a word like **gediyá**, "fruit," or **kællá**, "piece," to refer to actual food items. Consider the dialogue below.

11.9 School and Work

school	**iskōláyá, iskōlē**	**iskōlá**
pencil	**pænsálá**	**pænsal**
pen	**pǣná**	**pǣn**
notebook	Exercise **pothá**	Exercise **poth**
desk	**liyáná mēsē, liyáná mēsáyá**	**liyáná mēsá**

office	**kanthoruvā**	**kanthoru**
office	Office **kamarē, kanthoru kamarē**	Office **kamará**
report	Report/**Rapōrthu káránávā**	The second is nearly obsolete
report	Report **eká/ rapōrthuva**	Report, **rapōrthu**
meeting	**mītimá,**	**mītiṅ**
get together	**ræswīmá**	**ræswīm**
rally	**ræswīmá**	**ræswīm**
Political rally	**ḋeshápāláná ræswīmá**	**ḋeshápāláná ræswīm**

11.10 Places

beach	(usually **Muhuḋu**) **verálá, vælá**	**verálával, vælával**
river	**ga^{n}gá**, more formal **gangā**	**ga^{n}gával, gangāval**
sand	**væli**	
water	**vathurá**	
oil	**thel**	
Kind of oil	**thelá**	**thel**
milk	**kiri**	
A grain	**væli kætē**	**væli kættá**
hotel	**hōtáláyá**	

11.11 Exercises:

1-3: Translate the following dialogs into English:

Dialogue 28: At the Doctor's Office

A person who was in a major accident has recovered, and has come to the doctor's office for a final follow-up visit.

Riyá anáthurákátá mæḋivū/vuṇu minihek suváyá læbu pasu ḋostháráváá balanná āpu avasth^{h}āvá.

A: **Ḋæṅ kohomáḋá?**

B: **Hu^{n}gak ho^{n}ḋai, ho^{n}ḋátámá ho^{n}ḋai vagei.**

A: **Ho^{n}ḋai, kīpá ḋeyak kárálā balámu.**

A: **Ḋakuṇu athá ussanná.**

A: **vam athá ussanná**

A: **Riḋenávānam matá kiyanná. Monávath amāruvak ḋænuṇāḋá**?

B: **Næhæ**. This more formal version of the word **nǣ** is more likely to be used in a setting such as this.

A: **Kohomáḋá oḷuvá kækkum**?

B: **Ḋæṅ næhæ**.

A: **Æⁿgiliválin magē athá thaḋin allanná**.

A: **Hoⁿḋai**.

A: **Ḋaṇissá navánákotá riḋenávāḋá**?

B: **Giyá sumāne iⁿḋálā riḋennē nǣ**.

A: **Mūṇá vam athátá harávālā ītá passe ḋakuṇu athátá harávanná. Mūṇá harávánákotá bellá riḋuṇāḋá**?

B: **Næhæ**

A: **Ehenaṅ ḋæṅ sanīpái vage mamá ḋunnu** "exercises" **kárágená yanná. Kárágená yanná** - go on The **gená** form indicates continuation.

Dialogue 29: At a Restaurant

A group of friends have gone out to a restaurant and are ordering food. **Yaluvō kīpáḋenek hōtálēkátá gihillā kǣmá genná ganná lǣsthi venávā**.

A: **Api bath kamu nēḋá**?

B: **Ou, suḋu bathḋá rathu bathḋá** fried rice **ḋá kannē**?

C: **Suḋui rathui ḋekenmá gamu**.

A: **Ou, monāḋá elávālu gannē**?

B: **Parippu.**

C: **Bōñchi.**

D: **Bæḋápu miris karal.**

E: **Alá thel ḋālā.**

A: **vená monávāḋá?**

B: **Mas mālu monávāhari gamu.**

C: **thorá mālu bæḋálā.**

D: **Kukul mas kariyak.**

E: **Api sambōlēkuth gamuḋá?**

A: **Ou, bæḋápu mālu ekká sambōlē raha vei.**

B: **Ē æthi nēḋá?**

C: **Api parippu næthuvá polos kariyak gamuḋá?**

D: **Papáḋam tikákuth gamu, ethákotá æthi.**

The others agree, and that's what they order. After a while, they get the food and they are serving themselves.

E: **Matá mālu kǣlak beḋanná.**

A: **Mamá mālu ḋīsiyá ḋennaṅ, ethákotá ōgolantá kæmáthi viḋihátá mālu beḋā ganná puḷuvan.**

B: **Matá papáḋámak ḋenná.**

C: **Matath ḋenná.**

D: **Me miris karalnaṅ hari rahai. Matá thavá karálak ḋenná.** **Naṅ / nam** - used when describing something, implies comparison with other similar things.

B: **Me kukul mas kǣli hari lokui. Bāgeyak kǣvath aethi.**

E: **Matá bōñchi tikak beḋanná.**

C: **Apō, mē alánaṅ hariyátá katá ḋanávā. Ḋanávā** is commonly translated as "burning," but only in the sense of pain. It cannot be used with an actual fire.

Dialogue 30: What to wear

Some employees, while having lunch at the cafeteria are talking about what to wear to the office Christmas party. "Office" **ekē vædá kárání kīpá ḋenek kæmá kanágamaṅ Naththal utsáváyátá a^{n}ḋiná æ^{n}ḋuṅ gæná kath^{h}ā kárápu hæti.**

A: **Ōgollan sāriḋá a^{n}ḋinná hithannē næththan gaumḋá?**

B: **Mamánaṅ sāriyak a^{n}ḋinávā matá rathui koḷai sāriyak thiyenávā. Ēká naththal uthsáváyákátá ho^{n}ḋai.**

C: **Oyā sāriyak a^{n}ḋinávānaṅ mamath a^{n}ḋinávā. Matá kaḷui riḋī patai sāriyak thiyenávā. Eká ho^{n}ḋá vei.**

D: **Mamánaṅ gaumak a^{n}ḋinnē. Nil pātá ḋigá gaumak ho^{n}ḋá veiḋá næthaṅ rosá pātá kotá gaumákuth matá thiyenávā.**

E: **Ḋigá gaumá vædiyá ho^{n}ḋá vei.**

F: Mamá kaḷu ḋigá kalisámákui rathu shā́t ekak a^{n}ḋinávā. Oyā monávāḋá a^{n}ḋinnē?

G: Mamá thāmá hithánávā. Matá pātá pātá ḋigá sāyak thiyánávā. Maṅ hithannē eká a^{n}ḋinná.

A: Udátá mokáḋá a^{n}ḋinnē?

B: Mamá raththáran pātá hættáyak sæyath ekká a^{n}ḋinnam.

12
LOANWORDS

12.1 Late Loanwords

Usage of loanwords, particularly English ones, is increasingly common in modern times. There are fairly regular rules for converting an English word into a fully functional Sinhala one:

English adjectives may be imported directly, and English nouns can be made into adjectives with **vage**. Colors are an exception; these are suffixed with **pātá**.

Nouns are transformed based on their gender. Inanimate objects referring to discrete objects are imported with **eká.**

Desk **eká.** The desk

The indefinite form is **desk ekak**. The plural would just be **desk**, although a speaker fluent in English might say **desks**. Either way, the plural forms take the standard inanimate plural case endings.

Incidentally, place name loanwords are always plural, grammatically:

Mamá Wilmington **válin** Philadelphia **válátá giyā**. I went from Wilmington to Philadelphia.

Wilmington **válá i^{n}ḋálā** could be used here. This indicates that you stayed for a while. If it's a Sinhala place name, **i^{n}ḋálā** does not take a locative argument, but otherwise, it must.

These ***late loanwords***, which are basically just non-Sinhala words incorporated into Sinhala, are not to be confused with ***Sinhalized words***, which, though they are equally non-Sinhala in origin, have been adapted into the language and behave like ordinary words. For instance:

Mamá Maldives **válin Indiyāvátá giyā**. I went from the Maldives to India.

In the above sentence, **Indiyāvá** is an example of a Sinhalized word.

Animate nouns are imported differently. The singular form is just used "as is," with the regular singular definite endings tacked on:

Mamá ē prásiḋḋá rhinoceros**vá ḋækkā.** I saw that famous rhinoceros.

The indefinite form, however, is made by adding **kenek** to the word, so "a rhinoceros" would be rhinoceros **kenek**. The plural is formed by adding **-lā**, so the plural would be rhinoceros**lā**. Sometimes, the plural form of the loanword is used.

Curiously, the word **kangarū** has an indefinite form **kangarūvek**.

Animate nouns referring to people may also be made using certain other words:

Director **mahatháyā/nōnā.** The director (male / female)

A less formal version of this is:

Police **kāráyā.** The police person.

Verbs are imported as compounds, based on their meaning. **Káránávā** is the most productive in this respect. **Venáva** is also commonly used, often making passive verbs. **Gannávā** is used in some limited contexts, as is **gahanávā.**

"Petrol"**gahanávā.** pump gas - "gas" in SL English is gas for cooking.

These behave as ordinary compound verbs grammatically.

Examples:

1. **Mamá eyātá** vaccine **eká ḋunnā**.
2. **Apē iskōlētá aluth** teacher **kenek āvā.**
3. **Matath ēka** sure **næ**.

Answers:

1. I injected him with the vaccine.
2. A new teacher came to our school.
3. I'm also not sure about that.

12.2 Identifying loanwords

The above words are all late loans. As we have seen, they behave in a straightforward way. From a historical standpoint, we can group loanwords into three main categories. Early loans are not functionally distinct from native Sinhala words, and often cannot be distinguished from them; here we will treat them as being part of the "native Sinhala" category. Words borrowed in between these periods are the Sinhalized words (Many words in imitation of this style are still coined today, usually for technical purposes).

It turns out that, like late loans, Sinhalized words behave differently from native Sinhala words, and the main difference is that they behave much more regularly. Animate nouns which are Sinhalized words end in **-yā** or **-vā** unless they are feminine; in which case they end in **-ī**. The plurals are formed by replacing **ā** with **ō** or by adding **-yō**, respectively.

Inanimate Sinhalized words end in **-vá** or **-yá**; the plurals are formed by removing these endings.

There are several quick and easy ways to identify loanwords:

Eká type nouns are generally late loanwords, except when used to nominalize adjectives (e.g. **ḋuváná eká** "the run").

All words that end in consonants other than **k**, **ṅ**, **th**, **n**, **p**, **m**, **l**, or **s** are late loanwords. (In the Sinhalese script, **v** is also written at the end of words, as is **y**, usually as **-yi**. These are written as **-u** and **-i** here, as in all cases where they are at the end of syllables, except for the clusters **vv** and **yy**).

More generally, native Sinhalese words never have syllables that end in consonants other than the ones listed above.

All words with aspirates are loanwords, usually either from Pali or Sanskrit. Additionally, the letters **sh**, **ṣh**, and **ñ** are only found in loanwords. The long **á** sound is only found in late loans.

The **ch** and **j** sounds are found in a few native words and forms, especially as clusters. However, the vast majority of words with these sounds are loans.

Most non-literary words do not have even most of the possible consonant clusters; instead, they mostly have double consonants and the nasal clusters **ṅg**, **nḋ**, **nd**, and **mb**.

Loanwords only rarely have half-nasal sounds . Although the letter **ḷ** represents a sound that is found in several nearby languages, and is no longer pronounced differently than **l** in Sinhala, the vast majority of words spelled with it are not loans. The **æ** and **ǣ** sounds are also characteristic of Sinhala words, but these can be found in English and Dutch loanwords as well.

Many loanwords for family members occupy a place in between these categories. They have stems ending in **á**; like Sinhalized words, they are changed to form the singular (but by changing the ending to **ā**), and like late loans, form the plural by adding **lā** to the stem. Thus the plural of **ammā** is **ammálā**.

12.3 Summary:

	Singular	Indefinite	Plural
Native Sinhala/ Early loans	various	**-ek/ak**	various
Animate Sinhalized words	-**yā**, -**vā**, or -**ī**	-**yek**, -**vek**, or -**īyek**	-**yō**, -**vō**, or -**īyō**
Inanimate Sinhalized words	-**yá** or -**vá**	-**yak** or -**vak**	Remove -**yá** or -**vá**
Animate Late Loans	Unmarked	- **kenek**	Shorten final **ā** to **á** if present, then add **lā**. If an English loan, the English plural ending can optionally be added first
Inanimate Late Loans	- **eká**	- **ekak**	Remove -**eká**

Caution: These rules cannot reliably be applied in reverse; native Sinhala words may use the plural form rules above or some others (See sections X and Y). For instance, **-lā** plural endings appear on plenty of Sinhala words too, sometimes alongside an earlier plural form, sometimes with **ā** shortening, sometimes without.

Some Sinhalized words have also become irregular, e.g. **janēlē**, formally **janēláyá**; "window," pl. **janēl**.

12.4 Exercises:

Determine whether the word is identifiable as a loan or not. If it is; determine the plural.

1. **kar eká** "car"

2. **nāsikyáyá** "nasal"

3. **b^hāshāvá** "language"

4. **pi^mburā**, "python"

5. **jñāthiyā**; pronounced **ñāthiyā**; "relative"

6. **Væv**á "reservoir"

7. **kanthōruvá**, "office"

8. **jāthiyá**, "type."

9. **aḋáhasá**, "idea"

10. **Pacháyā**, "liar"

Translate the following sentences into English:

11. **Matá ēka** sure.

12. **Vædē ivárá vuṇáhamá** bell **eká gahanná**.

13. **Vathurá** leak **venávā**.

14. **Mamá** dinosaur **kenekge pinthūráyak ḋækkā**.

15. **Mamá** rhinoceros**lā godak ḋækkā**.

13
THE SINHALA ALPHABET

This final chapter will introduce the Sinhala alphabet. Although most texts in Sinhala will require knowledge of literary Sinhala to read, things like street signs, billboards, etc should be intelligible upon completing the problems in this chapter. Learning this script is also advisable if you are interested in continuing to study Sinhala, since many instructional texts do not use transliterations.

All the letters of the Sinhala alphabet, including the more obscure ones, have been provided here, so that if you do decide to learn literary Sinhala, you can focus on the language aspects and not have to learn a bunch of new letters. More usefully, if you happen to run into one of the rarer letters (probably in a name), you won't mix it up for a more common one.

13.1 General writing practices:

Writing in Sinhala is a bit different than it is in a language using the Latin script.Let's look at an example.

For the word **ahanávā**, “listen,”:

The first letter would be අ, which stands for the **a** sound. The next letter would be හ, which includes both the **h** and the **a** sounds. The next character is න, which stands for both the **n** and **á** sounds. Finally, we add වා. This letter has two components: he main body of the letter, ව, which alone would stand for **va** or **vá,** and the diacritic following it, ා, which indicates the **ā** sound.

A peculiarity is that each sound doesn't always get its own letter; **a** is represented by its own character in the first syllable, but is afterwards packaged together with other sounds. Why?

The rules here are rather simpler. If a vowel is before a consonant, it appears independently, but otherwise, it is bundled. In all other cases, consonant letters are used. If the vowel is **a** or **á**, the plain, unmarked form of the letter is used; for other vowels, or for writing a "pure" consonant without a bundled vowel, the letter is modified by a diacritic, as shown above. Certain consonant clusters have optional, special ways of being represented; we will deal with these later.

13.2 The (Relatively) Straightforward characters

Sinhala Letter	Pronunciation	diacritic
අ	a,á	-
ආ	ā	◌ා
ඇ	æ	◌ැ
ඈ	ǣ	◌ෑ
ඉ	i	◌ි
ඊ	ī	◌ී
උ	u	◌ු
ඌ	ū	◌ූ
එ	e	ෙ◌
ඒ	ē	ේ◌
ඔ	o	ො◌
ඕ	ō	ෝ◌
ඓ	ai	ෛ◌
ඖ	au	ෞ◌

These characters are "straightforward" in that they are only ever pronounced in a single way. The last two letters are mostly used for historical spellings. In fact, all the instances of **ai** and **au** that have been shown in this book up until now would have been written using **ayi** and **avu** instead, the **y** and **v** sounds being silent in those specific contexts. The vowel letters themselves are used only under the circumstances described in the last section; otherwise, the diacritic form is used with a consonant letter. A consonant without a vowel is written with a diacritic which can vary from sound to sound. The unambiguous consonants, with their pure forms and irregular forms, are given on the following page:

Sinhala letter	Pronunciation	Without vowel	Irregularities
ප	**pá**	ප්	
බ	**bá**	බ්	
ම	**má**	ම්	
ඹ	**^{m}bá**	ඹ්	
ව	**vá**	ව්	
ත	**thá**	ත්	තු=**þu**,තූ=**þū**
ද	**d̈á**	ද්	දු=**d̈u**, දූ=**d̈ū**
න	**ná**	න්	
ඳ	**^{n}d̈á**	ඳ්	ඳු=**^{n}d̈u**, ඳූ=**^{n}d̈ū**
ස	**sá**	ස්	
ශ	**shá**	ශ්	Often pronounced **sá** ශු=**shu**, ශූ=**shū**
ල	**lá**	ල්	
ර	**rá**	ර්	රැ=**ræ**,රෑ=**rǣ**, රු=**ru**,රූ=**rū***
ට	**tá**	ට්	
ඩ	**dá**	ඩ්	
ඬ	**^{n}dá**	ඬ්	
ච	**chá**	ච්	
ජ	**já**	ජ්	
ය	**yá**	ය්	
ක	**ká**	ක්	කු=ku,කූ=kū
ග	**gá**	ග්	ගු=gu,ගූ=gū
ඟ	**^{n}gá**	ඟ්	ඟු=^{n}gu,ඟූ=^{n}gū
හ	**há**	හ්	
ඤ	**ñá**	ඤ්	ඤු=ñu,ඤූ=ñū
ඥ	**(j)ñá****	ඥ්	ඥු=(j)ñu,ඥූ=(j)ñū
ඞ	**ṅa**	ඞ්	

*The **j** of this character is pronounced only when the letter is not at the start of a word.

There are also some characters that are unambiguously pronounced, though they have alternate pronunciations. This is because the alternate pronunciations are so obsolete that not even highly educated speakers will pronounce these letters historically.

ණ	ṇá	ණ්	ná
ළ	ḷá	ළ්	la (ළු=lu,ළූ=lū)

The **ṅa** character, as it turns out, is practically never used, as it has been superseded by a diacritic. For instance, see the spelling of **Laṅkā** below. The "n" in "Lanka" is represented by the small circle, which is known as the **binduvá**. This symbol, when added to a vowel or consonant letter, adds the **ṅ** sound after the vowel of the symbol (most of the time, see section 13.4). It turns out that this is the only position the **ṅ** sound can appear in Sinhala, which is probably why this diacritic is preferred.

Here is a table of additional commonly used diacritics:

diacritic	effect	example
ං	*Usually*, add an **ṅ** after the vowel	ලංකා= **lańkā**, “Lanka”
ඃ	Add an **h** after the vowel	අන්තඃපුරය = **anthahpuráyá**, “harem”
්‍ය	Insert a **y** between the consonant and the vowel	වාක්‍ය=**vākyá**, “sentence”
්‍ර	Insert a **r** between the consonant and the vowel	ග්‍රහයා=**grahayā**, “astrological sign”
ර්‍	Add an **r** before the consonant	කර්‍ම=**karmá**, “karma”

Aside from the sound mergers and historical spellings shown above, spelling in Sinhala is straightforward. One major exception is the **i** sound written at the end of clauses ended by most adjectives. Although spelled **yi**, it is pronounced as an **i** sound. So **sīthálai** is spelled {**sīthalayi**} (this book uses the more intuitive former spelling for transliteration). Likewise the **au** sound is typically written {**avu**}, when not using the vowel-letter, which is typically reserved for Sanskrit words..

In western loanwords, a lone “r” is indicated using the vowel-less letter. Sanskrit loans are the usually only words which use the syllabic r and l characters below, and then only in words that were historically spelled that way. Non syllabic r and y clusters in those words, and all other non-western words, generally the non syllabic diacritics above. These are not absolute rules though.

13.3 Ambiguous Characters:

The syllabic consonants of Sanskrit will be represented by their actual pronunciations rather than their nominal translations. The nominal pronunciations are never used, but the actual sound they represent can vary from word to word:

Sinhala Letter	Nominal Transliteration	Diacritic	Actual Pronunciation
ඍ	ṛ	◌ෘ	**ri, ir, ru,ur**
ඎ	ṝ	◌ෲ	**rī, īr, rū,ūr**
ඏ	*	◌ෟ	**li**
ඐ	*	ෳ	**lī**

These characters represent the syllabic "r" and "l" sounds of Sanskrit. Native Sinhala speakers pronounce these with either an **i**, **u**, **ī**, or **ū**, added, corresponding to the length or the original syllabic consonant. The choice of vowel type seems to be random, so the same word might be pronounced with an **i** by one speaker and with a **u** by another. The pronunciation of words written with these letters is not random, though.

The "l" sounds are exceedingly rare. They are presented here for the sake of completeness.

Sinhala letter	Educated Pronounciation	Without vowel	Colloquial Pronunciation
ඵ	**p^{h}á**	ඵ්	**pá**
භ	**b^{h}á**	භ්	**bá**
ෆ	**fá**	ෆ්	**pá**
ථ	**th^{h}á**	ථ්	**thá**
ධ	**ḋ^{h}á**	ධ්	**ḋá**
ඨ	**t^{h}á**	ඨ්	**tá**
ඪ	**d^{h}á**	ඪ්	**dá**
ෂ	**shá (ṣhá*)**	ෂ්	**sá**
ඡ	**ch^{h}á**	ඡ්	**chá**
ඣ	**j^{h}á**	ඣ්	**já**
ඦ	**^{n}já**	ඦ්	**
ශ	**shá**	ශ්	**sá**
ඛ	**k^{h}á**	ඛ්	**ká**
ඝ	**g^{h}á**	ඝ්	**gá**

* This letter represents the **ṣh** sound, which was distinct from **sh** in Sanskrit. Modern speakers may pronounce it **sh** or **s**.

** this letter is included here for completeness, but it does not seem to be used at all.

These letters are used for various historical spellings, especially loanwords from Sanskrit and Pali. Many native speakers will use the pronunciation given in the rightmost column, rather than that of the original sound.

13.4 The Binduva

The behavior of the binduva deserves more commentary. Although it is most often used to indicate the **ṅ** sound, it can, in fact, represent all five of the full nasals; that is, **m**, **n**, **ṇ**, **ñ** or **ṅ**. The sound it represents depends on the sound immediately after it. If it occurs at the end of a word or before a vowel, it represents **ṅ**. Otherwise, it will always be homorganic with the consonant after it.

It turns out that the sounds of Sinhala can be sorted into categories based on where they are articulated in the vocal tract. The consonants are traditionally divided into five categories:

ōṣhthájá (made with the lips): **p**, **p**^{h}, **b**, **b**^{h}, **m**, ^{m}**b**, **v**

ḋanthájá (made with the teeth): **th**, **th**^{h}, **ḋ**, **ḋ**^{h}, **n**, ^{n}**ḋ**, **s**, **l**, **r**

mūrḋ^{h}**ájá** (made with the tongue tip curled backwards): **t**, **t**^{h}, **d**, **d**^{h}, **ṇ**, ^{n}**d**, **ṣh**, **ḷ** (of course, in the modern language **ṇ**, **ṣh**, and **ḷ** are not pronounced in this manner).

thālujá (made with the palate): **ch**, **ch**^{h}, **j**, **j**^{h}, **ñ**, ^{n}**j**, **y**, **sh**

kaṇthájá (made with the throat): **k**, **k**^{h}, **g**, **g**^{h}, **ṅ**, ^{n}**g**, **h**

The real rule of the binduva is this: find the consonant that follows it in the table above; then find the full nasal in that row. That full nasal is the sound it represents in that word.

In practice, in modern Sinhala the binduva is usually used in contexts where it represents **ṅ**, however, other usages are not unheard of, especially in literary words.

13.5 Distinguishing Look-Alike Characters

Many of the letters are similar to each other. Unfortunately, except for most of the vowel variants and most of the prenasalized consonants, this graphical similarity rarely has any relationship to the actual pronunciation of the letters. As such, the small differences between pairs such as **k^{h}á** and **bá** must be memorized in order to properly read Sinhala. The tables below group letters based on their appearance, with their nominal pronunciation.

ට	ඨ	ව	ච	ඵ	ඏ	ඐ	එ	ඒ	ඓ
tá	**th^{h}á**	**vá**	**chá**	**p^{h}á**	**ḷu**	**ḷū**	**e**	**ē**	**ai**

These letters all have a simple curve as their skeleton.

ම	ඹ	ඔ	ඕ	ඖ
má	**^{m}bá**	**o**	**ō**	**au**

These letters all have a more complex inner curve.

ධ	ත	ඞ	ඪ	ඩ	ඬ
d̪^{h}á	**tá**	**ṅá**	**d^{h}á**	**dá**	**^{n}dá**

The letters above are two-lobed.

ය	ස	ඍ	ඎ	ඝ
yá	**sá**	**ṛ**	**ṝ**	**g^{h}á**

In addition to their two-lobed lower halves, these letters all have a small curve on their upper left.

ප	ජ	ඦ	ඡ	ඏ	ඐ	ෂ
pá	**já**	**^{n}já**	**ch^{h}á**	-	-	**ṣhá**

These letters have a single-lobed lower part, but a pair of small curves above.

ග	ශ	ඟ	හ	භ
gá	**shá**	**^{n}gá**	**há**	**b^{h}á**

These letters all share the spiral-like model of **gayanná.**

න	ත	ක
ná	**thá**	**ká**

These letters all have a long curve on the left, and a reduced main loop to compensate.

ඥ		ඣ		ඤ	
ග	ඳ	ක	ධ	ක	ද
jñá		**j^há**		**ñá**	

This table contains characters that are graphically the combination of two characters. The component characters are shown for comparison along with the transliterations. Curiously, **jñ** is frequently transliterated as "gn". Perhapsthis is because of the **^{n}g** component of this character.

The following four tables contain lookalike pairs.

ඊ	ර
ī	**ra**

ඛ	බ
k^há	**bá**

උ	ඌ
u	**ū**

ද	ඳ
d̈á	**^{n}d̈á**

The table below contains all of the a-like letters.

අ	ආ	ඇ	ඈ
a	**ā**	**æ**	**ǣ**

The last table here contains the few characters which have no lookalikes.

ඉ	ෆ	ළ	ල	ණ
i	**fá**	**ḷá**	**lá**	**ṇá**

Memorizing these characters table by table, taking note of the small differences which distinguish certain characters, is probably the most practical way to learn this alphabet.

13.6 Conflated Characters:

As a result of these spelling conventions, even native Sinhala speakers frequently produce typos as a result of mixing up letters which are pronounced identically in modern times. The aspirated consonants are rarely misused in this way, since they are used only in certain loanwords, so they are not listed in this table.

The letters listed in the first column are the most common ways to spell the listed sounds; if you have to guess, they will be your best bet. The letters in column 2 are

Colloquial Pronounciation	Letters		
sá	ස	ශ,ෂ	
l	ඏ	ඐ	◌ෟ
r	ඍ	◌ෘ	
ai	අයි	ඓ	
au	අවු	ඖ	
ná	න	ණ	
ṅ	◌ං		ඞ

used in various historical spellings; the **sá**-series is the only one here where any Sinhala speaker would pronounce the character in columns 2 differently from the corresponding entry in column 1. Letters in Column 3 are all but unused.

Distinguishing **a** from **á**

One big problem you have probably noticed is that in the Sinhala script, **a** and **á** are not distinguished. How, then, can one pronounce words written in Sinhala accurately?

It turns out that there are rules. The general rule is that the first "a" of a word will be pronounced **a**, and the subsequent "a"s will be pronounced **á**, with several regular exceptions. These are: 1). After "h," "a" is always **a**, *except* if it occurs in a syllable after the vowels **i** or **u**. 2) In a closed syllable(before a word final consonant, or a pair of two consonants), "a" is always **a**. 3). If a word begins with a consonant cluster and has a short "a," that "a" is **á**, unless exception 2) also applies.

The three rules above have exemptions in turn. **Káránávā** and its derivatives are exceptions to these rules in that the first "ka" will always be **ká**. Loanwords, especially recent English ones, tend to be exceptions also.

Examples:

Transliterate the following Sinhala words:

1. හදනවා
2. ප්‍රසිද්ධ
3. කරකර
4. මහනවා
5. සිංහයා

Answers:

1. haḋánávā

2. **prásiḋḋʰá**. Due to the intial pr-, the first "a" sound is **á**.

3. **kárákárá**. As a **káránávā** derivative, this ignores the rules for the first syllable.

4. **mahanávā**. In Sinhala words, short "a" after h is always **a**…

5. **siṇháyā**. … except if the previous syllable has **u** or **i**.

13.7 Exercises

1-30: Transliterate the following Sinhala words.

1.රෑ (night)

2.හුඟක් (much)

3.උයන්න (to cook)

4.හිඳ (because)

5.ඊට (that)

6. ඥාන (knowledge)

7. තාත්තා (dad)

8. එළු (An old name for Sinhala)

9. කණ්ණාඩි (glasses)

10. ෆෑන්(fan)

11. ලෝකු(big)

12. අඹ(mango)

13. ඔව් (yes)

14. වංස (chronicle)

15. කර්ම (religious concept)

16. වාක්‍ය(sentence)

17. ග්‍රහයා(astrological sign, a Sanskrit loan)

18. අං(horn)

19. විශ්වවිද්‍යාල (University)

20. වෘක(wolf)

21. බුද්ධධම්ම(Buddhism)

22. භාෂාව(language)

23. ශාක්‍ය(An ancient Indian state)

24. ලිච්ඡවී(proper noun)

25. මෞර්ය(dynasty name)

26. ථේරවාද(religious term)

27. දීඝවාපී(place name)

28. ප්‍රතිඵල(results)

29. රේඛාව(line, mathematics)

30. මනඃකල්පිත (imaginative)

Appendix I
ANSWERS TO END-OF-CHAPTER EXERCISES

Chapter 1:

1. **Īrī**-Shiny, **Minihā**-Pizza, **Gollō**-Show, **eḷu**-shoe
2. **Hædi**-paddy, **gedi**-ready, **podi**-Cody

3. **nil**-kill,**kakul**-cool,**mál**-political,**pol**-coal

4-6: The following are samples of casually romanized Sinhala. Convert them to the format used in this book.

4. **vei**

5. **bīlā**

6. **ūrū**

7. The "nd" here could represent either an **n** followed by a **d** or a prenasalized "d." The "d" could also be ambiguous, as there are two sounds which are commonly equated with it. The "a" is not ambiguous, it never takes its alternate value when followed by "i" or "u." This book represents this word as **ho^{n}ḋai**.

8. The "ng" could represent an **n** followed by a **g**, **^{n}g**, or **ṅ**. In fact it is the latter here. This example is not so ambiguous for anyone familiar with Sinhala, as half nasals and consonant clusters are not allowed at the end of native words (prenasals are also forbidden at the beginning of words). The "a"s are also ambiguous. This book represents this word as **parisámeṅ**.

9. The "d" could also be ambiguous, as there are two sounds which are commonly equated with it. The "a" not ambiguous: at the end of words, when not preceded by **h**, it is always pronounced as **á**.

10. **Pas**

11. **Æ^{n}ḋuṅ**, or more formally **Æ^{n}ḋum**

12. **bath**

13. **rilau**

14. **uḋavvá** (help)

15. **uḋau** pl. of 14

Note that if you have guess which sound a "d" in casually romanized Sinhala represents, you are generally better off guessing that it is **ḋ**. The **d** sound is commonly found in loanwords but is otherwise fairly rare. Some common Sinhala words with the sound are: **vædi**, **vædá**(**yá**), **vadā**, **adu**, **badá**(**gini**), **badu**, **podi**, **godak**, and **a^{n}dánávā**. Aside from these, the **d** sound is also found in some common Tamil loanwords: **kaṇṇādi**, "glasses," **ḋodam**, "oranges," for instance. In English loanwords, the English "d" sound is usually represented as **d**, not **ḋ**, so words like **desk eká**, "desk," are also a common source of this sound.

Chapter 2:

1. **Mamá bayá næ**. **Bayá** is one of the outliers with respect to the general trend for using **mamá** vs **matá**.
2. **Eyā mamá tharam bayá næ**.
3. **Ē mēsē suḋḋai**.
4. **Ē minihā tikak amuthui**.
5. **Gahá hu^{n}gak paráṇá næ.** Some people might use **vayásá** with trees.
6. **Ē ḷamáyā thamai mōdámá ḷamáyā.**
7. **Matá hari santhōsai.** I'm very happy. Needs correcting
8. **Matá harimá kēnthī**. **Tharáhá** is equally acceptable; **Matá hu^{n}gak kēnthi giyā** is a more common way to talk about having been angry.
9. **Matá rasne thē ḋenná**.
10. **Aluth báth paráṇá bathválátá vædiyá hari rahai**. Why is it **bathválátá**? The dative case ending is the same for animate

and inanimate *singular* nouns. **Bath** is plural, and so has a different ending.

11. **Ē killitu ballā hiyeṅ duvánávā.**

12. **Matá tuk gallá kæmá ḋenná. ikmánátá / ikmánin** could also be used.

13. **Ē gǣni issárá kettui**. The woman was thin.

14. **Ē ḷamáyā saḋḋáyak næthuvá niḋā gaththā**.

15. **Matá pāḷui**.

16. I'm very hot.

17. Clean that messy room.

18. Those men are extremely ugly. **Kæthá** can also mean "ugly" in the sense of their morality, and so this sentence could also be impugning their character.

19. I'm not hungry.

20. Many children are bad.

21. Give me a new house.

22. I'm a little thirsty.

23. Your house is very beautiful. Men might say **u^{m}bē** instead of **oyāgē**.

24. The child is tired and also sleepy.

25. That fast-walking man looks like he's angry.

26. I'm wrong.

27. It is dirty. Notes: **Kunu gǣvilā** - it was dirtied **Kunu velā** - rotted

28. I wasn't hungry so i didn't eat.

29. That short man is walking fast. (The word for "short," both with respect to height and length, is **kotá**)

30. It's not long enough. (The word for "long" is **ḋigá**)

31.**Ēká hu^{n}gak ḋurai**.

32. **Etháná kǣmá raha nǣ**.

33. **Etháná kǣmá hari rahai, hæbæi ēká hu^{n}gak ḋurai**.

Chapter 3:

1. **Mama ikmánátá ēká bonnaṅ**. Note: There is a certain amount of flexibility with word order here, though keeping **mamá** first is most natural, and **bonnam** has to be at the end.
2. **Kadētá yanná**.
3. **Matá yanná ōne**.
4. **Api ḋæṅ kamu**. **Api** is needed here.
5. **Mamá uyannaṅ**.
6. **Matá vathurá tikak bonná ōne**. Why does **tikak** come after **vathurá** here? It isn't saying that the speaker's desire for water is small; **tikak** is not an adverb here. In Sinhala, quantities, both definite and abstract, come *after* the items they quantify. Hence "a lot of water" would be **vathurá godak**. See Chapter 9.
7. **Kǣ gahanná epā**.
8. **Eyā thavá tikákin yanávā / yai**.
9. **Eyātá gæhuvalu**. (I was told) he was beaten.
10. **Eyā hetá kondē kapā ganná yai**.
11. **Eyā thavá tikákin iskōlátá yai / yanavā**. **Thavá tikakin** makes **yanavā** ok. If it was not present, **yai** would be required.
12. **Matá ēká káranná ōne nǣ**. Alternatively **ōnnǣ** could be used.

13. **Mamá passē enná puḷuvan**. Here **puḷuvan** means its possible.

14. **Ēká æththá venná æthi**.

15. I heard he didn't drink anything. A more literal translation would be "I was given to understand that he didn't drink anything." **Læbuṇē** is the past tense of **læbenávā**, a passive, transitive verb meaning "receive." **Matá balu pætiyek(vá) læbuṇā**, **Matá balu pætiyāvá læbuṇā**. **Pætiyā** in general means "little thing," **balu pætiyek** means "a puppy.

16. (Somebody told me that) They are going to Galle.

17. He likes his new computer.

18. I'm not saying that. What's the difference between **nemei** and **nǣ**? **Nemei** implies disagreement, **nǣ** indicates that you didn't perform the action at all, e.g. "I didn't see that": **Mamá ēká nemei ḋækkē**.

19. If you can't do it, I'll have to. Note that **ōne** is not required to express need here.

20. I don't need that book.

21. I don't need to read that book.

22. I want to eat now. **Ḋæmámá** would be used to say "right now;" this is the irregular **má** form of **ḋæṅ**.

23. Would you like to sit down? **Oyā i^{n}ḋá gannávāḋá**? / **i^{n}ḋá ganná kæmáthīḋá**? "Sit down" is **i^{n}ḋá gannávā**; this is the irregular **ganná** form of **innávā**.

24. I'm going to write the paper. There is a Sinhala word for "essay" as well, see chapter 12.

25. She'll understand it.

26. Stop hiding.

27. Don't stop running. **Navaththanná epā** by itself could be enough in context.
28. I need to buy some books. **Vagáyak** appears behind **poth** here for the same reason **tikak** comes after **vathurá** in problem 6.
29. I can do it. **Puḷuvan** is more common in this context, and has the exact same meaning.
30. She needs to study more. Compare **eyātá thavá pādaṅ káranná ōne** - she wants to study more. The absence of **-tá** conveys that she should be studying more vs. that she wants to study more.
31. He needs to eat.
32. He wants to eat.
33. I don't want to buy that.
34. I don't need to buy it. Unlike with the third person, there is no difference in **-tá** marking here.
35. I'll be able to swim.
37. I'm going for a walk.
38. I'm reading about it on the internet.
39. He only drinks water. Alternatively, **eyā vathurá vithárai bonnē**. Both are common.
40. You need to finish soon.
41. If the water is stopped, we can go.
42. He will be there.
43. **Matá vædá káranná ōná ḋēval ganná / gandá ōnē**.
44. **Api ḋæṅ kanávā**.
45. **Yanávā, yanávā**.
46. **Hōtálētá enávānaṅ parakku venná epā**.

Chapter 4:

1.**vætuṇā, vætilā, vætuṇá, vætichchá**

2.**biruvā, burálā, biruvá, burápu**

3.**erevvā, oroválā, erevvá, orovápu**

4. **thēruṇā, thērilā, thēruṇá, thērichchá**

5.**pænnā, pænálā, pænná, pænápu**

6. **nægittā, nægitálā, nægittá, nægitápu**

7. **imbā, i^{m}bálā, imbá, i^{m}bápu**

8. **kævvā, kaválā, kævvá, kavápu**

9. **æriyā, ærálā, æriyá, ærápu**

10. **nǣvā, nālā, nǣvá, nāpu**

11. **kiyuvā, kiyálā**

12. **Eyā ēká kivvē nǣ**. Eká might be omitted.

13. **Eyā kiyuvā eyātá igenáganná ōne kiyálā.**

14. **Mamá a^{n}duvē nǣ.**

15. **Eyā thē eká bonágamaṅ uththárá ḋunnā.**

16.**Apitá thavá godak ḋura avidinna thiyenávā.**

17. **Ē malá pipuṇā.**

18. **Banum ahuvātá passē, api niḋā ganná giyā**

19. **Mamá** TV **bæluvā**

20. **Ē golaṅ radio eká ahagáná hitiyā.**

21. **Mamá gē suḋḋá keruvā.**

22. **Mamá pothá arágená e gollantá ḋunnā.**

23. **Mamá mē pinthurē ændā.**

24. **E gollantá ē prashnētá uththárá ḋenná bæri vuṇā.**

25. **Eyā pārá pallehatá ævidálā ḋakuṇátá hæruṇā.**

26. **Eyā niḋā ganná issellā ḋath mæḋḋē næ**

27. **Mamá kadētá gihillā** (**ītá passe**) **iskōlētá yanávā** / **yannam.**

28. **Kǣmá kǣvātá passe pīnanná epa.**

29. **Mamá ehe hitiyā.**

30. **Ē gaha ikmánátá vævilā. Vævenávā** - growing; **vavánávā** is the transitive version.

31. I glared at them angrily.

32. I went to the store.

33. We didn't come

34. After eating rice and drinking water, the child fell asleep. **niḋā ganná** means "to go to sleep," as opposed to this example, where sleeping is a passive action.

35. Big brother repaired the bicycle. **Hæḋuvā** is the past tense of **haḋánávā**, which can mean both "make" and "repair"

36. The extremely angry man (gave someone) a thorough beating.

37. The literal translation suggests that the child will work themselves until they are tired, but a more idiomatic translation is just that the child likes to work hard

38. I was happy.

39. We have paid for that.

40.We paid for that.

41. **Mamá hæmáḋāmá mē viḋihatá hitiyē nǣ.**

42. **Hari lassánátá kárálā**. Omitting a **hu^{n}gak** word would just make it "nicely done"

43. (**Issálā**) **Hu^{n}gak sená^{n}gá hitiyā**. Including **issálā** is optional

44. **Mamá pothá metháná thiyálā giyā**.

45. **Mamá ḋækápu minihā ḋivvē nǣ.**

46. **Mamá eyātá kiyuvāhamá ē aḋáhasá ho^{n}ḋá næ kiyálā, eyātá tharáhā giyā. Eyā māth eká ho^{n}ḋá nǣ** - he is upset with me.

47.**Mālu allapu minihā geḋárá giyā**.

48. **Matá thē bonná ōne velā thibuṇē**.

49. **Ammā bath ivvā**.

50.**Matá káranná bari vechchá vædá amārui**. Or: **Matá amāru vædá kotásá** (piece of work) **ivárá káranná bæri vuṇā**.

51. **Mamá ēká ḋænágená hitiyā**. The past tense of d. Means i found out about it.

52. **Mamá issárá ēká ḋannágená hitiyā**.

53. Food

54. Drinks

55. Knowledge (literary)

56. **Ethákotá monávāḋá keruvē**? and **Ethákotá monávāḋá kálē**?

57. **Bērenávā**.

58. **Matath bayá hithuṇā**.

59. **Mathákáḋá Laṅkāvátá api giyápu velāvá**?

60. **Væssá adu vuṇoth, eyātá yanná puḷuvan vei**.

61. **Oyātá hetá yanná bæri veiḋá**?

62. I can help until the sun comes up.

63. **Mamá ḋivvē næ**.

64. **Mamá ho^{n}ḋátá pāḋaṅ keruvā**.

65. **Matá ikmánátá/ikmánin vædá káranná bǣ**.

66. **Mamá ho^{n}ḋátá pādam nokárātá, mamá** pass **vuṇā**.

Chapter 5:

Answer key:

1. (My) big sister gave Gunaratne medicine and made (him) well.

2. (My) big sister gave the medicine to Gunaratne and made (him) well. There is no meaningful difference between these two sentences, they are both equally valid.

3. (I) gave Gunaratne's medicine to (my) big sister and made (her) well. This kind of sentence would be appropriate in the middle of a conversation, after the sick person had been identified. Otherwise, that person's name would have to be included.

4. (I) got some medicine from Gunaratne, gave to (my) big sister, and made her well.

5. I had Gunaratne gave the medicine to (my) big sister and made her well.

6. (I) gave (someone) the medicine belonging to Gunaratne and made (that person) well.

7. While talking to b, I ran into c. (**hambenávā**, **hambá venávā** more formal)

8. I just ran into him.

9. I went to visit them after I got their letter. b. y. Is the "see" of going to visit. b.y. if going to visit.

10. I didn't borrow money from her. **Illá gannávā** means "borrow."

11. I didn't ask her a question.

12. I dropped him off at the station.

13. I'm near the junction.

14. I don't have the recipe on me. **Mē** would be used instead of **ē** if someone brought it up at that time.

15. Which one of you drew on the wall?

16. Did he cause his death?

17. Who broke this glass?

18. Who spilled this food?

19. I asked him to help wash the dishes.

20. I lent her a book. No distinction from "give"

21. I awarded him first place.

22. We went to see the elephants.

23. The leopard got very close to us.

24. The monkeys tried to steal our food.

25. The leopard chased a monkey up a tree.

26. The monkey screeched and escaped from the leopard. **Gagahā** is the continuous of **gahanávā**; **bērenávā** means escaping on one's own instead of á form, by someone else. **Mamá bērenávā** - I'm getting out of something. For humans this would be used also. I'm escaping - **pænálā**

yanávā - escaping from a non-dangerous situation, avoiding a situation, including a dire one like jail. **hiren hirá geḋárá, hirē** - jail. pl. **-ḋárával**

27. The leopard gave up and went to hunt something else.

28. The cat clawed at the dog.

29. The dog bit the cat.

30. I gave him some money.

31. I squashed a mosquito.

32. I told him to bring ice cream.

33. I told the students to come into the class. There is explicit Sinhala word for student: **shishyā**/ **shishyō** it is formal, mostly literary.

34. Kids, go to class.

35. Kid, do your work properly. **Ḷamáyō** would definitely be used if you didn't know the kid's name, but can also be used if you do. You might use **puthā**/**ḋuvá** even if it is not literally your child.

36. The boy threw the ball to the girl.

37. A dragged B away from C.

38. Let me buy you a drink.

39. The child is exhausted.

40. **Girávavá ussá ganná**.

41. **Naṅgiye, matá geḋárá yanná ōne**.

42. **Va^{n}ḋuru jāthi godak innávā**. The stem form of **va^{n}ḋurā**, **va^{n}ḋuru**, was given above. Unlike **girau**, the stem is different from the plural; this is normal for animate nouns.

43. **Iskōlē** (**yaná**) **kālē i^{n}ḋálā mamá mage yāḷuvavá ḋannávā**.

44. **Girávage kūduvá koheḋá thiyennē**?

45. **Mamá eyāgen ē gæná æhuvā**.

Chapter 6:

1. **Ēká Siṅhálen kiyanná**.
2. **Mē geḋárátá gal gahalā**
3. **Vaththē malak thiyenávā**
4. **Mamá vædá káranne geḋárá i^{n}ḋaṅ.**
5. **Oyá ē minihāge pænsálá**.
6. **Mamá eká potháká kiyevvā**
7. **Mamá'Ḋehiválin āvē**. Just **Mamá'Ḋehiválin** would mean that you are from Dehiwala.
8. **Mamá Kolá^{m}bá innē**.
9. **Mamá ēká mitiyen gahalā haḋannam**. Literally, I will use the hammer to hit and fix it.
10. **Mamá thamai eká kæḋuvē**.
11. I went from Anuradhapura to Nuwara Eliya. In Sinhala, Anuradhapura is called **Anurāḋ^{h}ápuráyá** or **Anurāḋ^{h}ápurē**.
12. I borrowed a pencil from him / her.
13. I went from Boston to Colombo.
14. I went from New York to Boston.
15. I went from Dehiwala to Kandy.
16. I went from Madras to Colombo. **Maḋurasiyá** is a Sinhalization of the name "Madras;" if the plain English name were used above, **válin** would have to be added.

17. We took a flight to Colombo.
18. We ate with our hands. More formally, **athválin** would be used instead of **athen**.
19. I fixed it with a screwdriver.
20. I left my bike in the front yard.
21. I passed the test. **Vib^{h}āgē** pass **vuṇā** could be used instead.
22. I tore that page out of my notebook.
23. Don't write on this paper with a pencil.
24. When I open the door, the alarm sounds.
25. I brought the bag of rice to the kitchen.
26. I swam in the ocean.
27. I found a shell on the shore. **Ḋi** means "at" or "on."
28. I cut down the trees with a saw.
29. There are some birds living in the trees.
30. That monkey is swinging from branch to branch.
31. The monkeys are jumping down from the trees.
32. That store usually closes early.
33. We relaxed on the beach for a while.
34. We need to replace these older books with new ones.
35. You can't go through those roads with a car.
36. There's a good smell coming from the kitchen.
37. I traded a banana for a mango.
38. My house has two bedrooms.
39. The school has four classrooms.
40.I practiced drawing with a pen.
41. I'll bring (it) from home
42. Its written on the wall.

43. The cat hit the dog with its tail.

44. In a little bit (we'll) need to ring the bell.

45. Turn to this side.

46. **Mē vaththē mal næ**. **Thiyennē** is not needed here.

47. **Va^{n}ḋurō kūduválá innávā**.

48. (**Oyā**) **kadētá velā monávāḋá kárannē**?

Chapter 7:

1. **Mē mokakḋá**? Alternatively **mēká**. **Mē monávāḋá**, "What are these things" cannot be used with **mēká**.

2. **Mēká haḋálā thiyennē monávāválinḋá**/ **monávainḋá**

3. **Ará mokaḋḋá**? Or: **Atháná thiyená ḋē mokakḋá**?

4. **Matá uḋau káranná kauruvathmá næ**.

5. Sir, can you do me a favor? **Mahaththáyō** is more respectful and less common. **Nonā** would be used when asking a woman. The female equivalent of **mahaththáyō**, **nonō**, is probably less common in this context. Both would be more common in rural enviornments.

6. I've heard about you (addressing a celebrity)

7. (Respectful) Did you call me? Used for some respected who you don't know well, ie not a friend or relative. Bosses, teachers, and senior ranked in general, sir is more common.

8. (Context: talking to a monk) Are you going to the temple? yannē is too impolite. Used for kings, nobles, priests.

Modern politicians? **Nu^{m}bá** is literary. **Obáthumā** - used for politicians, respectful, but less so than **vahanse**. **Obáthumiyá**. **Obáthumālā, obáthumiyálā**. **Obávahanselā** - pl. of **obávahanse**.

9. Are you studying? (Two male friends in the library studying) Might be used by village women. Devoid of respect, not explicitly insulting, never used for elders.

10. What do you know about this? Context: Someone roughly interrogating someone. Not used in polite circles. Used in anger. **Thopi** could also be used here

11. If you steal, I'll catch you. Context: threatening a suspected thief. **Thō** is usually not used in friendly situations.

12. I'll give you a good punishment. Something to say if you're very angry, with someone who has done something.

13. Who the hell is shouting? **Yakō** is used in fights, or when someone is really angry. It is very impolite, more so than **thō**

14. Are you going to hit me, you bastard? context, a fight that is escalating.

15. **Mē ayá monávahariværáḋi ḋeyak káránávā vagē**.

16. **Ē ḋennā vib^{h}āgáválá hæmávelēmá ho^{n}ḋátá káránávā**. Also **ho^{n}ḋin**, but in this context **-tá** is more common

17. **Eyā kohenḋá āvē**?

18. **Metháná kaváḋāvath ho^{n}ḋá kǣmá nǣ**.

19. **Metháná kǣmá kaváḋāvath ho^{n}ḋá nǣ**

20. **Mamá ḋannávā thænak, hæmá velēmá monávahari káranná puḷuvan.** Or **Mamá ḋannávā, hæmá velēmá monávahari káranná puḷuvan thænak.**

21. **Mē panthiyá samáhará velāvátá ho^{n}ḋai**.

22. **Ará gollō aḋá enávāḋá?** **Ará** can only be used if you already mentioned them in the conversation.

23. **Mē hōtáláyá kohomáḋá?** In villages, restaurants would be called **kǣmá kadē. Hōtáláyá** Is more common.

24. **Mē pothá anik ēvā/poth ekká thiyanná.**

25. **Mē vākyával pæhæḋili nǣ**.

26. **Apitá ēká ḋenná**. The word order could also be **e.a.d**.

27. **Eyā apeṅ uththáráyá labā gaththā**.

28. **Ē gollan apivá eḷevvā**.

29. **Ohe evā thiyenávāḋá?**

30. **Ohe evā pælá venávāḋá?**

31. **Ohe vahinávāḋá?**

32. **Oyá putuvá hari sanīpái vage**.

33. **Ará putuvá hari sanīpái vagē**.

34. **Mē putuvá hari sanīpái vagē**.

35. **Ē putuvá hari sanīpái vagē**.

36. **Ē putuvá mēkátá vadā ho^{n}ḋai**.

37. **Māvá kātávath navaththanná bæ**. The word order could also be **k. m. n. b**.

38. **Eyā samáhará velāvátá ehe yanávā**.

39. **Mamá hæmá velēmá mehetá enávā kæmá kanná**. Also, with **k.k.** after **mamá**

40. **Mē prashná giyá pārá prashnáválátá vadā hu^{n}gak lēsi vagē**.

41. **Kātávath bæri vuṇā matá ē prashnáválátá uḋau káranná**.

42. **Mamá metháná næthuvá vená kohē hari inná kæmáthī**.

43. I found out about that story yesterday.

44. It's different from the earlier report.

45. According to that story, this problem has been there for a long time.

46. Why is the eight o'clock train so late today? **-i** is not used because it's a question, contrast: **Aḋá atē kōchchiyá hu^{n}gak parakkui. -ḋá** is not used with **æi**. In this second example, **mē tharam** can't be used; on the other hand, it can be used in the following: **Aḋá atē kōchchiyá mē tharam parakku vei**

kiyálā mamá hithuvē nǣ. I didn't think today's eight o'clock train would be so late.

47. How did you find the house? **gē** = colloq. **geyá**

48. How did you make that food? **kohomáḋá oyātá ḋæṅ**? How are you feeling now.

49. It would be better to use red.

50. Stay the way you are for a bit.

51. No one is at this temple

52. There's no one in this house. Remember that **geḋárá** does not have a distinct locative case.

53. I can't even go there.

54. Has anybody rung the bell?

55. B **liyumá arágená āvā**.

56. B **liyumá athátá ḋunnā**. Adding mage before athátá would change the meaning of the sentence to "B handed the letter to me."

57. **Mamá oyá kiyápu kadētá giyā**.

58. By using **oyá**, A makes it clear that the flowers in question are the ones the shopkeeper just referred to.

Chapter 8

1. **Ḋæṅ ēká ivárá nisā, ī la^{n}gá vædē pataṅ gamu**.

2. **Mamá** "fail" **vuṇē næththaṅ ho^{n}ḋai.**

3. **Ḷāmáyā ē pārátá hærenávā mamá dækkā.** Or, less commonly but still correct: **mamá dækkā ḷāmáyā ē pārátá hærenávā.**

4. **Aḋá ahasē tharu hu^{n}gak pēnávā.** More formally, **thārákā** could be used.

5. **valākuḷu athárin avvá vætenávā.** Compare: **væssá thaḋinmá vætenávā.** It is raining really hard. **Me ḷamáyā loku minissu athárá/athárē gævásenávā. Athárá** means among here. This child associates - g. with adults. Or moves among. Can also be used literally: **Mē minihā mē pæththē gævásuṇā.** - This guy was wandering around here.

6. **Ḷamáyātá budágini nisā, báth/kæmá okkomá kǣvā.**

7. **Eyā ithin hæmá velēmá parakku velā ennē.**

8. **Eyā ithiṅ kæmá kanná ḋaksháyek ne.** The context of this sentence would be after someone said "Damn! He ate everything."

9. **Ithin ītá passē mokáḋá vuṇē?**

10. **Matá mahansī, hæbæi mamá ēká kárannaṅ.**

11. **Niḋā ganná yanná issellā ḋath maḋinna.**

12. **Api ē vadē passē kárámu.** The presence of **api** makes this sentence a promise, rather than a suggestion.

13. **Eyātá aurudu ḋahayak vithárá æthi**. **Æthi** emphasizes the imprecision here.

14. **Eyālātá mē kæmá æthi veiḋá**? Will this food be enough for them? When æthi is coupled with venávā it means "enough": **Oyātá sellań kárálā æthi velāḋá**? Have you played enough?

15. **Geḋárá thiyennē kærát vithárai elōḷuvákátá**.

16. **Mamá vithárai ēká ḋannē**.

17. **Mamá eyātá havásá pahatá vithárá enná kivvā**. Rember -**yánavā** type verbs typically have -**vvā** past forms, e.g. **uyánavā** - **ivvā**, not **iyuvā**.

18. **Mamath eyath ekká āvā**.

19. **Ḷamáyā ammath ekká iskōlē yanávā**.

20. The child is sitting on the chair. **i^{n}ḋágená innávā** = alternate.

21. Father is lowering the child from the tree slowly / carefully. **Parisámeń** could be used instead of **h**.

22. The grandmother is feeding the child.

23. The mother is giving the child water.

24. They get men to hit their foes.

25. The teacher got the students to tidy up the classroom. **Kárávágaththā** is the **ganná** causative form of **káránávā**.

Note the postpositional form of the word for "children." Likewise, if teachers were the ones being used **gurthuman lavvá** would be used.

26. He got the police to catch the burglar.

27. I understand it now.

28. It would be good if I could get that money this month.

29. I received that letter.

30. Because school is far away, its difficult to walk there.

31.I want to see Colombo, Galle, and Kandy.

32. I want to see Colombo, Galle, and Kandy. Less common than 31.

33. I want to go to Colombo, Galle, and Kandy. Less common than 31 or 32.

34. I can see the train as it arrives from far away. **Matá pēnávā** could also appear at the end.

35. I don't like to talk about that.

36. I have heard stories about that.

37. Who did this work before I came here?

38. Before the children come to class the classroom has to be swept.

39. This utterance was said sarcastically, commenting on uselessness of saying this or that.

40. Yes, I can see mother bathing the children.

41. You have to ring the bell when you want to get down. The bus will stop at the next bus stop. In Sri Lankan English, "halt" is used instead of stop.

42. You can't do that while I'm working.

43. Because I used my walking stick, I was able to get there. **Hærámitiyá pāvichchi keruvá nisā** could be said first. **Kárápu nisā** could be used instead.

44. **Oyā pādam káránávānam, ho^{n}ḋátá kanná ōne**.

45. **Mamá lūnui kiri piti tin ekakui gēnnáṅ**.

46. **Alath ivárá venná la^{n}gai**.

47. **Mamá ē taumē hæmáthænámá giyā**.

48. **Api okkomá pettiválath bæluvā**.

49. The example in the dialogue is a nested clause; it could be unpacked as **ammā kivvā, matá uḋau venná enávā kiyálā** or **matá uḋau venná enávā kiyálā ammā kivvā**. Note that unlike the dialogue example, the word **kiyálā** is not optional; without it, the sentences above would sound unnatural.

50. **Ōnenam mamá ēká háḋannam**.

51. **Eyā kadētá thaniyen giyā**.

Chapter 9

1. We need room for 15 people.
2. I couldn't answer four problems. Literally, “I couldn’t write answers for four problems.”
3. I bought six pencils.
4. Those two are inseparable.
5. This book is 391 pages long.The sentence **mē pothá pitu thun siyá anu ekak ḋigai** is more faithful to the English original, but less natural sounding.
6. I scored 80 points out of 100.
7. I scored 1 point out of one hundred.
8. She has 3 outfits for every day of the week.
9. His address is number 20 on Pieris street.
10. He lives in his house on number 20 Pieris street, Dehiwala.
11. Buy three loaves of bread.
12. That shirt costs 550 rupees.
13. This book costs 799 rupees.
14. Seven plus 8 is fifteen.
15. 111 plus 32 is 143.
16. 3 times 900 is 2700.
17. 100,000 times zero is zero.
18. 5 times zero is zero.
19. 100,000 + 100,000 = 200,000.
20. 100 times 100 is ten thousand.
21. 1000 minus 1 is 999.

22. **This thuná thuneṅ beḋuvahamá ekoḷáhai.**

23. **Lakshāyá lakshāyákin beḋuvahamá ekai.** Informally **beḋuvamá**

24. **Binḋuvá hayen beḋuvahamá binḋuvai.**

25. **Binḋuven beḋánnē epā.**

26. **Siyá ḋahayen beḋuvahamá ḋahayai.**

27. **Ḋaha ḋāha ḋāheṅ beḋuvahamá ḋahayai.**

28. **Api ḋinanná issellā thun særáyak pæráḋuṇā.**

29. **Matá** pass **venná thavá eká særáyai thiyennē.**

30. **Hæmá ḋētámá pæthi ḋekak thiyenávā.**

31. **Ē iskōlē innē teacherslā thun ḋenek vithárai.**

32. **Mamá va^{n}ḋuro hayá ḋenek ḋækkā.**

33. **Maṅ gāvá rupiyal hathárai panáhak thiyenávā.**

34. **Mamá thavá poth hayak kiyávanná ōne. Matá thavá poth hayak kiyávanná thiyenávā.** The first sentence slightly emphasizes the speaker; the second emphasizes the number of books that need to be read.

35. **Apitá thōrá ganná puḷuvan kōchchi ḋekak thiyenávā.**

36. **Ēkē gāná sathá anu namáyai.**

37. **Mage sahōḋáráyō thun ḋenāmá āvā.** This literary word must be used since the relative ages were not specified.

38. **Eyātá ḋuválā thun ḋenek innávā.**

39. **Eyātá eká puthai innē.**

40. **Eyātá eká ḋuvai innē.**

41.**Eyāgē siyálā ḋennāmá thāmá innávā.**

42. **Oyā giyāmá matá pāḷui.**

43. **Me uththárá dekē venaskam monávāḋá?**

44. A: It's good if we write down a list of things you will need for the hostel.
B: Oh, we have enough time to do that.
A: No we'll do it now, that way there'll be time to get anything that we're missing. How many uniforms will you need?
B: The hostel sent a list of items that I need to bring.
A: Then get it and read it to me.
B: 5 uniforms. Eight pairs of socks. Two ties. Ten notebooks. One box of colored pencils. 6 bars of soap. One comb. Two pairs of shoes. Five dresses.
A: Is that all?
B: No, there are a few other things. Here, take the list.
A: Okay, I'll look over the list, and add anything else that you might need.
45.
A: **Puthā chakkárá pādaṅ kárálā iváráḋá**?
B: **Ou, mamá ivárai**.
A: **Mamá chakkárá ahannaṅ balamu ḋannávāḋá kiyálā. Ḋolosvarak atá kīyáḋà**?
B: **Anu hayai**.
A: **Hathvarak namáyá? Kīyáḋà** is omitted because it is obvious.
B: **Panas hayai**.
A: **Næ panas hayá værádī.**
B: **Ā poddak inná… hætá thunai.**
A: **Hathárá varak ekoḷáhá**.
B: **Hathális hathárai**.

A: **Hayá varak thuná**?

B: **visi hathárai**.

A: **Næ ēkáværáḋi, oyā hariyátá pādaṅ káráIā næ, gihiṅ āyimath pādaṅ káranná**.

Chapter 10

1. A: Is it going to be very hot today, or will it rain?

B: Ugh, it's going to rain all day long.

A: Will the rain be heavy?

B: No, it's just going to drizzle.

A: Will it rain tomorrow?

B: No, it won't rain tomorrow, but it will be very windy.

A: Then it probably won't be very hot tomorrow.

2. My meeting is at 9:00 on Tuesday. Meeting **eká** could also be used.

3. Neil Armstrong went to the moon in 1969. If you wanted to talk about mankind getting to the moon, you might say: **minisā paḷámu/paḷáveni varátá ha^{n}ḋátá giyē ek ḋahas namá siyá hætá namáyē**. **Minisā** is otherwise literary, but is the only suitable word to refer to the collective of human beings.

4. My birthday is on the fifteenth of march.

5. School ends in December.

6. I'm on vacation for the next three weeks.

7. I'm scheduled (lit. I scheduled myself to be) to be on vacation for the next three weeks.

8. I work from 9:30 to 6:45 every day.

9. I will be working for the whole rainy season.

10. The southwestern monsoon is from May until September.

11. I get home from school around 2 o clock.

12. I'll be going shopping this weekend.

13. I bought these last week.

14. I left for Sri Lanka last month.

15. Next year, I'll be going to college. N.b. in Sri Lankan English, “college” is not used to refer to tertiary education; “university” is used instead. The word appears in the names of some high schools, and is otherwise unused.

16. I graduated from college last year.

17. Last night I went to bed at 12:05.

18. I received the results yesterday.

19. He is supposed to get here at 4:10 tomorrow.

20. Sri Lanka became independent on February fourth 1948.

21. **Ḋeveni lōká yuḋḋ[h]áyá ivárá vuṇē ek ḋahas namásiyá hathalis pahē Sæpthembár ḋeveniḋā**.

22. **Mamá ipáḋuṇē deḋáhas/deḋās thunē Mārthu visi thun venidā.**

23. **Kri. pu. hathárá veni siyávase Anuraḋ^{h}ápuráyá / ē lankavē agánuvárá vuṇā.**

24. **Ē golaṅ anthimá mohotheḋi āvē**. m. Means moment.

25. **Mē nuvárá hæḋuṇē pahaḷos veni siyávasēḋi**. **hæḋenávā** be made, **uná hæḋuṇē** became (made) sick. **Ē pælē ho^{n}ḋátá hæḋenávā**. That plant is growing well. **Ē ḷamáyā ho^{n}ḋátá hæḋilā thiyenávā. Eyā ho^{n}ḋátá hæḋichchá ḷamáyek**. He/ she was raised well. **Naráká** could be used with these

26. **Mamá mē rassāvá pataṅ gaththē auruḋu pahakátá issellā. Mamá mē job -eká/ rassāvá auruḋu pahakátá issellā pataṅ gaththē**. More natural with **pataṅ gaththē** not at end.

27. **Mamá thavá māsá ḋekak vishvá viḋyālē innávā.**

28. **Pusthákāláyá vahannē atátá namuth oyā hathai panáha venákotá yanná læsthi venná.**

29. **Mage nivādu kāláyá Jūnī ḋahathárá veniḋā i^{n}daṅ Julī hathveniḋā venákaṅ.**

30. **Mē rachánāvá ḋavas hayakin bārá ḋenná ōne.**

31. **Mamá this ek veni prashnáyátá uththárá liyánákotá, ræ ḋoḷáha vuṇā.**

32. **Sumāná gānak/kīpáyak** (more formal) **yanákotá, ēká lēsi vuṇā.**

33. **Thavá miniththu ḋahayákátá metháná inná.**

34. **Ī la^{n}gá pæyákuth miniththu visipahēḋi puḷuvan tharam prashnáválátá uththárá liyanná. Ī la^{n}gá pæyá eká hamāreḋi puḷuvan tharam prashnáválátá uththárá liyanná. Puḷuvan tharam** means "as much as possible". **Ḋi** specifies that the questions must be answered within the allotted time period. A very formal alternative to **ḋi** is **athuláthá.**

35. **Api atá hamārátá navaththámu.**

36. **Thappárá kīpáyákin ēká ivárá vei.**

37. **Ēká** recharge **venná pæyá kīpáyak yai.**

38. **Api māsá kīpáyak thissē gaman káránávā.**

39. **Api ḋoḷáhai hathá venákotá ethánā inná ōne.**

40. **Api ehātá yanákotá ḋoḷáhai kālá vithárá vei.**

41. **Mamá geḋárin yanákotá velāvá uḋē hathai.**

42. **Mē auruḋḋē eyātá auruḋḋu hathá labánávā.** This is one of the few contexts where **labánávā**, the un-umlauted version of **læbenávā** is used.

43. A: Let's check on your historical knowledge. I'm going to ask you questions about world history, (lit. World events) Those who know the answer, raise your hands. First question.
A: When did Sri Lanka become independent?

A: Why don't you answer the question?

B: February 4th, 1948.

A: Correct. Next question. When was Bastille day?

B: July 14th, 1769

A: Someone else try to answer

C: July 14th, 1789

A: Correct. Next question. When did the British Empire formally gain control of the whole country?

B: 10th of may, 1815.

A: No, that's wrong. Does anybody else know the answer?

C: November 5th, 1815.

A: That's also wrong. Any other answers?

D: August 10th, 1815.

A: All of you got the year correct, but the date wrong. The date should be March 2nd. Your knowledge is still not enough. So go home and study and we'll meet tomorrow.

44. A: Saman got the highest score in the exam . Saman was able to get the highest score because he studied well. If others study well like good kids, they can get better marks. How much time did you spend studying, Saman?

B: About an hour

A: Any child who studied for more than an hour, raise your hand.

(nobody raised their hands)

A: Those who studied for fourty-five minutes, raise your hand.

One person

A: See, your score depends on the amount of time spent studying. This child had the second best score. Those who studied for thirty minutes, raise your hand.

Several people.

A: You children need to study more. Now go out and play, but like good kids come back to the classroom in 15 minutes.

Chapter 11:

1.

A: How are you doing?

B: Much better, almost back to normal.

A: Ok, let's check a few things.

A: Raise your right arm.

A: Raise your left arm.

A: Let me know if there's any pain.

B: No pain.

A: Any headaches?

B: Not anymore.

A: Grip my hand with your fingers.

A: Good.

A: Is there any pain when you bend your knee?

B: Not since last week.

A: Turn your face right and then turn it left. Any pain in the neck when you do that?

B: No.

A: Ok, you look good to go. Keep doing the exercises I have prescribed.

2.

A: Shall we eat rice?

B: Yes, should we get white rice, red rice, or friend rice?

C: Let's get white and red.

A: Ok, what about the vegetables.

B: Lentils

C: Green beans

D: Fried chillies.

E: Fried potatoes.

A: What else should we get?

B: Let's get some fish or meat.

C: Fried seerfish.

D: Chicken curry

E: Shall we get some coconut sambol?

A: Yes, that will go well with the fried fish.

B: Isn't that enough?

C: Instead of dal, shall we get some jackfruit?

D: Let's add some papadum also.

E: Serve me a piece of fish.

A: I'll pass the dish to you, so you guys can serve yourselves.

B: Give me one papadam.

C: Give me one too.

D: These chillies are very tasty, give me one more.

B: These pieces of chicken are very big. Even half a piece will do.

E: Serve me some green beans.

C: Oh, these potatoes are very spicy.

3.

A: Are you planning on wearing saris or dresses?

B: I think I will wear a sari, I have a nice red and green one which is suitable for a Christmas party.

C: If you're wearing a sari I will too. I have a black and silver one which should do.

D: I am going to wear a dress. Do you think a dark blue long dress would be good? Or I also have a pink mini dress.

E: I think the long dress would be better.

F: I'm going to wear black pants and a red top. What about you? What are you planning on wearing?

G: I'm still trying to decide. I have a long multicolored skirt, maybe I will wear that.

A: What about the blouse?

B: I will wear a gold colored blouse with it. You could also use **a^{n}ḋinávā** here.

Chapter 12:

1. Late; **kar**(**s**)

2. Middle; **nāsikyá**

3. Middle; **b^{h}āshā**

4. The pre-nasal sound indicates that it is a native Sinhala word. The plural is **pi^{m}burō**, but note that native animate Sinhala words with a final consonant of r are *not* predictable; some have plurals ending in **ō**, others in **u**.

5. Even from the plain pronunciation; it should be clear that this is a loan due to the presence of **ñ**. It is Sinhalized word due to the **-yā** ending, so the plural is **jñāthiyō** (the initial **j** is written for orthographic reasons; but never pronounced).

6. Don't let the **-vá** ending fool you; the presence of **æ** suggests that this is a native Sinhala word. The plural is **væu** {**væv**}.

7. This word is indeterminate, unless you happen to be a Dutch speaker, in which case you will recognize it as a Sinhalized word. The plural is **kanthōru**.

8. A Sinhalized word; the plural is **jāthi**. Native Sinhala words do not begin with **j**.

9. Native Sinhala (actually a early loan); for inanimates; this is unambiguous if the word doesn't end in **-yá** or **-vá**, and isn't an English word. For inanimate nouns of this of this type that end in a single final permitted consonant or **h** followed by **á**, the plural is unambiguous; remove the final **-á** to get the plural, in this case, **aḋáhas**. Some of these words may have alternate **-val** type plurals in addition to these regular forms.

10. Native Sinhala words only have the **ch** sound doubled, and even many words with this cluster are loanwords. The -**yā** ending identifies it as a Sinhalized word. The plural is therefore **pacháyō**.

11. I am sure.

12. Ring the bell when the work is finished.

13. Water is leaking.

14. I saw a picture of a dinosaur.

15. I saw many rhinos. Note here that rhinoceros**lā** does not take the accusative ending because of **godak**.

Chapter 13:

Answers:

1. **rǣ**
2. **hu^{n}gak**
3. **uyanná**
4. **hi^{n}ḋá**
5. **ītá**
6. **ñāná** {**jñāná**}
7. **thāththā**
8. **elu** (strictly, **eḷu**)
9. **kannādi** (strictly **kaṇṇādi**)
10. **fæn**
11. **lōku**
12. **a^{m}bá**
13. **ou** {**ov**}
14. **vaṅsá**
15. **karmá**
16. **vākyá**
17. **graháyā**
18. **aṅ**
19. **vishvá viḋyālá**
20. **vṛká** (actually pronounced **vurká**)
21. **buḋḋ^{h}ád^{h}ammá**
22. **b^{h}āṣhāvá**
23. **Shākyá** (The name of an ancient Indian state)
24. **Lichch^{h}avī** (The name of another ancient Indian state)

25. **Mauryá** (An ancient Indian dynasty)

26. **T^{h}erávāḋá** (This is the dominant branch of Buddhism in Sri Lanka)

27. **Ḋīg^{h}ávāpī** (The name of a Sri Lankan shrine)

28. **prathip^{h}álá**

29. **rēk^{h}āvá**

30. **manahkalpitá**

Appendix II ENGLISH-SINHALA VOCABULARY

Nouns are given with their plural forms, adjectives without the final -i. Irregular, passive, and modal verbs are indicated. Compound are indicated, along with the non-verbal component, if that component is not separated from the base verb. A verb with a separate component can be assumed to be a compound verb.

Key: a= adjective, cc= clause conjunction, n = noun, num = numeral, pp = place postposition, post = postposition, v = verb

A

about(p): **gæná**
above(pp):**udá**

abundant(a):**sārá**

accept(v): **pili gannávā**

accustomed(a): **puruḋu**, **huru**, context: **oyātá mēká huruḋá** Are you accustomed / familiar / comfortable with this. **Matá mēká vædiyá hurui**. I'm more comfortable with this one.

ache(n): **kækkumá**, pl. **kækkum**

act(v):(formal) **ra^{n}gánávā**

add(v): (colloquial) **ekáthu káránávā**. In an academic setting, **ḋ^{h}aná** would be used, see section 9.5

address(v):(somewhat formal))(a crowd) **amáthánávā**

adorn(v): (somewhat common),(oneself) **palá^{n}ḋinávā**, (another) **palá^{n}ḋánávā**

afraid(a):**bayá**, does not take **tá**

again(post): **āyith**, **āyimath**, (more formally) **āpahu**

age(a?): **vayasáká**, i form **vayasai**

all(a):**okkomá**

and(post): **-i**, (more formally) **hā**, (very formally*)* **sahā**

angry(a):**kēnthi, tharáha**

animal(n): **sathā**, pl. **saththu**.

annoy(v):**karáḋárá káránávā**

annoyance(n):**karáḋáráyá**

answer(n): **uththáráyá**, pl. **uththárá**

answer(v): **uthárá ḋenávā**

ant(n): **ku^{m}biyā**, pl. **ku^{m}bi**

apple(n): **æpál gediyá**, pl. **æpál gedi**

appropriate(v): **suḋusu**

approval(n): **kæmæththá**, pl. **kæmæththával**

arm(n): **athá**, pl. **ath**

arrack(n): **arakku**, coll

Asiatic pennywort(n): **gotu koḷá**

ask(v): **illanává**

aspirated(a):**mahāprāṇá**, (informal) **māprāṇá**

associate(v): **gævásenává**

aunt(n):**næ^{n}ḋā** pl. **næ^{n}ḋálā**

B

bad(a): **naráká**

bark(v):**buránává**

bat(n): (the animal) **vaulā**, pl. **vaulō**

bat(v):**gahanává**

be(v)(animate): **innává** (irregular)

be(v)(inanimate): **thiyenává** (irregular)

be afflicted: (passive) **peḷenává**

be acquainted with(v): **a^{n}ḋunánává**

be broken(v): **kædenává**

be caught: (passive) **ahu venává**

be contagious(v):(passive) **bō venává,**

be cooled(v):(passive) **sīthálá venává**

be cut(v):(passive) **kæpenává**

be detected: (passive) **ahu venává**

be dried(v): (passive) **vēlenává**

be established(v): (passive) **pihitenává**

be exhausted(v): (passive) **hembath venává**

be fooled(v):(passive) **rævátenává**

be inflated: **pimbenává**

be irritated(v): (passive) (in the sense of minor physical pain) **ḋanávā**

be pleased: (passive) **pæhæḋenávā**

be scattered(v):(passive) **visirenávā**

be scratched(v):(passive) **hīrenávā**

be shattered(v): (passive) **bi^{n}ḋenávā**

be torn(v): **irenávā**

beach(n): **veráḷá**, pl. **veráḷával**, or **vællá**, pl. **vællával**

beach sand(n): **muhuḋu vællá**

beans(n): **bōñchi**, collective

bear(n): **valáhā**, pl. **valássu**

bear(v): **ḋaránávā**

beat(v): **gahanávā**

beautiful(a): **lassáná**

because(cc): **hi^{n}ḋá, nisā**

become(v): **venávā** irregular, past tense **vuṇā**

bee(n): **bamárā,ba^{m}bárā**

beef(n): **harak más**

believe in(v): **aḋáhánávā**

below(pp): **yatá**

bend(v): **navánávā**, (down) **nævenávā**

bestow(v): **piri namánávā**

big(a): **loku**

bill(n): (currency) **nōttuvá**, pl. **nōttu**

bind(v):**ba^{n}ḋinávā**

birth(v): **hambenávā**, (technical, for animals) **vaḋánávā**

bitch(n): **bælli**, pl. **bælliyo**

bite(v): **vikánávā**, **hapánávā,** equally common

bitter (taste)(a):**thiththá**

blind(a): **anḋá**

blow(v): **pi^{m}binávā**

bloom(v):**pipenávā**

blue: **nil**

boil(v):**thambánávā**, **uthurávánávā**

bone(v): **katuvá**, pl. **katu**

book(n):**pothá**, pl. **Poth**

bore(v): **viḋinávā**

bother(n):**karáḋáráyá**, pl. **karáḋárá**

bother(v):**karáḋárá káránávā**

bountiful(a):**sārá**

box(n): **pettiyá**, pl. **petti**

brain(n):**molē**, also **moláyá**, pl. **molá**.

branch(n):**aththá** pl. **athu**.

bread(n):**pān**, commonly **pāṅ**, collective

break(v):**kadá káránávā**, **kadánávā**, **bi^{n}ḋinávā**

bring(v): **gēnávā**, irregular. Past tense **gēnāvā**, past participle **genællā**.

brood(n):(derogatory) **hæththá**, pl. **hæthi**

brother(n):(elder) **ayyā**, pl.**ayyálā**, (younger) **malli** pl. **mallilā**

build(v): **thanánávā**

burn(v): (colloquial) **puchchánávā**

Buddhism(n):**buḋ^{h}á ḋ^{h}armáyá**, stem form **buḋ^{h}á ḋ^{h}armá**. Pali form used by monks

bush(n): **pa^{n}ḋurá**, pl. **pa^{n}ḋuru**

but(post):**hæbæi**

by(post): **lavvá**

C

cage(n): **kūduvá**, pl. **kūdu**

call(v): (to, out): **a^{n}dá gahanávā**

calm(a):**nisaṅsálá**

camel(n): **otuvā**, pl. **otuvo**

can(v):**puḷuvan**. Irregular; the plain negative form is **bǣ**, its inflected forms use **bæri**

candle(n): **itipanḋámá**, pl. **itipanḋam**

cannot bear(v): **russannē nǣ**

caste(n): **vansháyá**, pl.**vanshá**

cat(n): **pūsā**, pl.**pūsō**

catch(v):**allágannávā** (ganna compound)

cause to drink(v): **povánávā**

cease(v):**pāyánávā**

chair(n): **putuvá**, pl. **putu**

chase(v): **eḷávánávā**

chick peas (n): **kadálá**, collective

chicken (n): the food: **kukul más**, for the animal see rooster and hen.

child (n):**ḷamáyā**, pl. **ḷamai**

choose(v): **thōránávā**

chop(v): **paḷanávā**

city(n): **nuvárá**, pl. **nuvárával**

clarify(a):**pahaḋánávā**, **pahaḋálā ḋenna**, (more commonly) **therum kárálā ḋenná**

clean(a):**suḋḋá**

clear(a): **pæhæḋili**

clean(v):**suḋḋá káránávā**

clever(a): **ḋakshá**

climb(v): **Naginávā** intransitive nægenávā Rise

cling to(v): (a person) **ælenávā**

close(v): **vahanávā**

cloud(n): **valākuḷá**, pl. **valākuḷu**

coffee(n):**kōpi**, collective

cold(a):**sīthá**, **sīthálá**, both **-tá** marking

cold(n):**hembirissāvá**, pl. **hembirissā**

collect(v): **ekáthu káránávā**.

come(v): **enávā**,Irregular, past tense **avā**, past participle **ævillā**.

comfortable(a): (with doing something) **huru**

composite(a): (technical) **saṅyōgá**, (in prenasal names) **saññáká**

conquer(v): **abi bavánávā.**

consent(n): **kæmæththá**, pl. **kæmæththával**

constrict(v): (as a snake does) **velā gannávā**

cook(v):**uyanávā**, (somewhat uncommon) **pihánávā**, **viyánávā**

cool(v):**sīthálá káránávā**

copper(n): **tha^{m}bá**, collective.

correct(a):**hari**

cough(v): **kahinávā**

cough(n): **kæssá,** pl. **kæssával** (in this sense referring to kinds of coughs)

count(v): **gaṇinávā**. The past tense has an irregular spelling of **gænnā**

country(n): **ratá**, pl. **ratával**, (formal) **janápaḋáyá**, pl **janápaḋá** coup(n):**kumánthránáyá**, pl.**kumánthráná**

cover(v): (oneself) **porávánávā**, (something else) **vahanávā**

crazy(a): **pissu**, **-tá** marking

creeper(n): **vælá**, pl. **væl**

crime(n): **apárādḋē**, formally **apárāḋáyá**, pl. **apárāḋá**

crow(n): **kākkā**, pl. **kākkō**

crowd(n):**sená^{n}gá**, or **senágá** uncountable

cruel(a): **vasá**

cry(v): (as in weeping) **a^{n}dánávā** (intensely) **vælápenávā**

cucumber(n):**pipiññá**, collective

cultivate(v): **vavánávā**

curry(n):**kariyá**, pl.**kari**

cut(v): **kapanáva**

D

damage(v): **vanásánávā**

dance(v): **natánávā**

dancer(n): **nættuvā**, pl. **nættuvō**

dark(a): **kaḷuvárá,** takes **-in** instead of **in**

dark(n): **kaḷuvárá, -in** type, uncountable

daughter(n): **ḋuvá**, pl. **ḋuválā**

dawn: **pānḋárá**, uncountable, **-in** type

decay(v): **ḋiránávā**

decline(v): **pirihenávā**

decorate(v): **sarásánávā**

degenerate(v): **pirihenávā**

delegate(v): **pavárānávā**

demon(n): **yakā**, pl. **yakālā**

dental(a): (technical, of speech sounds) **ḋanthájá**

depart(v): **pitá venávā**

depend(v): **yæpenávā**

destroy(v): **nasánávā, vanásánávā**

detail(n): **visthááyá**, pl. **visthárá**

dew(n): **pinná**, uncountable

dewy(adj): **pini**

die(v): **marenávā** (passive)

difference(n): **venasá**, pl. **venaskam**

different(a): **venas**

difficult(a): **amāru**

difficulty(n): **amāruvá**

diffuse(v):**vihiḋánávā**

dirty(a): **kuṇu**, **kiliti**, insulting to use on humans.

dig(v):**kotánávā**

disembark(v): **bahinávā**

distribute(v): **beḋánávā**

dive(v):**kimiḋenávā**

divide(v): **beḋánávā**

do(v):**káránávā**

doctor(n):**ḋosthárá**, pl. **ḋōsthárávarun**

dog(n):(male?) **ballā**, pl. **ballō**

don't: **epā**

drag(v):**aḋinávā**

draw(v): **a^{n}ḋinávā,**

dress(n): **gaumá** ,pl. **gaum**

dress(v): (somebody else) **a^{n}ḋánávā**, (yourself) **a^{n}ḋinávā,**

drink (v):**bonávā**. Irregular, past tense **bivvā**, past participle **bīlā**.

drip(v):**galánávā**

drop(n): **binḋuvá**, pl **binḋu**,

drop(v):**halánávā**

drop off(v): **bassánávā, bassávánávā**

drown(v): **gilenávā** (passive)

dry(v): **vēlánávā**

E

ear(n):**kaná, pl.kan**

early(a): **vēlasáná**, adverbial form **vēlasánin**, see "early morning"

early morning: **uḋē pānḋárá**, may be shortened to just **pānḋárá**. -**in**-type

earn(v): **hambá káránávā**

earring(n):**karābuvá**, pl. **kárābu**

east(n): **nægenáhirá**, uncountable

easy(a): **lēsi**

eat(v): **kanávā**. Irregular, past tense **kævā**, past participle **kālā**, (honorific) **vaḷá^{n}ḋánávā**, (with a mocking subtext in some dialects) **buḋinávā**

eight(num): **atá**

eighty(num): **asūvá**

eke out(v):**piri mahanávā**

elephant(n): **aliyā**, pl. **aliyo**. For elephants with tusks, see "tusker"

empire(n): **aḋ^{h}irājyáyá**, pl. **aḋhirājyá**

end(v): **nivánávā** extinguish - passive **nivenávā** -cooling or me, **má not used** endure(v): **ivásánávā**

enemy(n): **tharáha kāráyā**, pl. **tharáha kāráyo**

enjoy(v):(uncommon) **pinávánávā**

enough(a): **æthi**

envelop(v): **velā gannávā**

era(n):**kāláyá**, pl. **kālá**?

erase(v): **makánávā**

err(v): **varáḋinávā**, irregular, past tense **væráḋuṇā**, (more formal) **væráḋenávā**

essay(n):(school) **rachánāvá**, pl. **rachánā**

establish(v): **pihitánávā**

evening(n):**havásá**, pl.**havás or -val**; **hæ^{n}ḋǣvá**, pl. **hæ^{n}ḋǣ**

every(a):**hæmá**

evil(a):**ḋuṣhtá**

exam(n): **vib^{h}āgē**, formally **vib^{h}āgáyá**, pl. **vib^{h}āgá**

excrement(n):**gū**, **kakka**. Both are collective.

exist(v):(animate) **innávā**, (inanimate) **thiyenávā**. They are most often used to indicate location; Sinhala does not have an independent copula. For **thiyenávā** with an animate dative noun, see "have"

expand(v): **bælumá pimbenávā** somebody's inflating the balloon.

expensive(a): **ganaṅ**

explain(v): **thōránávā**

explode(v): **pupuránávā** ,mildly irregular past form **pipiruvā**. Some dialects may have a regular past tense.

eye(n):**æhá**, **æhæ**, pl. **æs**

F

face(n): **mūṇá**,pl. **mūṇával, mūṇu** (more formally) **muhuṇá**,pl. **muhuṇával**?

false(a):**boru**

familiar(a): (with doing something) **huru**

fan(n):**fæn eká**

far(pp): **ḋurá**

fat(a):**mahathá**

father(n):**thāththā**, pl. **thāththálā**

feature(n):**aṅgáyá**, pl. **aṅgá** formal

feel(v): (commonly used with ḋuk (sadness) or sæpá (happiness) cannot be used with hunger or thirst) **vi^{n}ḋinávā**, (**Eyā issárá kárápu vædá válátá ḋæng ḋuk vi^{n}ḋinávā** He's suffering due to what he previously did). (to be aware of) **ḋænenávā**, (**matá rasne ḋænenávā**, I feel hot), **hithenávā** (**ḋuká hithenávā**, but not **sæpá**. Used when feeling for someone else)

few(a):**tikak**, less commonly **tiká**

fifty: **panáha**

fight(v): (people) **gaha gannávā**, (animals) **porá kanávā**

fill(v): **purávánávā**

final(a):**anthimá**

find(v): **hoyā gannávā**

fire(n):**ginná**, pl. **gini**

firewood(n):**ḋará**, collective, commonly used with **godá** , **kællá**

first(a):**paḷáveni,** (more formal) **paḷámu**

finger(n):**æ^{n}gillá**, pl. **æ^{n}gili**

fish(n):**māḷuvā**, pl. **māḷu**

fish, dry(n):**karáválá**. collective

fish, Maldive - little pieces of dried fish used as seasoning: **u^{m}bálákadá**, collective

fit(v):**gaḷápánává**

five: **paha**

fix(v):**haḋánává**

flow(v):**galánává**

flower(n):**malá**

fly(n): **mæssā**, pl. **mæssō**

fly(v): **piyā^{m}bánává**. For humans flying on a plane, use **yanává**

foe(n): **tharáha kāráyā**, pl. **tharáha kāráyo**

fold(v): **navánává, akuḷánává**

folk(n):**ayá**, collective

follow(v): (the rules) **pili paḋinává.**

food(n): **kǣmá**, uncountable

fool(v): **ravatanává**

foot(n):**kakulá**, pl. **kakul**

foreign(a): **pitá**

forest(n): **kæḷáyá, kæḷǣval,** formally **vanáyá, vanáyával**

form(v): **thanánává**

forty: **hathálihá**

four: **hathárá**

fracture(v):**bi^{n}ḋinává**

fragrance(n): **suva^{n}ḋá** pl. **suva^{n}ḋával** General term for pleasant smells

fragrant(a): **suva^{n}ḋá**

fridge(n):**frij eká**

from(i): (for a journey or time interval "from" A to B) **i^{n}ḋaṅ, i^{n}ḋála**. (for other uses, use the ablative case).

front(a): **issáráha**

fruit(n): (a type of plant, distinct from vegetables) **pælē**, formally **pæláyá**, pl. **pælá**, (plant matter that can be easily consumed) **gediyá**, pl. **gedi**

fry(v): **baḋinávā**

G

garden(n): **vaththá**, pl. **vathu**

get(v): (as in take) **gannávā**, (as in receive, passive) **læbenávā**

get wet(v): (passive) **themenávā**

giant(n): **yōḋ^{h}áyā**, pl. **yōḋ^{h}áyō**

give(v): **ḋenávā**. Past tense **ḋunnā**, past participle **ḋīlā**, (a prize) **piri namánávā**

glass(n): (the material) **vīḋuruvá**, pl. **vīḋuru**

glasses(n):**æs kaṇṇadiyá**, pl.**æs kaṇṇadi**

grain(n): (of sand, etc) **kætē**, more formally **kætáyá**, pl. **kættá**

go(v): **yanávā** (irregular)

goat(n):**eḷuvā**, pl. **eḷuvō**

god(n):**ḋeviyā**, pl. **ḋeviyō**

gold(n):**raththáran**, collective

good(a): **ho^{n}ḋá**, adverbial form **ho^{n}ḋin**

grandfather(n):**sīyā**, pl. **sīyálā**

grandmother(n):**āchchi**, pl. **āchchilā**

great(a): **maha**

green(a): **koḷá**

ground(n):**bimá**, pl. **bim, bimával**

group: **kattiyá**, pl. **katti**, (derogatory) **hæththá**, pl. **hæthi**

grow(v)(animate): **loku venávā**

grow(v)(inanimate): **vævenávā**

guttural(a): **kaṇthájá**, technical

H

hand(n): **athá**, pl. **ath**

happy(a): **santhōsá**, **-tá** marking

hard(a): **thaḋá**

harem(n): (literary) **anthahpuráyá**, pl. **anthahpurá**

have(v): **thiyenávā**; the dative ending is used to mark the noun that possesses the inanimate subject.

he(pn): **eyā**, literary **ohu**

hen(n):**kikiḷi**, pl. **kikiḷiyo**

head(n):**oḷuvá**, pl. **oḷu**

headache(n):**oḷuvá kækkumá**, pl. **oḷuvá kækkum**

healthy(a):(of food or drink) **guná**

heavy(a):**bará**

hell(n): **apāyá**, (formal) **narákā ḋiyá**

hero(n):**vīráyā**, pl.**vīráyō**

heroic(a):**vīrá**

hide (yourself or another person)(v): **hæṅgenávā**

hide (someone or something) (v): **haṅgánávā**

hint (n): (nonverbal) **æ^{n}gávīmá**

hint (v): (nonverbally) **a^{n}gávánávā**

historical(a): **aithihāsiká**

history(n): **ithihāsáyá**, pl. **ithihāsá**

hoot(onomatopoeia): **hū**

hope(v): **balaporoththuvenávā** (venna compound)

horn(n):**a^{n}gá**, pl. **aṅ**, **a^{n}gával**

hot(a): **rasne**, **-tá** marking

hotel(n): **hōtálē**, formally **hōtáláyá**, pl. **hōtál**

hour(n): **pæyá**, pl. **pæyával**

house(n): **geḋárá**, pl. **geḋárával**, **gē**, **geyá**, **getá**, **geyin** pl. **geval**

humble(a): **yatath** formal **yatathvá**

hunger(a): **badáginná**,

hungry(a): **badágini**, **-tá** marking

hurt(v):(passive) **riḋenávā**, (due to the entrance of an external irritant) **kævenávā**

I

I(pn): **mamá**, inflects as if it were [ma],(informal) **maṅ**

idea(n): **aḋáhasá** pl **aḋáhas**

illegal(a): **thahanam**

illness(n)**:** **asanīpē**, more formally **asanīpáyá,** pl. **asanīpá**

imaginative(a):**manahkalpitá**

impel(v): **polá^{m}bánávā**

inadequate(a): **maḋi**

incite(v): **polá^{m}bánávā**

incorrect(a): **væráḋi**

indeed(post): **thamai**

infinity(n): **anantháyá**, pl. **ananthá**

inside(pp): **æthuḷá**

interrupt(v): **bāḋ^{h}ā káránávā**

it(pn): **ēka** (inanimate), **eyā** (animate), **ū** (for animals, used as an insult for humans)
item(n): **baduvá**, pl. **badu**

J

job(n): **rassāvá**, pl. **rassā**
join(v): **gaḷápánávā**
joke(n): **vihiḷuvá**, pl. **vihiḷu**
journey(n): **gamáná**, pl. **gamán**
jump(v): **paninávā**

K

karma(n):**karmá**, collective
keep(v):**thiyánávā**. Irregular, past tense **thibbā**, participle **thiyálā**, formal **thabánávā**. The first two are conflated with **thiyenávā** and **thibenávā**, respectively, in modern speech
key(n): **yathurá**, pl. **yathuru**
kill (v):**maranávā**
kind(n): **jāthiyá**, pl. **jāthi**
kindle(v):(candle or a lamp, only rarely for a cooking fire) **ḋalvánávā**. For a cooking fire, **molávánávā** is common
kiss(v):**i^{m}binávā**
kitchen(n):**kussiyá**, pl, **kussi**
knee(v): **ḋaṇissá**, pl. **ḋaṇissával**
knit(v): **gothánávā**
knock(v): **happánávā**

know(v):**ḋannávā**. Irregular; no future, past or past participle forms, **ḋænágannávā** can be used to express these meanings, (a person) **a^{n}ḋunánávā**
knowledge(n):**jñāná** pronounced **ñāná**, uncountable

L

labial(a):(technical) **ōṣhthájá**
lady(n):**nōnā**, pl. **nōnálā**
language(n):**b^{h}āṣhāvá**, pl. **b^{h}āṣhā**
late(a): **parakku**
launch(v): (taking off to fly) **igilenávā**, only used with animals
leaf(a): **koḷáyá**, pl. **koḷá**
learn(v):**igenágannávā** (**gannávā** compound)
leave(v): **pitá venávā**
left(a): **vam**
left-handed(a): **vamath**
leftovers(n): **ithuruvá**, pl. **ithuru**
leg(n):**kakulá**, pl. **kakul**
leopard(n): **ḋiviyā**, pl. **ḋiviyō**
letter(n):(character) **akurá**, pl. **akuru**, (a message) **liyumá**, pl. **liyum**
liar(n):**pacháyā**, pl. **pacháyō**, **boru kāráyā** A prolific liar: **tompacháyā**, pl.**tompacháyō**
lick(v): (more commonly used for people) **levinávā**, (more commonly used for animals),**levá kanávā**
lie(n):**boruvá**, pl. **boru**.
lie down(v): **hānsi venávā** (with animals) **laginávā**

lift(v): **ussánávā**, less commonly and more formally,**osávánávā**

light(v):(candle or a lamp, only rarely for a cooking fire) **ḋalvánávā**. For a cooking fire, **molávánávā** is common

lightning(v): (weather forecasting) **akuṇu**, uncountable

lightning striking(v): **akuṇu gahanávā**

like(a): **vagē**

like(v): **kæmáthi**. Irregular modal, subject is not marked with **-tá**

little(a):(size) **podi**, (quantity) **poddak**, **tikak**, less commonly **tiká**

live(v): (be alive) **jivath venávā**, (dwell) **innávā**

load(v): **patávánávā**

lonely(a): **pāḷu**

long(a):**ḋigá**

look(v): **balánávā**

loud(a):**suḋḋá**

loudly(adv):**suḋḋen**

low(v): **adu**

lower(v): **bahinávā**, **bānávā**, (a price) **adu káránávā**

luggage(n): **baduvá**, pl. **badu**

M

maid(n):**āyā**, pl. **āyālā**

make(v):**haḋánávā**, (slightly less common) **thanánávā**

make do(v):**piri mahanávā**

man(n):**minihā**,pl. **minissū**, (respectful) **æththō**

mango(n): **a^{m}bá gediyá**, pl. **a^{m}bá gedi**

many(a):**hari, hu^{n}gak, godak, bohō**. These are interchangeable; the non indefinite forms **hu^{n}gá** and **godá** are also used, but less frequently. **Hō gālā** indicates even larger amounts.

marry(v):**ba^{n}ḋinávā**

match(v):**gaḷápánávā**

measure(v): **maninávā**

meat(n): **mas**, collective

medicine(n): **behethá**, pl. **beheth**. Used both in writing and colloquially; the plural is informally **bēth**

meet(v):**hambá venávā**

melt(v):(active) **ḋiyá kárānávā,**(passive) **ḋiyá venávā**

memorialize(v): **samáránávā**

messy(a):**hædi**

middle(pp): **mæḋá**

might be(v): **æthi**

milk(n): **kiri**, uncountable

milk(v): **ḋovánávā**

minute(n): **miniththuvá**, pl. **minithth u**

mixed(a): **mishrá**

moisten(v): **themánávā**

moment(n): **mohothá,** at that moment **mohotheḋi**. pl. **mohothával**

money(n): **salli**, collective

monkey(n): **va^{n}ḋurā**, pl. **va^{n}ḋuro**. Used for monkeys other than the toque macaque.

month(n): **māsáyá, māsē**, pl. **māsá**

moon(n): **ha^{n}ḋá**, pl **ha^{n}ḋával**

morning(n): **uḋē**, formally, **uḋáyá**, pl. **uḋá**

mother(n): **ammā**, pl. **ammálā**

much(a):**hari**, **hu^{n}gak**, **godak**, **bohō**. These are interchangeable

goat meat(n): **eḷu más**

N

name(n): **namá**, pl. **nam**

nasal(a):(technical) **nāsikyá**

nasal(n):(technical)**nāsikyáyá**, pl. **nāsikyá**

near(pp): **la^{n}gá**

neck(n): **bellá**, pl. **beli**

necklace(n): **māláyá**, pl. **mālá**

need(v):**ōne**, adjectival form **ōná**. See "require"

new(a): **aluth**

night (n): **rǣ**, pl. **rǣval**, less commonly **ræyá**, pl. **ræyával.**

no: **næ**, **nǣ**, formally **næhæ**

north(n): **uthurá**, uncountable

northern(a): **uthuru**

nose: **nahayá**, pl **nahayával**

not:(for adjectives): **næthi**, (do not): **epā**, (if not): **næththan**, (cannot): **bæ**, for general verbs in the emphatic form, **næ**, **nǣ**, formally **næhæ**

note(n): (currency) **nōttuvá**, pl. **nōttu**

O

occur(v): (formal) **siḋu venávā**

ocean(n): **muhuḋá**, pl. **muhuḋu**, **muhuḋával**

odd(a):(animate) **amuthu**, (in an amusing way) **vikārá**

office(n):**kanthōruvá**, pl. **kanthōru**

oh(interjection): **ā**

oil(n): (variety of oil) **thelá**, pl. **thel**, (a single actual oil) **thel**, collective

old(a):(animate) **nāki**, **vayásáká** (i-form **vayásai**), (inanimate) **paráṇá**

only(post):**vithárai**

open(v): **arinávā**

overflow(v): **uthuránávā**

or(post):**hari**, **hō**

orange(a): **thæ^{m}bili**

order(n): **ajñāvá** pl. **ajñā**

organize(v): (items) **ahuránávā**

outing(n): **gamáná**, pl. **gamán**

outside(pp): **eḷiyá**

owl(n): **bakámūṇā**, pl. **bakámūṇō**

P

pace(v):(formal) **særisaránávā**

page(n):**pituvá**, pl. **pitu**

pain(n): **kækkumá**, pl. **kækkum**

palatal(a):**thālujá**

party(n): **uthsáváyá**, pl. **uthsává**

pay(v): **gevánávā**

peek(v): **ebenávā**

pen(n):**pǣná**, pl. **pǣn**

pencil(n):**pænsálá**, pl. **pænsal**

people(n):**ayá**, uncountable

perform(v):(formal) **ra^{n}gánávā**

person(n):**kená**, pl. **minissū**

picture(n):**pinthūráyá**, pl. **pinthūrá**

piece(n): (as in a small bit of something) **kǣllá**, pl. **kǣli**, **kotásá** pl. **kotas** interchangeable

pierce(v): **viḋinávā**

pig(n):**ūrā**, pl. **ūro**

pink(a): **rōsá**

place(n): **thæná**, pl. **thæn**

place(v):**ḋānávā**. Irregular, past tense **ḋæmma**

plait(v): (hair) **gothánávā**

plant(v):**vavánávā**

play(v):**sellam káránávā**, (less common) **keḷinávā**

pleasing(a): **pranīthá**

pluck(v): (tea leaves) **nelánávā**, (otherwise) **kadánávā**

point(n): **lakuṇá**, pl. **lakuṇu**

poisonous(a): **visá**

polish(v):**maḋinávā**

pork(n): **ūru mas**, collective

pour out(v):**vakkáránávā**

practice(n): **puruḋḋá**, pl. **puruḋu**

practice(v): **puruḋu venávā**

prawn(n): **issā**, pl. **issō**

pray(v):**yaḋinávā**, **pathánávā**

preach(v):**ḋesánávā**

press(v): **obánávā**

price(n): **Gāná**, (highly formal) **milá**. Both are grammatically uncountable, and can be used in situations where an English speaker might use the plural "prices."

produce(v): **niṣhpāḋánáyá káránávā**
project(v): (technical) **neránávā.**
prosperous(a): **isuru**
protect(v): **rakinávā**
protrude(v): (technical) **neránávā.**
pull(v):**aḋinávā**.
puppy(n): **pætiyā**, pl. **patavu**
put(v):**ḋānávā**. Irregular, past tense **dæmma**
put together(v):**haḋánávā**
python(n): **pi^{m}burā**, pl. **pi^{m}burō**.

Q

question(n): **prashnē**, formally **prashnáyá**, pl. **prashná**
quickly(adv): **hayyen**
quiet(a): **nissáḋḋá**

R

race(n):(derogatory) **hæththá**, pl. **hæthi**
rain(n): **væssá**, uncountable, stem form **væhi**
rain(v): **vahinávā**
read(v):**kiyávánávā**
receive(v):**læbenávā**
red(a): **rathu**
reduce(v): **adu káránávā**
regard(v):**salákánávā**
relative(n):**næyā**, pl. **næḋæyō**; more formally **jñāthiyā**
pronounced **ñāthiyā**, pl **ñāthi**

remainder(n): **ithuruvá**, pl. **ithuru**

remove(v): **gaḷávánávā**

repose(v):**sætheápenávā**

require(v):(formal) **uvámánai**, (even more formal) **avashyai**. **ōne** is used in casual speech

rescue(v): **bēránávā**

reside(v): **vasánávā**

restaurant(n): **hōtálē**, formally **hōtáláyá**, pl. **hōtal**

result(n):**práthiphaláyá**, pl. **práthiphalá**

retroflex(a):(technical) **mūrḋ^{h}ájá**, (colloquial) **mūthtthájá**

revolve(v): **kærákenávā**

rice, cooked(n):**bathá**, pl **bath**. The plural is usually used in a collective sense.

rice, uncooked(n):**hāl**, collective. +**atē** - "bean"

right(n): **aithiyá**, pl. **aithi**

ripen(v):(passive) **iḋenávā**

right(a):(direction) **ḋakuṇu**

right-handed(a): **ḋakuṇu athá**

ring(n):**muḋḋá**, pl. **muḋu**

rise(v):**nægitinávā**

river(n):**ga^{n}gá**, pl. **ga^{n}gával**, more formally **gaṅgā**

road(n): **pārá**, pl. **pārával**

rooster(n): **kukulā**, pl. **kukullu**

root(n): **mulá**, pl. **mul**

rose(n): **rōsá malá**, pl. **rōsá mal**

rosebush(n): **rōsá pa^{n}ḋurá** pl. **rōsá pa^{n}ḋuru**

royal(a):(descent) **kæth**

rub(v): **gānávā**

run(v): **ḋuvanávā**

rupee(n): **rupiyálá**, pl. **rupiyál**

S

sad(a): **ḋuká**, **-tá** marking

salty(a):**lunu raha**

sand(n): **væli**, collective

savings(n): **ithuruvá**, pl. **ithuru**

say(v):**kiyanávā**, (formal, rare) **pavásánávā**

scratch(v):**hūránávā, kahánavā**

school(n): **iskōláyá**, pl **iskōlá**

scissors(n): **kathurá**, pl. **kathuru**

scold(v):**baṇinávā**, (formal) **bæṇávaḋinávā**, past tense **bæṇávæḋuṇā**

sea(n): **muhuḋá**, pl. **muhuḋu, muhuḋával**

see(v): **ḋakinávā**

sell(v):**vikuṇánávā**

send(v):(1st person) **yavánávā**, (otherwise) **evánávā**

sentence(n): **vākyá**, pl **vākyával**

serve(v):(a portion of food) **beḋánávā**, (oneself) **beḋā gannávā**,

set fire(v):**paththu káránávā**

set up(v):(items) **ahuránávā**

settlement(n): **janápaḋáyá,** pl **janápaḋá**

seven: **hathá**

sew(v):**mahanávā**

shake(v):**holávánávā, hollánávā, halánávā**

shameful(a):**læjjá**

shark(n): **mōrā**, pl. **mōru**

shine(v): **ḋilisenávā**

she(pn):(Literary):**ǣ**, in speech **eyā** is used.

shoe(n): **sapáththuvá**, pl **sapáththu**

short(a):(in general) **podi,** (height) **kotá**, (length), (time, formal) **keti**

shout(v): **kǣ gahanávā**

shy(a):**læjjá**

sickness(n):**ledá**, pl. **ledával**

side(n):**pæththá**, pl. **pæthi**

sieve(v):**halánávā**

sift(v): (through grains) **poḷánávā**

sign, astrological(n):**grahayā**,pl. **grahayō**, planet - animate, presumably for superstitious reasons **lagná**

silver(n): **riḋī**, collective

sink(v): (while stuck in mud, sand etc) **erenávā**

sister(n):(elder) **akkā, pl. akkálā**, (younger) **naṅgi**, pl. **naṅgilā**

six: **hayà**

sixty: **hætà**

sleep(v): (formal): **niḋá gannávā**, (informal) **buḋiyánávā**, (somewhat formal) **sæthápenávā**

sleepy(a): **niḋimathá**, **-tá** marking

slipper(n): **sereppuvá,** pl. **sereppu**

slowly(adv):**hemin,hemihitá**

small(a): **punchi**, **podi**, **chuti**

smart(a): **molē thiyená**

smell(n): **ga^{n}ḋá, pl. ga^{n}ḋával.** Only for unpleasant smells, see "fragrance"

smell at(v): **pusu^{m}bá balánávā**, **suvá^{n}ḋá balánávā**

smelly(a): **ga^{n}ḋá**.

sneeze(n): **kimumá**, pl. **kimu**, baby-talk **hachis**, collective

sneeze(v): **kimumak yánávā**

solve(v): **visá^{n}ḋánávā**

son(n): **puthā**, pl. **puthālā puththu**

sound(n): **sváráyá**, pl. **svárá**

sour(a):**æ^{m}bul rahá**

south(n): **ḋakuṇá**

southern(a):**ḋakuṇu**

sow(n):**īri**, pl **īriyo**

sow(v):**vapuránávā**

speak(v): **kath^{h}ā káránávā**, (formal) **vaḋāránávā**

spectacle(n): **kaṇṇadiyá**, pl. **kaṇṇadi**

spend time(v): **gevánávā**

spill(v): (passive) (accidentally) **ihirenávā**

spoon(n): **hænḋá**, pl. **hæ^{n}ḋi**

spread(v): **pathuránávā**, (condiments on food) **gānávā**, (light) **vihiḋenávā**, (intangible things): **pæthirenávā**

spread out(v) **vihiḋánávā**

spring(v):(liquid) **unánávā**

sprinkle(v): **ihánávā**, **isánávā**,(less common) **ihinávā**

split(v): **paḷanávā**

spotted seerfish(n): **thōrā**, pl. **thōru**

squeeze(v): **obánávā**

star(n): **tharuvá**, pl. **tharu**, less commonly **thārákāvá**, pl. **thārákā**

stare(v): **ravanávā**, **orovanávā**

step on(v): **pāgánávā**

stern(a): **særá**

stick to(v): **ælenávā**

stitch(v): **mahanávā**

strange(a):(in an amusing way) **vikārá**

strength(n):**hayyá**,uncountable

string(n): **laṇuvá**, pl. **laṇu**

stomach(n):**badá**,pl. **badával**

stone(n):**gálá**,pl. **gál**

stop(v): **navátháná vā**

story(n):**kathʰāvá**,pl. **kathʰā**

string(v): (a needle) **amuṇánávā**

stuff(n): **baduvá**, pl. **badu**

stupid(a): **mōdá**

subdue(v): **damánáyá káránávā**

submissive(a): **yatath**

subtract(v): **adu káránávā**

sun(n): **irá**, pl. **irával**

sunshine(n): **avvá**, uncountable

supply(v): **genath ḋenávā**, (formal) **sapáyánávā**

support(n): **kæmæththá**, pl. **kæmæththával**

surround(v): **vatá káránávā**

suspicious (a): **sæka**, **-tá** marking

swallow(v):**gilinávā**

sweep(v): **athu gānávā**

sweet(a):(taste) **pæni rahá**

swell(v): (passive) **iḋimenávā**

swim(v):**pīnánávā**

T

tail(n): **valigē**, formally **valigáyá**, pl. **valigá**

take(v): (from some place) **gannávā**, (to a place) **geniyánávā**. Both are highly irregular

take responsibility(v): **bārá gannávā**

talk(n):**kath^{h}āvá**, pl.**kath^{h}ā(val)**

talk(v): **kath^{h}ā káránávā**

tall(a): **usá**

tasty(a):**rasá, rahá**

teach(v):**ugannánávā, uganvánávā**

tear(v): **iránávā**

tear out (v): **irā gannávā**

test(n): **vib^{h}āgē**, formally **vib^{h}āgáyá**, pl. **vib^{h}āgá**

that: **ōká**, **araká**, **ēká**,(as in "before that" or "after that") **ītá**, ('said that") **kiyálā**

they(pn): **arayalā**, **ēyalā**, **aragollō**, **ēgollō**

think(v): **hithánávā**, **kalpánā káránávā**. These can be used interchangeably

thirsty(a): **thibáha**, **-tá** marking

this: **mēká**

thread(v): **amuṇánávā**

throat(n): **ugurá**, pl. **ugurával**

throw out(v): **visi káránávā**

tie up(v):**ba^{n}ḋinávā**

time(n): (era): **kalē**, formally **kaláyá**, pl **kalá**, (this time) **pārá**, pl. **pārával særáyá**, pl. **særá**

tired(a): **mānsi**, **-tá** marking

train(n): **kōchchiyá** pl. **kōchchi**

tree(n): **gahá** pl. **gas**

trip(n): **gamáná**, pl. **gamán**

trouble(n):**karaḋárá**

today(n):**aḋá**

tomorrow(n):**hetá**

tooth(n): **ḋathá**, pl. **ḋath**

toque macaque(n): **riḷavā**, pl. **riḷau**

torture(n):**vaḋáyá**, pl. **vaḋá**

town(n):**taumá**, pl. **taum**, (large) **nuvárá**, pl. **nuvárával**

trample(v): **pāgánávā**

true(a):**æththá**

turn: (yourself) **hærenávā**, (something else) **harávánávā**, (involuntarily) **hærávenávā**

tusker(n):**æthā**

type(n): **jāthiyá**, pl. **jāthi**

U

ugly(a):**kæthá**

unaspirated(a):**alpaprāṇá**

uncle(n):**māmā**, pl. **māmálā**

uncultivated land(n): **mudubim**, collective

under(pp): **yatath**

understand(v):**thērenávā**

unfortunate(a):**apárāḋá**

unhealthy(a):(of food or drink) **aguná**

unite(v):**gaḷápánávā**, **ekáthu káránávā**.

unload(v): **bānávā**, past tense **bǣvā**

unmoving(a):**nisal**
unpalatable(a):**pál rahá**
until(post):**venákal**
uproot(v): **ugullánávā**
use(v): **pāvichchi káránávā**
using(post): **lavvá**

V

vacation(n):**nivāduvá**, pl. **nivādu**
variety(n): **jāthiyá**, pl. **jāthi**
vegetable(n): **elōḷuvá**, pl. **elōḷu**; formally **eláváḷuvá**, pl. **eláváḷu**
vermin(n): **gullā**, pl. **gullo**
very(a):**hari**, **hu^{n}gak**, **godak**, **bohō**. These are interchangeable
village(n):**gamá**, pl. **gam**
villainous(a):**ḋuṣhtáyā**, pl.**ḋuṣhtáyō**
villainous(a):**ḋuṣhtá**
vomit(v): **vamáne ḋānávā**, (formal, literary) **vamāránávā**
vowel(n): **sváráyá**, pl. **svárá**

W

wake up(v): **nægitinávā** (more formal, less common) **pibiḋenávā**
walk(v): **ævidinávā**,(back and forth, formal) **særisaránávā**
walking stick (v): **hærámitiyá**, pl. **hærámiti**
wall(n): **biththiyá**, pl. **biththi**
want(v):**ōnē**

warm(a):**rásne**, **-tá** marking

warm(v):(an area of the body for healing purposes) **thavánávā**

wash(v): **hōḋánávā**, (clothes by beating) **apullánávā**

water(n): **vathurá**, uncountable

water buffalo(n): **mī harákā**, pl.**mī harák**

wave(n): **rællá**, pl. **ræli**

wave(v): **athá vanánávā**

way(n): **viḋiyá**, more formal **viḋihá** pl.**viḋi**, **hætiyá**, pl. **hæti**. The latter is more commonly used in its plural form as a postposition

wear(v):(somewhat common) **palá^{n}ḋinávā**

weave(v):**viyánávā**

week(n): **sumānáyá**, pl. **sumāná**, a bit more formally **sathiyá**, pl. **sathi**

weep(v): **a^{n}dánávā**, (intensely) **vælápenávā**

weight(n):**bará**, pl. **barával**

weld(v):**pāhánávā**

well(a):(healthwise) **sanīpá**, **-tá** marking

well(v): **unánávā**

west(n): **basnāhirá**, uncountable

wet(a):**thethá**, **-in**

what(int):**monávā**,(without understanding) **mokakḋá**

where(int):**kō**. Does not require **ḋá**

which(int):**moná**

whip(n):**sæmitiyá**, pl.**sæmiti**

whole(a):**muḷu**. no i-form

why(int): **æi**, does not require **-ḋá**, (equally common) **mokáḋá**, emphatically **æi mokáḋá**

win(v): **ḋinánáva**:

wing(n): **pihātuvá**, pl. **pihātu**, (less common) **piyāpathá**, pl. **piyāpath**

wipe(v): **pihinávā**

wilt(v): **pará venávā**

window(n): **janēláyá**, pl.**janēlá**

with(post):**ekká**, **lavvá**

write(v): **liyanávā**

wrong(a): **væráḋi**

wolf(n): **vṛkáyā**, pl.**vṛkáyō**

woman(a):**gǣni**, uncommonly **gǣniyá** pl. **gænu**

word(n): **vachánáyá**, pl.**vachánáyá**

work(n): **vædá**, uncountable

work(v): **vædá káránávā**

world(n): **lokáyá**, pl.**lokával**

worship(v): **va^{n}ḋinávā**, **aḋáhánávā**

Y

year: **auruḋḋá**, pl. **auruḋu**

yes: **ou**

yesterday: **īye**, uncountable

you(pn): **oyā**, also see section

Z

zero: **binḋuvá**

Appendix III
SINHALA-ENGLISH VOCABULARY

This dictionary order is based on that of English, with modifications to account for the extra letters used by this transliteration. Digraphs (th, ch, aspirates and prenasals) are treated as two letters for this purpose. The order is:

Á, A, Ā, Æ, Ǣ, B, C, D, Ḋ, E, Ē, F, G, H, I, Ī, J, K, L, Ḷ, M, ᴍ, N,ɴ, Ṅ, Ṇ, O, Ō, P, R, S, Ṣ, T, U, Ū, V, Y

The romanizations are written using the notation of this book, along with usage peculiarities.

A

abi bavánávā. v. subdue, conquer

adu. a. low

adu káránávā. v. reduce, (math) subtract

aḋá. n. today, uncountable. **Beheth arágená aḋátá ḋavas kīyáḋá** how long has it been since started taking medicine?

aḋáhánávā. v. believe in, worship

aḋáhasá. n. idea, pl. **aḋahas**.

aḋinávā. v. pull, drag

aḋ^{h}irājyáyá. n. empire, pl. **aḋ^{h}irājyá**

aguná. a. (of food and drink): unhealthy

ahanávā. v. hear, ask.

ahu venávā. v. (passive) be caught, be detected

ahuránávā. v. set, organize (items)

aithihāsiká. a. historical

āpahu : post. (formal) again

āyimath : post. again

āyith : post. again

ajñāvá. n. order, pl. **ajñā**

akkā. n. older sister, pl. **akkálā**

akuḷánávā. v. fold, reduce in size(as in folding a blanket, closing an umbrella, or rolling up a sleeping bag)

akuṇu. n. (weather forecasting) lightning, uncountable

akuṇu gahánávā. v. lightning striking

aliyā. n. Elephant pl. **aliyō, ali**

allágannávā. v. catch (a ball), grab, grasp. **Ganná** form of **allánávā**

allánávā. v. catch, touch

alpaprāṇá. adj. unaspirated. The full names of the unaspirated consonants are formed by prefixing their **-yanná** names with this word.

aluth. adj. new

amáthánávā. v. (somewhat formal)) address (a crowd)

amāru. adj. difficult

amāruvá. n. difficulty, pl. **amāru**

amuṇánávā. v. thread, string (a needle)

amuthu. adj (animate) odd

ammā. n. mother, pl. **ammálā**

a^{m}bá. 1. mango, sg. **a^{m}bá gediyá**, pl. **a^{m}bá gedi**

ananthává. n. infinity, pl. **ananthá**

anthimá. a. final.

anthahpuráyá. n. harem, pl. **anthahpurá**

a^{n}dá gahanávā. v. call (out, to)

a^{n}dánávā. v. cry, weep

anḋá. adj. blind. The Sanskrit loan **anḋ^{h}á** is used in literary Sinhala. Can be used in a figurative sense like in English

a^{n}ḋinávā. v. draw, dress

a^{n}ḋunánávā. v. know, be acquainted with. Irregular, past tense **æ^{n}ḋinnā**

a^{n}gávánávā. v. (nonverbally) hint

a^{n}gá. horn, pl. **aṅ**, **a^{n}gával**

aṅgáyá. n. feature. pl. **aṅgá**

apárāḋá. adj. unfortunate

apáráḋē, formally **apárāḋáyá.** noun. crime, pl. **apárāḋá**

apāyá. n. hell

apullánávā. v. wash clothes by beating

arakku. n. arrack

arinávā. v. open. Older pronunciation **harinávā**,

asanīpē, formally **asanīpáyá.** n. illness, pl. **asanīpá**

n. illness, pl. **asanīpá**. More commonly used than **asanīpáyá**.

asūvá. eighty, stem form **asū**

atá. eight.

athá. n. arm, hand, pl. **ath**

athá vanánávā. v. wave. From **athá** + **vanánávā** "spread, waggle, wave"

aththa: n. branch, pl. **athu**

athu gānávā. v. sweep

athulá. n. inside, collective

auruḋḋá. n. year, pl. **auruḋu**

avashyai. v. (modal) require, need. In literature, used instead of **ōnē**

avvá. n. sunshine, uncountable

ayá. n. people, folk, uncountable

ayyā. n. older brother, pl. **ayyálā**

Ā

ā. interjection. oh

āchchi. n. grandmother, pl. **āchchilā**

āyā. n. maid, pl **āyālā**

Æ

æi. int. why. Does not require **-ḋá**

ælenávā. v. stick to, cling to (a person)

æ^{m}bul rahá. adj. sour

æ^{n}gávīmá. n. (nonverbal) hint. pl.**ængávīm**. Noun form of **a^{n}gávánávā**

æ^{n}gillá. n. finger. pl.**æ^{n}gili**

æhá, æhæ: n. eye, pl. **æs**. From literary **æsá**

æpál: n. apple, collective (as in, "shall we eat some apples")

æpál gediyá. n. apple, pl. **æpál gedi**.

æthā. n. tusker, pl. **æththu**. The general word for elephant is **aliyā**

æthi. 1. modal verb. might be. 2. adj. enough

æththá. 1. a. true. 2. n. fact, pl. **æththával** Cf. **æthi**.

æththō. n. (respectful) person. Can be used to address one or many people. It was originally the plural/vocative of **æththā**, a word meaning "owner" or "possessor," and so declines like a plural noun

æthuḷá. pp. inside

æviḋinávā. v. walk

Ǣ

ǣ.Literary Sinhala third person female pronoun

B

badá. n. stomach, pl **badával**

baduvá. n. stuff, luggage, item, pl **badu**

badágini. a. hungry, **-tá** marking.

badáginná. n. hunger.

baḋinávā. v. fry

bahinávā. v. disembark, lower (oneself). Literary form **basinávā**

bakámūṇā. n. owl pl. **bakámūṇō**

balánávā. v. look. Can refer to "looking" with the eyes or other kinds of investigation.

balāporoththu venávā. v. hope. Compound with **venávā**

ballā. n. male dog, pl. **ballō**

bamárā. n. bee pl. **bamáru**

ba^{m}bárā. n. bee pl. **ba^{m}báru** From earlier **bamárā**; both are used today, but **bamárā** is more formal

baṇinávā. v. scold. The past tense is **bænnā**

ba^{n}ḋinávā. v. bind, tie up, marry

baṅ An indeclinable word used for addressing people in a somewhat impolite manner. It is similar in tone to **u^{m}bá**

bará. 1. a. heavy 2. n. weight, pl. **barával**

basnāhirá. n. west, uncountable. See **bahinávā** and **irá**

bassánávā. v. drop off. Causative of **bahinávā**

bassávánávā. v. drop off. Double causative of **bahinávā**

báthá. n. cooked rice, pl. **báth**

bayá. adj. afraid

bāḋ^{h}ā káránávā. v. interrupt

bānávā. v. lower, unload

bārá gannávā. v. take responsibility

bælli. n. bitch, pl. **bælliyo**. From **ballō**

bæṇávaḋinávā. v. (formal) scold, past tense **bæṇávæḋuṇā**

bæ^{n}ḋenávā. v. be bonded. Passive of **ba^{n}ḋinávā**

beḋā gannávā. v. take one's portion, (of a meal) serve oneself.

beḋánávā. divide, distribute, (of a meal) serve

behethá. n. medicine, pl. **beheth**, informally **bēth**

bellá. n. neck, pl **beli**

bēránávā. v. rescue.

bēthá. n. medicine, pl. **bēth**. Informal version of **behethá**

b^{h}āṣhāvá. n. language, pl. **b^{h}āṣhā**

bimá. n. ground pl, **bim**, **bimával**

bi^{n}ḋenávā. v. Be shattered. Passive of **bi^{n}ḋinávā**

bi^{n}ḋinávā. v. fracture, break

binḋuvá. 1. n. drop, pl **binḋu**, 2. zero

biththiyá. n. wall, pl. **biththi**

bohō. adj. many, much

bonávā. v. drink. Irregular, past tense **bivvā** (literary **bīvā**), past participle **bīlā**, continuative **bibi**, causative **povánávā**

boru. adj (inanimate) false

boruvá. n. lie, pl **boru**

bō. 1. adj. Lit. Many, much. From earlier **bohō**. 2. n. enlightenment

bō venávā. v. be contagious, propagate; from **bō**[1]

bōñchi. n. beans, collective

buḋḋʰá ḋʰarmáyá. n. Buddhism, uncountable; stem form **buḋḋʰá ḋʰarmá**

buḋinávā. v. eat. Has a mocking subtext in some dialects

buḋiyánávā. v. (informal) sleep

buránávā. v. bark

C

chuti. adj. small

D

desk eká. n. desk

Ḋ

ḋá. the question particle

ḋahayá. ten

ḋakinávā. v. see

ḋakshá. a. capable

ḋaksháyā. a. clever / able person

ḋakuṇá. n. south, uncountable. From the stem **ḋakuṇu**

ḋakuṇu. 1. adj. right. 2. southern

ḋakuṇu athá. adj. right handed. From **ḋakuṇu** and **athá**. Literary form **suráthá**, from **suru/huru**, "dextrous, right" and **ath**

ḋalvánávā. v. (candle or a lamp, only rarely for a cooking fire) light, kindle

ḋamánávā. v. 1. (uncommonly) put, 2. (very rarely) tame

ḋanávā. v. (passive) be irritated, burn, sting. **Matá ḋanávā** "I feel irritated"

ḋannávā. v. know. Irregular, no future, past or past participle forms; for these, see **ḋænágannávā**

ḋaṇissá. n. knee, pl. **ḋaṇissával**

ḋantháјá. adj. (of speech sounds) dental, used for alveolar sounds as well

ḋa^{n}duvámá. n. punishment, pl. **ḋa^{n}duvam**

ḋaránávā. v. bear

ḋathá.n. tooth, pl. **ḋath**

ḋānávā. put, place. Irregular past form **ḋǣmā**

ḋænágannávā. v. know, understand. Irregular **ganná** compound form of **ḋanávā**

ḋænenávā. v. feel.

ḋeká. num. two, stem form **ḋe**

ḋenávā. v. give. Past tense **ḋunnā**, past participle **ḋīlā**

ḋesánávā. v. preach

ḋeviyā. n. god, pl. **ḋeviyō**

ḋeyá, ḋē. thing. **ḋeyátá/ḋētá**, **ḋeyin**, **ḋē**. pl. **ḋēval**

ḋigá. adj. long

ḋilisenávā. v. shine

ḋinánáva: v. win

ḋiviyā. n. leopard, pl. **ḋiviyō**.

ḋiyá káránávā. v. melt

ḋiyá venávā. v. (passive) melt. Archaically **virenávā**

ḋosthárá. n. doctor, pl. **ḋōsthárávarun**. The **-yā** form is disrespectful

ḋovánávā. v. milk

ḋurá. pp. far

ḋuṣhtá. adj. evil, villainous.

ḋuṣhtáyā. n. villain, pl.**ḋuṣhtáyō**

ḋuvá. n. daughter, pl. **ḋuválā**

ḋuvánávā. v. run.

E

ebenávā. v. peek

eká. num. one

ekáthu káránávā. v. collect, unite, (mathematics, colloquial)

ekká. post. with. From **ek venávā** "unite"; in turn from **eká**

eḷiyá. pp. outside

eḷávánávā. v. chase

Eḷu. a literary word used to refer to Sinhala, especially with respect to the archaic language, also spelled **Heḷu**

eḷu mas. n. goat meat, collective

eḷuvā. n. goat, pl.**eḷuvō**

enávā. v. come. Irregular, past tense **āvā**, past participle **ævillā**

epā. (interjection, auxillary) don't

erenávā. v. be stuck and sinking (in mud or sand)

evánávā. v. send. Causative of **enávā**. This word is only used if the item was sent by someone to the speaker. It could be used in the first person only if, say, the speaker sent something to themselves or a group to which they belonged. See **yavánávā**

eyā. pn. he, she, it (animate). Cf. Sinhala **ē**

Ē

ē. That (near or far)

ēká. pn. it (inanimate)

F

fæn eká. n. fan

frij eká. n. fridge

G

gaha: n. tree. pl.**gas**

gaha gannávā. v. (humans) fight

gahanávā. v. hit, bat

galá. n. stone. pl. **gal**

galánávā. v. motion of any liquid, such the flowing of a river or the dripping of a faucet

gaḷápánávā. v. join, fit, unite, match

gaḷávánávā. v.remove

gamá. n. village, town. pl. **gam**

gamáná. n. outing, trip, journey. pl. **gaman**

ganaṅ adj. expensive

gannávā. v. take, get. Irregular, past tense **gathā**, past participle **arágená**.

gaṇinávā. v. count. The past tense has an irregular spelling of **gænnā**

ga^{n}ḋá. adj. bad-smelling. Stem of **ga^{n}ḋē**

ga^{n}ḋē, more formally **ga^{n}ḋáyá.** n. (foul) smell, pl. **ga^{n}ḋá**

ga^{n}gá. n. river, pl. **ga^{n}gával**, (more formal) **gaṅgā**

gaumá. n. dress, pl. **gaum**

gāná. n. price, uncountable

gānávā. v. rub, spread (condiments on food)

gæná. post. about

gævásenávā. v. associate, move (among)

gǣni. n. woman. pl.**gǣnu**

gediyá. n. fruit, in the sense of a fruiting body, and can be applied to certain vegetables and loaves of bread, pl. **gedi**

geḋárá. n. house, pl.**geḋárával.** Irregular singular ablative **geḋárin**, locative **geḋárá**. Equivalent to **geyá**

genath ḋenávā. v. bring, supply

geniyánávā. v. Take (to a location). Irregular, past tense **genichchā**; the regular perfect form is used along with an irregular variant **genihillā**.

geyá. n. house, pl. **geval.** Irregular singular ablative **geyin**. Equivalent to **geḋárá**

gēnávā. v. bring, irregular. Past tense **gēnāvā**, past participle **genællā**.

gilenávā. v. drown, passive.

gilinávā. v. swallow

ginná. n. fire. pl. **gini** Alternatively: **gini godá**, pl **gini godával**; only **ginná** can be used with **pæthirenávā**

giyá. adj. previous. Adjectival form of **giyā**

godá. 1.n. land, uncountable 2. n. lot, much

godával. n. A pile (of something), collective.

godak. adj. a lot

gothánávā. v. plait (hair), knit, make lace

gotu koḷá. n. *Centella asiatica,* Asiatic pennywort.

grahayā. n. (*animate*) planet, pl. **grahayō**. The irregular animacy is probably due to ancient beliefs regarding the divinity of planets

guná. a. (of food and drink): healthy

gullā. n. vermin, pl. **gullo**

gū. n. excrement, collective

H

hā. post. (formal) and. **-i** is more common. Cf. **sahā**

hachis eká. n. (used with little children) sneeze, pl. **hachis**.

haḋánávā. v. make, put together, fix

halánávā. v. drop, shake, sieve

hambá káránávā. v. (colloquial) earn. The literary equivalent is **upáyánávā**

hambá venávā. v. meet, find, birth; **hamu venávā** is slightly formal

hambenávā. v. birth

ha^{n}ḋá. n. moon, pl. **ha^{n}ḋával**

hapánávā. v. bite

harávánávā. v. turn (something). Cf. **hærenávā**

harak más: n. beef, collective

hari. 1. adj. correct 2. adj. very 3.post. or

hathá. seven. Stem form **hath**, literary form **sathá**

hathálihá: forty. Stem form **hathális**, literary form **sathálisá**

hathárá. Four

happánávā. v. knock

havásá. n. evening, pl. **havás, havásával**

hayà: six. Literary form **sayá**

hayyá. n. strength, uncountable.

hayyen. adverb. Quickly

hāl: n. uncooked rice. collective

hæbæi. post. but

hædi. adj.messy

hæmá. adj. every.

hænḋá. n. spoon, pl. **hæ^{n}ḋi**

hæ^{n}ḋǣvá. n. evening, pl. **hæ^{n}ḋæ.** Literary forms **sæ^{n}ḋǣvá, sa^{n}ḋává, sanḋ^{h}yāvá**

hælenávā. v. drop. Passive of **halánávā**

hærámitiyá. n. walking stick, pl. **hærámiti**

hærávenávā. v. Be turned, moved involuntarily

hærenávā. v. turn

hætà: sixty. Literary form **sætà**

hæththá. 1. n. (derogatory) group, race, brood, pl. **hæthi** 2. Variant stem of **hæththǣvá**

hæththǣvá. seventy. Stem form **hæththæ**, (less formally) **hæththá**

hætiyá. n. way, method, pl. **hæti**

hetá. n. tomorrow, uncountable

hembath venávā. v. be exhausted

hembirissāvá. n. cold, pl. **hembirissā**

hemihitá. adverb. slowly

hemin: adverb. slowly

hinḋá. cc. because.

hithánávā. v. think

hithenávā. v. feel

hīrenávā. v. be scratched. Passive of **hūránávā**

holáváná vā. v.shake

hollánávā. v.shake

ho^{n}ḋá. adj. good

hoyā gannávā. v.find

hō. or

hō gālā. a. a lot (more than **hu^{n}gak** and co.)

hōḋánávā. v. wash

hōtálē, formally **hōtáláyá.** n. hotel, restaurant, pl. **hōtal**

hu^{n}gá. adj. many. Uncommon

hu^{n}gak. n and adj. a lot

huru. 1. adj. used to, accustomed. 2. (Literary) See **ḋakuṇu athá**

hūránávā. v. scratch.

I

-i. 1. (at the end of nouns) and. 2. (at the end of vowel-final adjectives) to be. 3. (at the end of verb roots) the non-first person future form

iḋimenávā.v. (passive) swell.

iḋenávā.v. (passive) ripen.

igilenávā. v. launch, take off, start to fly. Only used with animals flying using their own wings.

ihánávā. v. sprinkle

ihinávā. v. sprinkle. Less common than **ihánávā**

ihirenávā. v. (passive) (accidentally) spill

igenágannávā.v. learn. **Ganná** compound, derived from **ugannávā**

illánávā. v. ask

i^{m}binávā.v. kiss.

i^{n}ḋálā.post. from, used only in to-from statements. Perfect tense of **innávā**

i^{n}ḋaṅpost. from, used only in to-from statements. Informal form of **i^{n}ḋálā**

innávā.v. (for animates and animate-composed groups) exist. Irregular past tense **hitiyā**, perfect **i^{n}ḋálā**.

irá. n. sun, pl. **irával** Earlier, literary forms are **iri** (only in **iriḋā**, "Sunday"), **iru**, **hiru** and **hirá**

iránávā. v. tear

irā gannávā. v. tear out

irenávā. v. be torn

isánávā. v. sprinkle. Less common than **ihánávā**

iskōláyá. n. school, pl. **iskōlá**

issáráha: a. front

issā. n. prawn, pl. **issō**

isuru. adj. prosperous

ithihāsáyá. history, pl. **ithihāsá**

aithiyá. n. right, pl. **aithi**

ithuruvá. remainder, leftovers, savings, pl. **ithuru**

itipanḋámá. n. candle, pl. **itipanḋam**

ivásánávā. v. endure

Ī

īri. n. female pig, pl **īriyo**. Feminine form of **ūrā**

ītá. that, as in "before that," or "after that".

īye: n. yesterday, uncountable

J

janápaḋáyá. settlement, country pl. **janápaḋá**

janēláyá. window, plural **janēlá**

jāthiyá. n. kind, variety, type, pl. **jāthi**

jivath venávā. v. live, be alive

jñāná pronounced **ñāná.** n. (formal) knowledge, uncountable.

jñānámavá pronounced **ñānámavá.** n. godmother, pl. **ñānámavváru**

jñānápiyā pronounced **ñānápiyā.** n. godfather, pl. **ñānápiyáváru**

jñāthiyā pronounced **ñāthiyā.** n. (formal) relative, pl **ñāthi**. **Næyā**/**nǽḋæyō.** is more common

K

káránávā. v. do

kadálá. n. chick peas, collective

kadá káránávā. v. break.

kadánávā. v. break, pluck (plants other than tea leaves)

kahánavā. v. scratch

kahinavā. v. cough.

kakulá. n. leg, foot pl. **kakul**. **Pāyá**, "foot" is literary.

kakkā. n. excrement, collective.

kalpánā káránávā. v. think

kaḷuvárá. adj. (inanimate) dark, takes **-in**.

kaná. n. ear, pl. **kan**

kanávā. v. eat. irregular, past tense **kǽvā**, past participle **kālā**

kanthōruvá. n. office, pl. **kanthōru**

kaṇṇādiyá. n. spectacles, pl.**kaṇṇādi**

kaṇthájá. adj. guttural, traditionally used for both velar and glottal sounds

kapánávā. v. cut

karáḋárá káránávā. v. annoy, bother.

karáḋáráyá. n. annoyance, bother, nuisance, pl. **karáḋárá**

karáválá. n. dry fish, collective

karābuvá. n earring pl. **kárābu**

kariyá. n curry pl. **kari**

karmáyá. a supernatural moral force, pl. **karmá**

katá. n. mouth pl. **katával**

kathurá. n. scissors pl. **kathuru**

kattiyá. n. group, pl. **katti**

katuvá. n. bone,pl.**katu**

kākkā. n. *Corvus splendens*, aka the crow, pl. **kākko** Onomatopoeic

kath^{h}ā káránāvā. v. talk

kath^{h}āvá. n. story, pl. **kath^{h}ā**

kavánavā. v. feed. Causative of **kanávā**.

kāláyá. era, time. pl. **kālá**

kāmáráyá. n. room, plural **kāmárá**. Alternatively, **kā^{m}bárá**, **kā^{m}bárē**

kædenávā. v. be broken. Passive of **kadánávā**

kæmáthi. v. (modal). Like. Does not use a dative subject; the object of affection is so marked instead

kæmæththá. n. approval, consent, support. pl. **kæmæththával.**

kæpenávā. v. be cut. Passive form of **kapánávā**

kærákenávā. v. (Passive) revolve.

kætē. grain (of sand, etc), more formally **kætáyá**, pl. **kættá**

kæth. adj. (*archaic*) of royal or noble blood

kæthá. adj. ugly

kævenávā. v.1. (Passive): feel pain or irritation (due to the penetration of an object into the body, such as dust in an eye or a splinter in a finger). 2. accidentally eat. Passive of **kavánávā**.

kǣ gahanávā. v. shout

kǣllá. n. piece, as in a bit of, pl. **kǣli**

kǣmá. n. food, uncountable. Gerund of **kanávā.**

keḷinávā. v. play. Less common than **sellam káránávā**

kenā. n. person, pl. **minissū**

keṭi. adj. (time, formal) short

kēnthi. adj. Angry

kikiḷi. n. hen, pl. **kikiḷiyo**. From **kukuḷá**.

kiliti. adj. dirty, insulting to use on humans.

kimiḋenávā. v. dive

kimumá. n. sneeze, pl. **kimu**. Formally **kimuhumá**, **kimuhum**

kimumak yánávā. v. sneeze

kiri. n. milk, collective.

kiyánávā. v. say.

kiyálā. (having said) that. Perfect form of **kiyánávā**

kiyávánávā. v. read

koḷá. adj. green. cf. **koḷáyá**

koḷáyá. n. leaf, pl. **koḷá**

kotá. adj. short (height)

kotánávā. v. dig

kotásá. n. piece, pl. **kotas**

kō. int. where (does not require **ḋá**)

kōchchiyá. n. train, pl. **kōchchi**

kōpi. n. coffee, uncountable

kūduvá. n. cage, pl. **kūdu**

kukuḷ más. n. chicken (as in the meat), collective

kukuḷā. n. rooster, pl. **kukuḷo**

kumánthránáyá.n. coup

ku^{m}biyā.n. ant, pl. **ku^{m}bi**, (more formal) **ku^{m}biyō**

kuṇu. adj. dirty

kurullā. n. bird, pl. **kurullō**

kussiyá.n. kitchen, pl. **kussi**

L

labánávā. v. attain. Used to refer to the number of years attained by someone, i.e. their age

lakuṇá: n. point, pl. **lakuṇu**

laginávā. v. lie down

laṇuvá. n. string, pl. **laṇu**

la^{n}gá. pp. near

lassáná. adj. beautiful

lavvá. pp. by, with, using

læbenávā. v. receive, get. Passive of **labánávā**

læjjá. adj. (animate) shy, (*in some contexts*) shameful

ledá. n. sickness, pl. **ledával**

levá kanávā. v. (more commonly used for animals) lick

levinávā. v. (more commonly used for people) lick.

lē: n. blood, collective

lēsi. adj. easy

liyánávā. v. write

loku. adj. big. Possibly a loan related to **lōkáyá**

loku venávā. v. (animate) grow

lōkáyá. n. world, pl. **lōkával.**

luṇu rahá. adj. salty

Ḷ

ḷamáyā. child, pl. **ḷamai**

M

má. (with nouns) the emphatic particle, (with adjectives) the superlative particle

maḋi. a. inadequate

maḋinávā. v. polish, brush (teeth)

mahá. adj. great

mahanávā. v. stitch, sew

mahansi. adj. tired.

mahathá. adj. fat, related to **mahá**

mahāprāṇá. adj. aspirated

makánávā. v. erase.

malá. n. flower, pl. **mal**

malli. n. younger brother, pl. **mallilā**

mamá. I. Highly irregular declination: accusative **māvá**, dative **matá**, genitive **magē**, ablative **magen**, instrumental **ma(ge) athin**, **mā lavvá**, locative **mā la^{n}gá**

manahkalpitá. adj. imaginative

maninávā. v. measure

manussáyā. n. person pl. **manussáyō**

maṅ pn. (informal) I. Irregular instrumental form **manlauvá**. From **mamá**

maránávā. v. kill

mas. n. meat, collective

māláyá.n. necklace, pl.**mālá**

māḷuvá.n. fish, pl **māḷu**. The stem is used in a collective sense when referring to the food

māmā. n. uncle, address for significantly older ~20+ yrs male. pl. **māmálá**

mānsi. adj. tired. From the more formal but commonly used **mahansi**

māsáyá, māsē. n. month, pl. **māsá**

mæḋá. pp. middle

mærenávā. v. (not passive - **vá** would be incorrect) die

mæssā. n. fly, pl. **mæssō**

milá. n. (highly formal) price, uncountable

minihā.n. man, pl. **minissū**

miniththuvá.n. minute, pl. **miniththu**.

mishrá. a. mixed. Used to describe the full set of characters needed to write Literary Sinhala.

mī harákā.n. water buffalo, pl. **mī harak.**

mohothá. n. moment pl. **mohothával**

mokáḋá.int. why

mokakḋá. int. what

moḷē, also **moḷáyá.** n. brain, pl. **moḷá**

moḷē thiyená. adj. smart, intelligent. Literary form **buḋḋʰimath**.

moná.int.which

monávā.int.what (general)

molávánávā.v. start a cooking fire

mōdá. adj. stupid

mōrā. n. shark, pl.**mōru**

mudubim:n. uncultivated land, collective

muḋḋá.n. ring, pl. **muḋu**

muhuḋá. n. ocean, sea pl. **muhuḋu, muhuḋával**

muhuḋu vællá.n. Beach sand.

muhuṇá. n. face, pl **muhuṇával**, **muhuṇu**

mulá.n. root, pl **mul**.

muḷu. adj. whole. no i-form

mūṇá. n. face, pl. **mūṇával**, **mūṇu**

mūrḋʰájá. adj. retroflex, cerebral

mūththájá.(*colloquial*) adj. retroflex, cerebral

N

naháyá. n. nose, pl **nahayával**

namá.n. name, pl. **nam**

naṅgā. n. younger sister, younger woman, more commonly the former. Uncountable, used mainly as a mode of address

naṅgi. n. younger woman, younger sister more commonly the former. More common than **naṅgā**. Pl. **naṅgilā**.

naráká. adj. bad

narákāḋiyá. n. (formal) hell

nasánávā. v. destroy

natánávā.v. dance

nættuvā. n. (professional) dancer, pl. **nættuvō**

navánávā. v. bend, fold

navaththánávā. v. stop

nāki. adj. (animate, informal) old

nāsikyá. adj. nasal

nāsikyáyá. n. nasal (speech sound), pl. **nāsikyá**

nægenáhirá. n. east, uncountable. Literally "rising sun"

nægitinávā. v.rise, wake up.

næⁿd̊ā. n. Aunt pl. **næⁿd̊álā**

nævenávā. v. bend (down)

nǣ. no, not. Also **næ**, formally **næhæ**

nelánávā. v. pluck (tea leaves)

neránávā. v.(technical) project, protrude

nid̊á gannávā. v. (formal) sleep.

nid̊imathá. adj. Sleepy

nil: the color blue

nimánávā, also **nivánávā.** v. end

nissád̊d̊á. adj. quiet

nisal: 1. adj. unmoving

nisaṅsálá. adj. (inanimate) calm

nisā. cc. because

niṣhpād̊ánáyá káránávā. v. produce. The literary equivalent is **nipád̊ánávā**

nivāduvá. n. vacation, pl. **nivādu**

nōnā. n. lady, pl. **nōnálā**

nōttuvá. note, bill, in the sense of a paper unit of currency, pl. **nōttu**

nuvárá. n. large town, city, pl. **nuvárával**

O

o: irregular form of **oyá**. Related to **ō**. See. **ochchárá, otháná**, **ohe**, etc

obá. pn. you, honorific

obánávā. v. squeeze, press

okkomá. adj. all

oḷuvá.n. head,pl. **oḷu**. The literary Sinhala word is **sirásá**

oḷuvá kækkumá.n. headache, pl. **oḷuvá kækkum**.

orávánávā.v. stare

osávánávā.v. lift. Irregular, past tense **issevvā**.

otuvā. n. camel, pl. **otuvō**

ou. yes

oyā. pn. you.

Ō

ō.that (near addressee)

ōká. pn. it (near addressee).

ōnē. v. want or need.

ōṣhthájá. adj. labial

P

pacháyā. n. liar, pl.**pacháyō**

paha: five, stem form **pas**.

pahaḋánávā. v. clarify. **pahaḋálā ḋenna**, (more commonly) **therum kárálā ḋenná**

pal rahá. adj. unpalatable

palá^{n}ḋánávā. v. (somewhat common) wear, adorn (another person).

palá^{n}ḋinávā. v. (somewhat common) wear, adorn (oneself).

paḷámu. a. (formal) first. The literary version is **paḷámuveni**

paḷánávā. v. chop, split

paḷáveni. a. first. Less formal than **paḷámu**

panáha: fifty, stem form **panas**, literary form **panása**

paninávā. v. jump

panthiyá. n. class, pl. **panthi**

pa^{n}ḋurá. n. bush, pl. **pa^{n}ḋuru**

pará venávā. v. wilt

paráḋánávā. v. defeat

paráṇá. adj. (inanimate) old

parakku. adj. late

patávánávā. v. load

paththu káránávā. v. set fire

pathuránávā. v. spread. For spreading condiments on food, see **gānávā**

paváránávā. v. delegate.

pavásánávā. v. (formal, rare) say

pāgánávā. v. trample, step on

pāhánávā. v. weld

pāḷu. adj. lonely

pān: n. bread, commonly **pāṅ** collective

pānḋárá. n. dawn, uncountable, **-in** type

pārá. n. 1. road, 2. time. Pl. **pārával**,

pāvichchi kárānávā. v. use

pāyánávā. v. cease, brighten up. usage: rain ceases; but **avvá pāyanávā** = "the sun is coming up."

pæhæḋenávā. v. (passive)(somewhat common) be pleased

pæhæḋili. adj. clear

pæṇi rahá. adj. sweet

pænsálá. n. pencil, pl. **pænsal**

pæyá. n. hour, pl. **pæyával**

pǣná. n. pen, pl. **pǣn**

pæthirenávā. v. (of intangible things, like ideas or diseases) spread.

pæththá. n. side, pl. **pæthi**

pætiyā. n. puppy, pl. **pætau**,

pettiyá. box, pl. **petti**.

peḷenávā. v. (passive) be sick, be afflicted

pibiḋenávā. v. wake up, less common and more formal than **nægitinávā/nægittā**

pihánávā. v. (uncommon) cook

pihātuvá. wing, pl. **pihātu**.

pihinávā. v. wipe

pihitánávā. v. establish

pihitenávā. v. be established

pili gannávā. v. accept

pili paḋinávā. v. follow (the rules)

pimbenávā. v. be inflated

pi^{m}binávā. v. blow

pi^{m}burā. n. python, pl. **pi^{m}burō**

pinávánávā. v. (uncommon) enjoy

pini. adj. dewy

pinná. n. dew, uncountable

pinthūráyá. n. picture, pl.**pinthūrá**

pipenávā. v. bloom; expand

pipiññá. n. cucumber, collective

piri mahanávā. v. make do, eke out

piri namánávā. v. bestow, give (a prize)

pirihenávā. v. decline, degenerate

pissu. adj. crazy, **-tá** marking

pitá. adj. foreign

pitá venávā. v. leave, depart

pituvá. n. page, pl. **pitu**

piyāᵐbánávā. v. fly. For humans flying on a plane, use **yanávā**.

piyāpathá. n. wing, pl. **piyāpath**. Less common than **pihātuvá**

pīnánávā. v. swim

puchchánávā. v. (colloquial) burn; the literary equivalent is **pulussánávā**

poddak. n. a few things.

podi. adj. little

puḷuvan: v. can. The negative form is **bǣ** (formal) **bæhæ**; and inflects as **bæri**

pumbánávā. v. inflate

punchi. adj. small

pupuránávā. v. explode. Mildly irregular past form **pipiruvā**. Some dialects may have a regular past tense

purávánávā. v. fill

purudu. a. accustomed

puruḋu venávā. v. practice

puruḋḋá. n. practice, pl. **puruḋu**

pusu^{m}bá balánávā. v. smell at

puthā. n. son, pl. **puththu, puthālā**

putuvá. n. chair, pl. **putu**

pūsā. n. cat, pl. **pūso**

podi. adj. small, short

polá^{m}bánávā. v. incite, impel

poḷánávā. v. sift (through grains)

porá kanávā. v. (animals) fight

porávánávā. v. cover oneself

pothá. n. book, pl. **poth**

povánávā. v. cause to drink. Aberrant causative of **bonávā**

prashnē, formally **prashnáyá.** n. question, pl. **prashná**

pránith. adj. pleasing, good

práthip^{h}aláyá. n. result, pl **prathip^{h}alá**

prāṇá. Sanskrit loanword used in letter names

R

rachánāvá. n. (academic) essay, pl. **rachánā**.

rahá. adj. tasty. From **rasá**

rakinávā. v.protect

ra^{n}gánávā. v. perform, act

rasá. adj. tasty.

ratá. n. country, pl. **ratával**

rathu. a. red

raththáran: n. gold, collective

rassāvá. n. job, pl. **rassāvál,** less commonly **rassā**

ravanávā. v.stare

ravatanávā. v.fool

ræḷlá. n. wave, pl. **ræli**

ræ^{n}ḋenávā. v. get stuck

rævætenávā. v. be fooled. Passive form of **ravátánávā**

ræyá. n. night pl. **ræyával.** Less common than **rǣ**

rǣ. n. night pl. **rǣval.** From earlier **ræyá**

riḋenávā. v. (passive) hurt

riḋī. n. silver, collective

riḷavā. n. *Macaca sinica,* the toque macaque, pl. **riḷau**

rōsá. 1. adj. pink

rōsá malá. n. rose, pl. **rōsá mal**

rōsá pa^{n}ḋurá. n. rosebush, pl. **rōsá pa^{n}ḋuru**

rupiyálá. n. rupee, pl. **rupiyál**

russánávā. v. (*obsolete*) bear. The negative form, **russannē nǣ** is still in use.

S

saḋá. adj. loud

sahā. post. (very formal) and. Less common than **-i** or **hā**

sahōḋáráyā. n. brother, pl. **sahōḋáráyō**. Literary, but the most common way to refer to brothers without specifying their relative age. See **ayyā** and **malli**

sahōḋárī. n. sister, pl. **sahōḋárīyō**. Literary, but the most common way to refer to sisters without specifying their relative age. See **akkā** and **naṅgi**

salákánávā. v regard

salli. n. money, collective

samáránávā. v. memorialize

sanīpá. adj. well, as in healthy.

santhōsá. adj. happy

sañyōgá. adj. composite. Loan from Sanskrit

saññáká. the Sinhala name for the prenasal sounds

sapáththuvá.n. shoe. pl. **sapáththu**

sapáyánávā.v. (formal) supply, **genath ḋenávā** is more common

sarásánávā.v. dress, decorate

satháyá. n. cent, pl. **sathá**.

sathā. n. animal, pl. **saththu**.

sathiyá. n. week, pl. **sathi**. More formal than **sūmánáyá**

sārá.adj. abundant, bountiful

sæka: a. suspicious, **-tá** marking, adverbial form is with **viḋiyá**. Curiously, this word is similar to the English equivalent in that saying "I am suspicious" / **matá sækai** implies that the speaker is suspicious of another person, not a description of their own trustworthiness.

sæmitiyá.n. whip, pl.**sæmiti**

særá.adj. 1. stern 2. swift

særáyá. n. time, pl. **særá**

særisaránávā .v. (formal) pace, walk back and forth

sætháp enávā.v. (somewhat formal) repose, sleep

sellam káránávā.v. play

sená^{n}gá.n. crowd. Uncountable, though **sená^{n}gával** is uncommonly used. Alternatively **senágá**, this word is animate, but the irreg plural is inanimate

sereppuvá.n. slipper. pl.**sereppu**

shrī, usually pronounced **srī** even by educated speakers. sacred, beautiful

siḋu venávā. v. (formal) occur. Used frequently when discussing historical events.

siṅháyā. n. lion, pl. **siṅháyō**

sīthá. adj. cold

sīthálá. adj. cold

sīthálá káránávā.v. cool

sīthálá venávā.v. be cooled

sīyā.n. grandfather, pl **sīyálā**

suḋḋá.adj. clean

suḋḋá káránávā.v. clean

suḋusu.adj. appropriate

suvá^{n}ḋá balánávā. v. smell at

sumānáyá. n. week, pl. **sumāná**

sváráyá. n. vowel, sound pl. **svárá**

T

tá. the dative case marker.

tak gālā. a. right away

thabánávā.v. keep. Less common than **thiyánávā**

thaḋá. adj. hard

thahanam. adj. illegal

thambánávā. v. boil

thaᵐbá. n. copper, collective.

thamai. post. indeed

thanánávā.v. build, make, form. Common, but less so than **haḋánávā**

tharáhá. adj. angry

tharáha kāráyā. n. enemy, foe, pl. **tharáha kāráyo**

taumá. n. town, pl. **taum**

thavánávā. v. warm

tharuvá. n. star, pl. **tharu**

thālujá.adj. palatal

thārákāvá. star, pl. **thārákā**. **tharuvá** is more common

thāththā. n. father, pl.**thāththálā**

thæᵐbili. adj. orange

thæná. n. place, pl. **thæn**

thethá. adj. wet

themenávā. v. get wet. Passive of **themánávā**

themánávā. v. moisten

thel: n. oil, collective

thelá. n. (a variety of) oil, pl. **thel**

thē. n. tea, collective. **thēválátá sīni vædi**

thērenávā. v. understand. Passive of **thōránávā**.

Thʰērávāḋá. The dominant branch of Buddhism in Sri Lanka.

thibáhá. adj. thirsty

thiththá. adj. bitter

thiyánávā. v. keep. Irregular, past tense **thibbā**

thiyenávā. v. 1. (inanimate) exist, have. Irregular, past tense **thibuṇā**, past participle **thibilā**, past participle adjective **thibichchā**

tholá. n. lip, pl. **thol**

thoráthurá. n. information, pl. **thoráthuru** - piece of information. Sing. def. not normally used, instead pl. or indef.

thō. (rude) you

thōránávā. choose, explain

thōrā. n. *Scomberomorus guttatus*, the spotted seerfish, pl. **thōru**.

tiká. adj. few, little. **tikak** is more commonly used.

tikak. adj. a few

tompacháyā. n. (rude) prolific liar, pl.**tompacháyō**. From English *ton* and **pacháyā**

U

udá. pp. above

uḋē. n. morning. Formally **uḋáyá**, pl. **udá**

uḋē pānḋárá. n. dawn, uncountable, **-in** type

ugánnánávā. v. teach

ugánvánávā. v. teach

ugullánávā. v. uproot

ugurá. n. throat, pl. **ugurával**

u^{m}bá. pn. you, pl. **u^{m}bálā**

u^{m}bálákáḋá. n. Maldive fish, a kind of garnish, collective

unánávā. v. spring, well

usá. adj. tall

ussánávā.v. lift. From **osávánávā**

uthsáváyá. n. party, pl. **uthsává**

uththárá ḋenávā. v. answer.

uththárē. n. answer, formally **uththáráyá**, pl. **uththárá**

uthurá. n. north, uncountable. From the stem **uthuru**

uthuránávā. v. overflow

uthurávánávā. v. boil. Causative of **uthuránávā**.

uthuru. adj. northern.

uvámánai. v. require. More formal than **ōne**, but less so than **aváshyai**

uyanávā. v. cook

Ū

ū. Third person pronoun used for animals, or derogatorily for humans. Pl. **ūn**. See also **mū** and **arū**.

ūrā. n. pig, pl **ūro**

ūru mas. n. pork, collective

V

-vá. the accusative case marker. Not to be confused with the common singular ending of many inanimate nouns with back vowel-final stems.

vachánáyá. n. word. pl. **vacháná**

vaḋáyá. n. torture, pl. **vaḋá**. Can refer to any kind of inflicted pain, ranging from an annoyance to full blown torture

vaḋánávā. v. (technical, for animals) birth

vaḋāránávā. v. (formal) speak

vagē. adj. like

vahanávā. v. close, cover

vahinávā. v. rain

vakkáránávā. v. pour out.

val. an inanimate plural marker, commonly used after certain consonants

valáhā. n. bear, pl. **valássu**

valākuḷá. n. cloud, pl. **valākuḷu**

valigē, formally **valigáyá.** n. tail, pl. **valigá**

vaḷá^{n}ḋánávā. v. (honorific) eat.

vam. adj. left

vamáne ḋānávā. v. vomit

vamath. adj. Left-handed.

vamāránávā. v. (formal, literary) vomit

vanásánávā. v. damage, destroy

va^{n}ḋinávā. v. worship

va^{n}ḋurā. n. monkey, pl. **va^{n}ḋuro**. For the toque macaque, see **riḷau**

vaṇsháyá. 1. n. caste. pl. **vanshá** 2. n. chronicle. pl.**vanshá**

vapuránávā. v. sow

varáḋinávā. v. make a mistake, err. Irregular, past tense **væráḋuṇā**

vas vasánávā. v. (honorific) live (in the forest during the rainy season)

vasá. a. cruel, used generally with negative adjectives to amplify them

vatá káránávā. v. surround

vaththá. n. garden, pl. **vathu**.

vathurá. n. water, collective

vaulā. n. bat, pl. **vaulo**.

vavánávā. v. plant, cultivate

vayásáká. adj. (animate) age, i-form **vayásai**

vākyáyá. n. sentence. pl.**vākyá**

vædáyá.1. n. work, job. pl. **vædá, vædával** 2. adj. more n. increase, work, uncountable

vædá káránávā: v. 1. increase, 2. work.

vælápenávā. v. cry, weep (intensely)

vælá. n. creeper, pl. **væl**

væli. n. sand, collective

vællá. n. beach, pl. **vællával**

væráḋenávā. v. (formal) make a mistake, err.

væráḋī. adj. incorrect.

væssá. n. rain. Uncountable, stem form **væhi**

vævenávā. v. (of plants) grow. Passive of **vavánávā**.

vib^{h}āgē, formally **vib^{h}āgáyá.** n. test, exam, pl. **vib^{h}āgá**

viḋihá. n. way, pl. **vidi**

viḋinávā. v. bore, pierce

vihiḷuvá. n. joke, pl. **vihiḷu**

vihiḋánávā. v. diffuse, spread out

vihiḋenávā. v. (of light) spread

vikánávā. v. bite

vikārá. adj. amusingly odd, strange

vikāráyá. n. an amusingly odd action, pl **vikārá**

vikuṇánávā. v. sell

vi^{n}ḋinávā. v. feel

visá. a. poisonous

visá^{n}ḋánávā. v. solve

visi káránávā. v. throw out

visirenávā. v. (passive) be scattered

visthááyá. n. detail, pl. **visthárá**

vithárá. post. about

vithárai. post. only

viyánávā. v. weave, (less commonly) cook

viyath. adj. (Literary) wise, learned.

vīḋuruvá. n. glass, pl. **vīḋuru**

vīrá. adj. heroic

vīráyā. n. hero, pl.**vīráyō**

velā gannávā. v. envelop, (as snakes do) constrict

vēlánávā. v. dry

vēlenávā. v. be dried. Passive of **vēlánávā**

venákal:post. until.

venákaṅpost. until. From **venákal**

venas. adj. different

venasá. n. difference, pl. **venaskam**

venávā. v. become. irregular, past tense **vuṇā**

veráḷá. n. beach, pl. **veráḷával**

vṛkáyā. n. wolf, pl.**vṛkáyō/vṛkáyan**. The **ṛ** here is pronounced **ur**

Y

yaḋinávā. v. pray.

yanávā. v. go. Irregular: past tense **giyā**, past participle **gihillā**, past participle adjective **giyápu**

yanná. 1. a suffix in the formal names of letters 2. Infinitive of **yanávā**

yakā.n. demon pl. **yakālā**

yatá. pp. below"

yatath. adj. under, humble, submissive

yathurá. n. key, pl. **yathuru**

yavánávā. v. send. Generally used with **mamá** and **api**, for non-first person usages, see. **evánávā**.

yæpenávā. v. depend

yōḋʰáyā. n. giant, pl. **yōḋʰáyo**

GLOSSARY

Ablative case: Converts a noun into an adverb, indicating that the action took place from it. For inanimates, this is usually identical to the instrumental case, but in certain contexts **i^{n}ḋálā** must be used instead.

Accusative case: Indicates that the verb affected the animate noun directly. This is distinct from the nominative for animate nouns only.

Adjectival form: A verb form which is an adjective. Identical in use to standard adjectives, except that they may be modified by adverbs. Present, past, and past participle forms have corresponding adjectival forms.

Adjective: a word which modifies the subsequent noun or adjective.

Adverb: an adjective which only modifies verbs and verbal adjectives.

Animate: One of the two grammatical genders in Sinhala. Includes all nouns which are sentient beings, such as people, deities, and animals.

Causative: A verb type which expresses causation of an action.

Clause: A part of a sentence which could either stand on its own without modification, or could do so after conversion of a final adjective to its corresponding verb/i-form adjective

Collective: Nouns which only have a plural form.

Conjunctions: words which link two clauses together.

Dative case: Converts a noun into an adverb, indicating that the action affected the noun indirectly.

Definite: A noun which is specific, i.e. "the chair" rather than "a chair." The "default," dictionary form of Sinhala nouns is definite. Singular nouns may be definite or indefinite.

Doubling: When a consonant is duplicated, a process which is common in forming i-stem past forms and in forming u-type plurals. Half nasals form nasal-stop pairs instead. If **h** would double, **ss** is formed instead. If r or ḷ would double in an i-stem verb, a y is added before the final **ā**.

Fronting: When a back vowel is changed to a front vowel. In the context of Sinhala, this converts **u** to **i**, **ū** to **ī**, **o** to **e**, **ō** to **ē**, **á** to **e**, **a** to **æ**, and **ā** to **ǣ**, while leaving the front vowels unchanged.

Gerund: The noun form of a verb. May be formed by adding **īmá** (polite) or **illá** (impolite) to the past root; or more colloquially, by prefixing **eká** with a verbal adjective

Half-nasal: The sounds ^{m}**b**, ^{n}**d**, ^{n}**d**,^{n}**g**. Also called pre-nasals. When they double, they form a full nasal-stop pair; that is, ^{m}**b**, ^{n}**d**, ^{n}**d**,^{n}**g** form **mb**, **nd**, **nd**,**ṅg**, respectively.

I-form: An adjective form which can stand on its own, effectively containing a copula. Generally only exists for adjectives ending in vowels, formed by adding a final **i**.

Inanimate: One of the two grammatical genders in Sinhala. Includes all nouns which are not animate.

Indefinite: A noun which is not specific, i.e. "a chair" rather than "the chair," a state which is marked with **-ek** for animates and **-ak** for inanimates. Singular nouns may be definite or indefinite.

Infinitive: A verb form used for giving commands and coupling with modal verbs.

Interrogative: A question word. These typically behave like the nouns they inquire about, and except for **ko**, they require use of the question particle.

Intransitive: A verb type which just takes a subject. For active verbs, the subject is nominative. For passive verbs the subject is accusative. For modal verbs (except **kæmáthī**), the subject is dative.

Instrumental case: Used with inanimate nouns to indicate the noun was used to perform an action. For animates, a comparable meaning can only be expressed via postpositions. With the postposition **athin**, used to express the marked animate noun's responsibility for an action without implying voluntary action; **lavvá**, on the other hand implies active participation in an action.

Locative case: Used with inanimate nouns to indicate that something takes place in, on, or around the marked noun, and identical to the genitive case. For animates, certain postpositions or **innávā** can convey a comparable meaning

Modal: A verb type which is often coupled with infinitive forms of verbs.

Nominative case: The case typically used for the subject of a sentence, except with passive, modal, and causative verbs,

Passive: These verbs indicate that the action occurred without without intent on the part of the subject.

Past participle: In Sinhala, a verb form used to indicate that an action was completed prior to action described by the sentence's main verb.

Past tense: The form of a verb used to refer to an action that has already occurred. Regular verbs form the past tense based on three different paradigms, based on their stem vowel. Irregular verbs do not have a predictable past tense form.

Plural: The noun form indicating that there are multiple instances of it. Formed irregularly in Sinhala.

Postposition: A word which modifies the preceding word, the Sinhala equivalent of prepositions.

Pre-nasal: see Half nasal

Predicate: A clause, frequently ending in a verbal adjective, which modifies the subject of sentence

Question particle: Required for all questions without interrogatives and with all interrogatives except **ko**.

Root: the part of a verb preceding the navā stem. The final vowel determines the which class the verb belongs to.

Singular: The noun form indicating that there is just one of it.

Stem: (of nouns) a reduced form of a noun, which can be derived from knowledge of the singular and plural; for inanimates, often identical to the plural. The stem generally forms a related adjective, and may be used in compound words. (of present-tense verbs) the final **-navā** found on non-modal verbs, preceded by a stem vowel for regular verbs

Stem vowel: The vowel just before the -navā stem. A-theme verbs may have **a**, **á** or **ā**; **i** and **e** themes have only the named vowels as possibilities. Irregular verbs may have **o**, or no vowel (instead having an **-n-**)

Subject: The noun which is the main topic of the sentence. Which case it is in is dependent on the verb type. See transitive and intransitive.

Transitive: A verb which, in addition to involving a subject, has another noun as an object. For active verbs, the subject is nominative and the direct object is accusative. For passive verbs the subject is accusative, while the object is dative.

Type: A word in Sinhala that must generally be coupled with a generic noun in order to function, such as colors, many kinds of plants, and most tastes.

Umlaut: A sound change caused by a subsequent vowel (which is sometimes lost afterwards) in a word. In

Sinhala, this typically takes the form of vowel fronting, and occurs when forming regular past tenses, passive verbs, regular u-type plurals, and feminine nouns.

Uncountable: A noun which only has a singular definite form.

Verb: A word expressing action. In Sinhala, there are four major types: active, passive, causative, and modal.

Vocative case: A marginal, somewhat archaic case, which effectively converts a noun into a second-person nominative pronoun. Family words form this case with **-e**, words in general do so with **-o**.

ABOUT THE AUTHOR

The author graduated from Cornell University in 2013, having completed, among other things, the full sequence of Sinhala courses offered there, taught by Bandara Herath. Some years later, he wrote a blurb about himself in the third person.

Printed in Great Britain
by Amazon

65015834R00246